JUST ORDINARY CITIZENS?

Towards a Comparative Portrait of the Political Immigrant

Since the 1960s, the number of immigrants living in liberal democracies has been steadily rising. Despite the existence of numerous studies on social, economic, and geographic integration, few books have addressed the integration of immigrants into the politics of their host countries. When it comes to politics, are immigrants just ordinary citizens?

This collection considers the political integration of immigrants in a number of liberal democracies. *Just Ordinary Citizens?* offers a behavioural perspective on the political integration of immigrants, describing and analysing the relationships that immigrants develop with politics in their host countries. The chapters provide both unique national insights and a comparative perspective on the national case studies, while editor Antoine Bilodeau offers both a framework within which to understand these examples and a systematic review of 288 studies of immigrant political integration from the last sixty years.

ANTOINE BILODEAU is an associate professor in the Department of Political Science at Concordia University and a member of the Centre for the Study of Democratic Citizenship.

Just Ordinary Citizens?

Towards a Comparative Portrait of the Political Immigrant

EDITED BY ANTOINE BILODEAU

UNIVERSITY OF TORONTO PRESS
Toronto Buffalo London

© University of Toronto Press 2016
Toronto Buffalo London
www.utppublishing.com

ISBN 978-1-4426-4648-3 (cloth)   ISBN 978-1-4426-1444-4 (paper)

Library and Archives Canada Cataloguing in Publication

Just ordinary citizens? : towards a comparative portrait of the political
immigrant/edited by Antoine Bilodeau.

Includes bibliographical references.
ISBN 978-1-4426-4648-3 (cloth). – ISBN 978-1-4426-1444-4 (paper)

1. Immigrants – Political activity – Case studies.   2. Emigration and
immigration – Political aspects – Case studies.   3. Social integration –
Political aspects – Case studies.   4. Immigrants – Political activity – Canada –
Case studies.   5. Social integration – Political aspects – Canada – Case studies.
I. Bilodeau, Antoine, 1976–, editor

JV6124.J88 2016   325'.1   C2015-907274-3

University of Toronto Press acknowledges the financial assistance to its
publishing program of the Canada Council for the Arts and the Ontario
Arts Council, an agency of the Government of Ontario.

Canada Council Conseil des Arts
for the Arts   du Canada

ONTARIO ARTS COUNCIL
CONSEIL DES ARTS DE L'ONTARIO
an Ontario government agency
un organisme du gouvernement de l'Ontario

Funded by the   Financé par le
Government   gouvernement
of Canada   du Canada

Canadä

Contents

Acknowledgments

Putting together *Just Ordinary Citizens? Towards a Comparative Portrait of the Political Immigrant* has been quite a lengthy process, and it would not have been possible without the support of many people and organizations.

Before evolving into an edited volume, the project started as a two-day workshop, which was held in November 2011 at Concordia University and which benefited from the financial support of the Social Sciences and Humanities Research Council of Canada (Aid to Research Workshops and Conferences Grant), the Centre Métropolis du Québec – Immigration et métropoles, the Centre for the Study of Democratic Citizenship, and Concordia University and its Vice President, Research and Graduate Studies (Aid to Research Related Event Grant). Organizing such an event was a time-consuming task, one that required a great deal of planning and coordination, and I would like to thank Soheyla Salari for having made it possible.

Beyond organizing the workshop itself, the even larger task of making this project possible was identifying and codifying the 288 existing peer-reviewed articles on immigrant political integration that serve as the basis for the Introduction to this volume. For this task, I am grateful to Christiane Perreault for her initiative, rigour, patience, and thoughtfulness in piloting this task.

Many thanks to the authors for their cooperation and patience; this edited volume would certainly not have been possible without their ideas and inspired contributions. I am also grateful to the anonymous reviewers for their thorough and swift review and to Daniel Quinlan and the University of Toronto Press for their continued support throughout the process.

Very sincere thanks also to Luc Turgeon and Stephen E. White, my inspiring colleagues and friends, for their comments and suggestions for the Introduction and Conclusion of the manuscript. Your insights are always helpful and thoughtful.

Finally, very special thanks to Anne-Sophie Hébert for her precious help in the final stage of the process, attending to all of the details necessary for ensuring the cohesion of the volume.

JUST ORDINARY CITIZENS?

Towards a Comparative Portrait of the Political Immigrant

Introduction: Just Ordinary Citizens? Towards a Comparative Portrait of the Political Immigrant

ANTOINE BILODEAU

The number of immigrants living in more developed countries has been steadily rising since the 1960s, from about 29 million in 1965 to almost 100 million in 2010. How well do these newcomers integrate into their host country? While over the last several decades a significant amount of research has been conducted to better understand the successes and challenges of immigrants in gaining access to employment, housing, and education, our efforts to assess the success of immigrants in acquiring a political voice of their own, and the impact of newcomers on the political affairs of their host country, has been far more limited. Are immigrants just like other citizens when it comes to politics? Up until recently, very few accounts of how newcomers relate to politics in their host country have been available.

Yet these questions have been increasingly salient since the 1990s, with the growth and diversification of migration flows. On the one hand, concerns have been expressed regarding the political, social, and economic barriers to the integration of newcomers into the political affairs of the host country. These concerns have led some observers to question whether newcomers are striving or struggling to navigate various political institutions to voice their needs and demands. There have also been debates about the best policies for helping newcomers articulate a political voice of their own. On the other hand, concerns have been expressed as to whether newcomers from increasingly diverse origins are a "good fit" in liberal democracies. These concerns have generated questions about how strongly newcomers adhere to liberal democratic principles and whether they are loyal and committed citizens like any others. They have also led to debates about whether immigrants are contributing to the greater public good or building parallel societies within their own ethnic communities. In the late 1990s, these anxieties about immigrant exclusion and social cohesion became more acute and sparked an interest in academic research on immigrant political integration. Nearly 20 years later, what have we learned?

Despite the booming literature on the topic over the last decades, we still lack a general portrait of the political immigrant. The main objective of this volume is to begin drawing such a portrait – or different portraits - of immigrants as citizens. Given the complexity of the phenomenon, and given the variety of national experiences and the diversity of immigrant groups in each country, it would be premature to draw generalized conclusions. Accordingly, the main objective of this volume is to take us a step closer towards a comparative portrait of immigrant political integration in Western democracies.

But first, what do we mean by *immigrant political integration*? For several reasons, there is no straightforward answer to this question. First, people disagree on what terminology to use. Some like the term *integration* (Garcia 1987), others prefer the term *incorporation* (Bloemraad 2006), and many others avoid using any terminology at all, limiting themselves instead to the expression *immigrant political behaviours and attitudes*. Second, it is often difficult to clearly identify a specific substantive definition that cuts across the varying terminology. Some researchers talk about "the extent to which self-identified group interests are articulated, represented, and met in public policymaking" (Ramírez and Fraga 2008, 64), others prefer to talk about "cohesiveness" (Garcia 1987), while some refer to the idea of a "two-way process" in which both immigrants and the host population are transformed (Biles, Burstein, and Frideres 2008).[1] It is not the objective of this volume to resolve this debate about the most appropriate terminology or conceptualization. It seems, however, that the definition provided by Irene Bloemraad corresponds to the approach that drives the present volume. She describes it as

> the process of becoming a part of mainstream political debates, practices, and decision-making. The end point of the process is difficult to identify, but incorporation is generally achieved when patterns of immigrant participation are comparable to those among the native born, although different individuals and groups might privilege certain forms of participation over others. (2006, 6–7)

To this definition, we would add that the focus is not limited to participation but also includes emotional attachments to the host country;

relationships with the political system of the host country, such as trust and political efficacy; as well as support for the core political values of a country, such as democracy, tolerance, and freedom of speech and equality between men and women.[2] Accordingly, the review that follows, along with the 11 chapters, work broadly from the above definition. As it mentions, the notion of comparison with the local population is quite central to understanding immigrant political integration. Hence, almost all chapters in this volume use the local population of the host country as a benchmark, not so much because immigrants ought to become more like the host population but rather because the comparison helps us to assess where immigrants suffer from political marginalization and where they fare better.

Using the above definition, we can then state that the volume aims to draw a preliminary cross-national portrait of how immigrants relate to politics in their host countries in comparison to native-born populations. It considers the ways in which they participate in the political process, their political preferences, their relationship with government authorities and political institutions, their attachment and identification with the host country, and their support for the core political values of the host country. It also examines the extent to which immigrants are represented in the political institutions of the host country.

Beyond the terminology used with regard to political integration, it is also important to clarify this volume's specific object of study. As readers will notice, the terminology used to describe the population studied will vary across the chapters. Some chapters will refer to "immigrants," others to "ethnic minorities," and finally others will refer to "visible minorities." These different terms refer to different objects of study; they are not meant to be synonyms. They reflect the different realities in the national case studies examined in this volume and the specific questions asked in each chapter. The object of study is thus not exactly the same across the chapters. Imposing a common object of study would not have done justice to the diverse realities in each case study, and imposing a common terminology would not have allowed the endeavour of each chapter to be adequately reported. Accordingly, the decision was made to allow each contributor to define his or her own object of study and use the terminology most appropriate to describe that object of study in that particular national context.

To pursue this objective, the volume proposes three main avenues. The first avenue is a brief review of how scholars in the field have addressed the question of immigrant political integration. Through this review, presented in the later part of this Introduction, the task is to identify the numerous questions that have been raised and the various perspectives that have been used to answer them over the last 60 years. This task is performed through an analysis of all articles addressing the political integration of immigrants (from an attitudinal and behavioural perspective) in 55 scientific journals for the period from 1955 to 2011. This review allows us to not only identify when, where, and in which countries research was conducted on immigrant political integration but also see the trends in the perspectives that scholars have used to reach a better understanding of the political immigrant.

After taking a broad look at the field of immigrant political integration over a period of close to 60 years, the second avenue we take in drawing a portrait of the political immigrant is to take a closer look at more recent research being conducted on the topic in different countries. Through this second strategy, Part One of the volume proposes key lessons from various national experiences in Anglo-democracies and continental Europe. To do justice to the diversity of interests and approaches when studying immigrant political integration, each of these seven chapters examines its own dimension of newcomers' relationship to politics in their host country.[3]

Chapters 1 through 3 on the Netherlands, Belgium, and the United Kingdom examine a trio of questions that are often the first to come to mind when thinking about immigrant political integration. First, do immigrants in each of these three countries take part in the electoral process? Do they vote? All three chapters indicate gaps in the levels of voter turnout between immigrants and the local population of the host countries, highlighting an initial challenge for immigrants in acquiring a political voice of their own through the most important democratic channel in Western democracies. Moreover, these three chapters reveal significant variations in levels of electoral turnout across groups of immigrants, thus highlighting the critical need for researchers to avoid thinking of immigrants as a homogeneous category and to become more systematic in analysing distinctive immigrant communities within a single country.

The second question asked in these three chapters concerns the partisan preferences of immigrants. When engaged in the electoral process, which party do immigrants tend to vote for? These chapters highlight a common trend also observed in other national settings (White and Bilodeau 2014) – namely, a tendency to support large centre-left parties. Immigrants are not unanimous in their electoral preferences, nor do the majority of them systematically cast their vote for a left-leaning party.

In each of the three countries examined, however, immigrants appear to have a clear preference for a large centre-left party, a preference systematically stronger than that expressed among the rest of the population. The question is, why do immigrants express such consistent political preferences across many countries? In Chapter 1, Anja van Heelsum, Laure Michon, and Jean Tillie discuss the role that ethnic networks in the Netherlands play in mobilizing immigrants and shaping their political preferences. In Chapter 2, Dirk Jacobs, Celine Teney, Andrea Rea, and Pascal Delwit examine the role that ethnic voting plays in attracting immigrants to certain parties in Belgium, a role that may explain the left-leaning tendency of the political immigrant. In Chapter 3, Shamit Saggar provides a broader reflection on the roots of such political preferences among immigrants and ethnic minorities in the United Kingdom, what he calls the "iron law" of immigrant political integration.

As a third question, these three chapters examine the extent to which immigrants are represented in political institutions in the Netherlands, Belgium, and the United Kingdom. All three chapters provide crucial cross-time evidence to assess the progress made, and the lasting deficiencies, in the representation of immigrants in the elected bodies of their host countries. It is interesting that commonalities in the findings emerge despite the focus of the analyses on both local and national politics. In Chapter 1, Anja van Heelsum and her colleagues provide a general examination of immigrant political participation and representation at the local level in Amsterdam and Rotterdam, along with some comparative evidence at the national level. In Chapter 2, Dirk Jacobs and his colleagues provide an in-depth examination of immigrant ethnic voting in local elections in Brussels. And in Chapter 3, Shamit Saggar describes the participation of ethnic minorities in British elections and their representation at Westminster.

The subsequent three chapters address newly emerging questions about the political integration of immigrants. In Chapter 4, Michael Jones-Correa, in keeping with the previous chapters, examines the political participation of immigrants in the American context. His focus, however, is solely on Mexican immigrants, the largest and most rapidly expanding subgroup of the American immigrant population. Echoing concerns about the various political experiences that immigrants bring with them and their impact on the politics of the host country, Jones-Correa's chapter investigates the extent to which immigrant political participation is structured by their cumulative political experiences in Mexico. The chapter seeks to determine whether immigrants' political socialization evolves once in the host country or remains crystallized around pre-migration experiences. This question is especially relevant given the variation in the successes and challenges of political integration observed across groups of immigrants in the first three chapters. Jones-Correa highlights the potential role of pre-migration experiences in making sense of the varying successes and challenges faced by different immigrant communities.

In a similar vein, Juliet Pietsch and Ian McAllister in Chapter 5 address the question of lasting pre-migration influences on immigrant political integration in the Australian context. Pietsch and McAllister, however, set aside immigrant political participation to instead examine the levels of confidence immigrants express in Australian political institutions. As discussed in the review of the field below, the growing interest in research on a wide range of dimensions in immigrant political integration, which include – but also go beyond – political participation has been a key feature of the field over the last decades. And echoing the debate about the impact of immigrants on the politics of their host country, Pietsch and McAllister examine whether immigrants from authoritarian political regimes – the majority of newcomers nowadays – exhibit higher or lower levels of confidence than immigrants from other political backgrounds. They also provide evidence about second-generation immigrants in Australia – those born in Australia of foreign-born parents – thus beginning to fill one of the most glaring gaps in the immigrant political integration literature.

In Chapter 6, Chris Haynes and S. Karthick Ramakrishnan also move beyond the issue of political participation to investigate immigrants' knowledge of politics in the United States. Though it is a key component of citizen competence, political knowledge has rarely been studied in the context of immigrant political integration. Recognizing that immigrants are not a homogeneous group, Haynes and Ramakrishnan describe the levels of knowledge of American politics among the three main ethnic-minority groups in the United States – namely, Latinos, Asian Americans, and African Americans. Haynes and Ramakrishnan also provide an innovative approach to the field of immigrant political integration by examining the role of the ethnic media in structuring the levels of knowledge of American politics among these three groups; this is an increasingly salient question in the United States with the growth in the number and popularity of such media.

This volume could not aspire to provide a comparative portrait of immigrant political integration without including a chapter that systematically compares immigrants in different countries. Accordingly, to conclude Part One of the volume, Marc Helbling, Tim Reeskens, Cameron Stark, Dietlind Stolle, and Matthew Wright compare, in Chapter 7, immigrants' political orientations and participation in 18 European countries. As indicated in the review below, such comparative assessments are rare; the vast majority of studies on immigrant political integration have focused on single countries or, in some cases, on two-country comparisons; comparisons involving multiple countries are still an exception.

Moreover, Helbling and his colleagues further contribute to our understanding of immigrant political integration by investigating the impact of immigration policies and integration regimes. The debate as to what are the best policies to welcome newcomers has been quite intense over the last 20 years; the last decade alone has seen a dramatic rise in the number of publications describing, comparing, and analysing the policies relating to immigration across countries. Very few studies, however, have taken up the challenge of assessing the impact of these policies on immigrant political integration (see Bloemraad 2006). This is precisely the question that Helbling and his colleagues tackle in Chapter 7, finding evidence to support the view that immigration policies have a significant impact on newcomers' integration into the political affairs of their host country.

Part Two of the volume presents the third avenue for drawing a portrait of the political immigrant. It provides an in-depth look at immigrant political integration in a single country: Canada. There are numerous reasons for focusing on Canada. First, aside from the United States, Canada is the country for which we find the largest number of studies on the topic of immigrant political integration.[4] Over the last 30 years especially, the topic has been on the radar of political scientists in Canada, and this interest crystallized after the publication of several studies on the topic by Jerome H. Black in the 1980s. The reasons for this marked interest in the topic in Canada may be linked to several factors. For instance, like the United States, Canada is a settler society, one that still receives large flows of immigrants. The historical importance of immigrants, and their considerable impact on the contemporary demographics of the country, may partly explain the high level of interest in how newcomers integrate politically in Canada. Canada's multiculturalism policy may also account for the greater research interest in the topic: with ethnic diversity at the heart of the country's identity since the early 1970s, it has made sense for scholars to assess the successes and challenges of newcomers in acquiring a political voice of their own.

Another reason for choosing Canada relates to the perceived success it has had with immigrant integration, so much that Canada is sometimes presented as a "model" for other countries in the area of immigration and diversity. In this context, it is worth taking a closer look to assess the validity of that claim. The various contributions on Canada provide evidence of some of the challenges that immigrants still face in spite of this "champion" reputation. The final reason for looking at Canada is that the strong interest in newcomers' political integration has meant that, over the years, scholars have employed a multiplicity of perspectives and strategies to study the topic. This does not mean that Canadian scholars have always been the first to propose novel approaches to the study of immigrant political integration or that these approaches are absent from other national contexts. The advantage of looking at Canada, however, is that we can find so many of these novel approaches. They provide a good sense of where the field is heading.

In Chapter 8, Elisabeth Gidengil and Jason Roy answer one of the most policy-relevant questions in the Canadian context: is there a racial divide in the political integration of immigrants? With the accumulated evidence that Canadians of non-Caucasian backgrounds were experiencing greater difficulty in finding employment, the federal government passed the Employment Equity Act in 1986, which made the category *visible minority* an official and salient statistical category in Canada.[5] Today, however, the dynamics of social and economic integration remain more challenging for immigrants from visible minority backgrounds than they are for other segments of the population (Biles, Burstein, and Frideres 2008). Gidengil and Roy examine whether this same dynamic holds when it comes to their political integration and investigate whether immigrants of visible minority background participate in politics to the same extent as other groups of immigrants.

Stephen E. White, in Chapter 9, takes another strategy to uncover the challenges faced by specific groups of immigrants – challenges often hidden when investigating "immigrants" as a homogeneous category. Grounded in political socialization research, like Chapter 4 on Mexican immigrants in the United States and Chapter 5 on immigrants in Australia, Chapter 9 examines whether immigrants who arrived at a younger age tend to integrate more easily than those who arrived later in life. White also transforms the research question; he leaves aside the matter of whether immigrants hold a specific set of political orientations and instead investigates whether and how younger and older immigrants rely on their political orientations to relate to the politics of their host country. For instance, White investigates whether the sense of civic duty among younger immigrants exerts a stronger influence on their propensity to vote – as it does for the local population – than among older immigrants.

In Chapter 10, Karen Bird presents another dimension of immigrants' integration, examining their political representation at the municipal level in Ontario. Bird's chapter sheds light on both the extent of immigrants' representation on municipal councils in Ontario and the public opinion barriers they face when running for office. It clearly lays out the challenge of immigrant political representation from both the supply and the demand side. It then takes a closer look at the demand side of the equation through an innovative experiment: investigating how Canadians' evaluations of candidates in municipal elections in Ontario change according to the ethnicity and sex of the candidates. The chapter reveals significant ethnicity-affinity bias, with voters preferring same-ethnicity candidates to different-ethnicity candidates. Interestingly enough, Bird uncovers an ethnic-affinity effect among both majority and minority ethnic groups, thus contributing to the larger discussion about ethnic votes presented in chapters 1 and 2.

To end Part Two, in Chapter 11, Jerome H. Black challenges our perspective of immigrant political integration. Rather than asking the standard question of whether immigrants and ethnic minorities win seats in Canada's political institutions, he examines the extent to which immigrants and ethnic minorities' interests are discussed in the Canadian House of Commons. He asks, using a systematic analysis of Question Period in the House of Commons, who speaks up for immigrants and ethnic minorities. In a first-of-its-kind study, Black investigates which members of Parliament (MPs) – and under what circumstances – ask questions concerning immigrants and ethnic minorities. He demonstrates that matters of strong interest to immigrants and ethnic minorities do get raised during Question Period, primarily those relating to immigration and refugees. Echoing broader work on constituency representation (Blidook 2012), Black shows that not just MPs of ethnic-minority background raise issues relating to the minority agenda; indeed, the presence of an ethnically diverse population in electoral districts seems to ensure that even "non-ethnic" representatives raise these issues, especially when their electoral victory was the result of a close race. Black shows how and when MPs speak up for immigrants and ethnic minorities during Question Period and thereby help uncover the conditions favouring immigrant political empowerment.

Immigrant Political Integration: A Look Through 288 Studies

Let us now begin with a look at the field of immigrant political integration. To explore the ways in which the field has been studied over time, 288 studies published between 1955 and 2011 in 55 academic journals were coded according to their year of publication, journal of publication, national focus, and main dependent and independent variables.[6] To be selected, a study had to have as dependent variables the political behaviours or political attitudes of immigrants. Accordingly, the review is not concerned with research that examines issues relating to immigration policies, integration regimes, or a conceptual discussion of immigrant political integration. The list of journals was selected to include the main journals in ethnic and immigration studies, political science, and social sciences. Given the number of studies involved and the diversity of approaches to measuring or explaining immigrant political integration, the objective here is not to synthesize the findings of these 288 studies but rather to present how the field is structured and how it evolved between 1955 and 2011.

A New and Fast-Growing Field of Research

As mentioned, the field of study of immigrant political integration is relatively new. Up until the late 1990s, there were very few peer-reviewed articles published on the topic. This reality is quite apparent in the data presented in Figure 1 below, which tracks over time the number of articles appearing on the topic of immigrant political integration. The numbers are quite telling. Up until the mid-1980s, no more than one or two articles per year were published on the topic in the 55 journals reviewed; between 1955 and 1985, a grand total of only 25 studies were identified. After 1985, the pace of publication started to rise to a few articles per year, but we have to wait until the very late 1990s and early 2000s to see studies on immigrant political integration develop rapidly, resulting in between 10 and 15 publications per year. The volume of publications has now risen to more than 20 peer-reviewed articles every year. In terms of sheer numbers, the field is booming.

What are the causes of such an expansion of the field of immigrant political behaviours and attitudes? The answer to this question is not easy to provide, but a quick look at changing migration trends in Western democracies may help to provide the beginning of an answer. The increasing number of publications on immigrant political

Figure 1. Number of Articles on Immigrant Political Integration by Year of Publication (1955–2011)

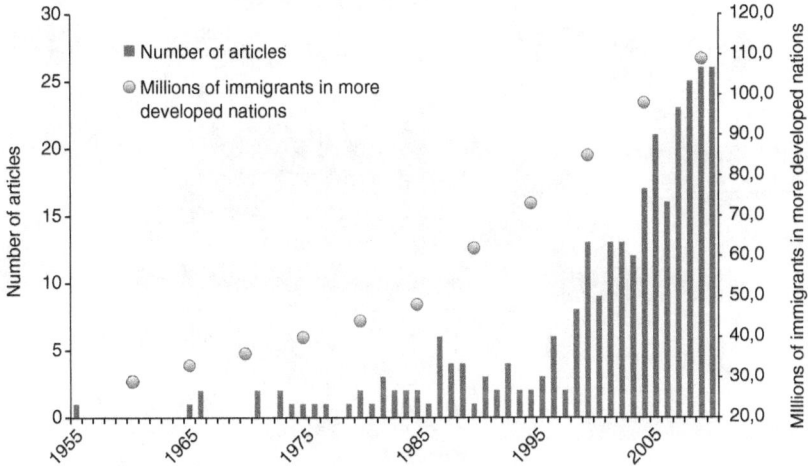

integration seems to follow – with a lag of about five to 10 years – the increasing flows of immigrants to Western democracies from 1985 to 2010. We observe a lag effect here, but this may not come as a big surprise. Indeed, peer-reviewed academic research takes quite some time to develop, from the moment a research project is conceived to final publication. Whatever the cause, however, the trend is clear. Starting in the late 1990s, the number of peer-reviewed articles on the topic of immigrant political integration grew significantly.

Although this surge in interest in the topic of immigrant political behaviour and attitudes is observed in many Western democracies – as indicated in Figure 2 below – the field has taken root more deeply in the United States than anywhere else. Perhaps because of the English-language bias of our review, we found a total of 176 studies aimed at providing a better understanding of immigrant political integration in the United States, the majority of these articles more specifically studying Latinos. The next three countries where research on immigrant political integration has been most prolific (Canada, the United Kingdom, and Australia) are also (primarily) English-speaking. This observation is important and further raises the question of whether these numbers reflect a broad interest in immigrant integration in Anglo-democracies or are rather a mere reflection of the English bias of our review. Nevertheless,

Figure 2. National Focus of Research in Reviewed Scholarly Sample

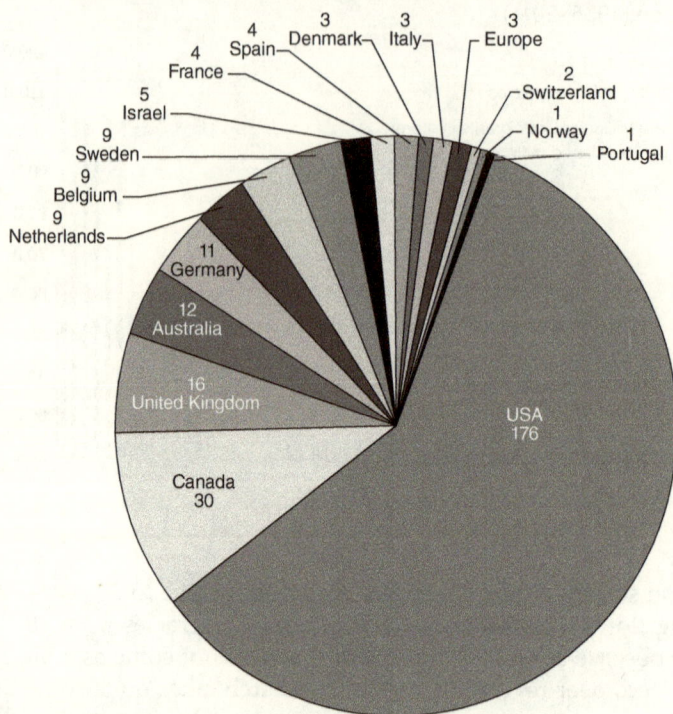

the field has also taken root in continental Europe. We do not present the findings here, but it is important to note that the number of publications on immigrant political integration started to increase broadly at the same time for Anglo-democracies and continental Europe. Overall, six of the eight countries where research on immigrant political integration has been most prolific are represented in this volume (United States, Canada, the United Kingdom, Australia, the Netherlands, and Belgium), leaving only Germany and Sweden not represented.

Where has this research been published? This question is important as it arguably reveals the breadth of the interest in, or the normalization of, research on immigrant political integration. If the research is primarily published in journals specializing in the topic of immigrants and ethnic diversity, then one could argue that immigrant political integration remains a topic of interest to only a small community of immigration experts. If, however, the research is also published in journals with

Figure 3. Where Was Immigrant Political Integration Research Published?

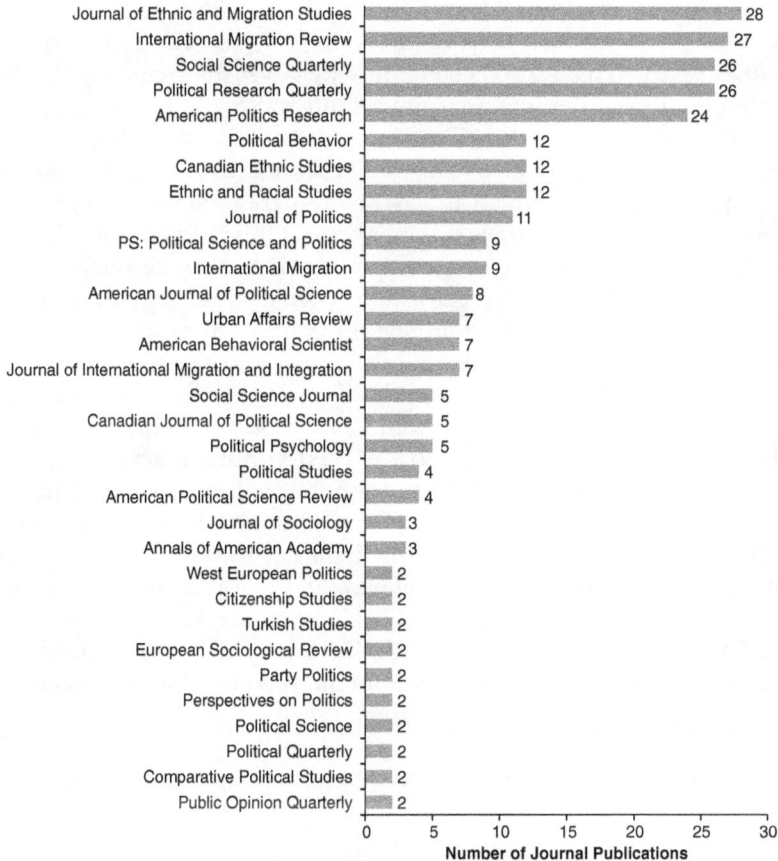

Journal	Number of Journal Publications
Journal of Ethnic and Migration Studies	28
International Migration Review	27
Social Science Quarterly	26
Political Research Quarterly	26
American Politics Research	24
Political Behavior	12
Canadian Ethnic Studies	12
Ethnic and Racial Studies	12
Journal of Politics	11
PS: Political Science and Politics	9
International Migration	9
American Journal of Political Science	8
Urban Affairs Review	7
American Behavioral Scientist	7
Journal of International Migration and Integration	7
Social Science Journal	5
Canadian Journal of Political Science	5
Political Psychology	5
Political Studies	4
American Political Science Review	4
Journal of Sociology	3
Annals of American Academy	3
West European Politics	2
Citizenship Studies	2
Turkish Studies	2
European Sociological Review	2
Party Politics	2
Perspectives on Politics	2
Political Science	2
Political Quarterly	2
Comparative Political Studies	2
Public Opinion Quarterly	2

Number of Journal Publications

Note: Journals with fewer than two articles are not reported.

a broader focus, then it might indicate that the field has indeed reached a certain level of maturity and that it appeals to a broader community of scholars. To answer this question, each of the 288 studies was codified based on the type of journal in which it was published. We created three categories: immigration and ethnic studies journals, political science journals, and other social science journals.

As seen in Figure 3 above, the journals that published the largest number of studies on the topic are those specializing in issues of immigration and ethnic studies (*Journal of Ethnic and Migration Studies* and

International Migration Review). It is interesting to note, however, that some general social science and even political science journals (such as the *Social Science Quarterly, Political Research Quarterly,* and *American Politics Research*) have also been quite active over the years in publishing on the topic of immigrant political integration. In fact, among the top 10 journals that published the largest number of articles on immigrant political integration, five are political science journals. The diversity of publications in which articles on immigrant political integration appear is a sign of the growing importance of this field of research.

Moreover, research on immigrant political integration is widely read when it is published in political science journals. Table 1 below reports the 10 most cited studies on immigrant political integration, eight of which have been published in political science journals. One could certainly argue that such high citation levels primarily reflect the prestige of some of these journals (*American Political Science Review, American Journal of Political Science,* and *Journal of Politics*), but the fact that articles on immigrant political integration are published in such top journals speaks not only to the quality of the topic but also to the interest that it generates. Moreover, Table 2 below indicates the average number of citations for articles in each type of journal. Clearly, it appears that research published on immigrant political integration in political science journals is read and cited (on average, 43.5 times) more often than when published in journals specializing in immigration and ethnic diversity issues (32.3) or in social science journals (23.9).

How Have Scholars Addressed, Measured, and Explained Immigrant Political Integration?

How many studies, about which countries, and published in which journals are certainly important questions to ask in order to draw a picture of the field of immigrant political integration. These questions, however, provide us with only limited substantive insights. The present section examines how scholars have addressed, measured, and explained immigrant political integration over the last 60 years. This in turn can help us address the question of how to define immigrant political integration.

One worthy observation relates to the type of methodology scholars have employed to study immigrant political integration. The field of political behaviours has been traditionally marked by a reliance on mass survey research and quantitative analysis. Given that we decided

Table 1. Ten Most Cited Peer-Reviewed Articles (1950–2011)

Author(s)	Title	Journal	Year	Number of citations
R. Wolfinger	"The Development and Persistence of Ethnic Voting"	American Political Science Review	1965	282
J. Leighley and A. Vedlitz	"Race, Ethnicity and Political Participation: Competing Models and Contrasting Explanations"	Journal of Politics	1999	275
M. Fennema and J. Tillie	"Political Participation and Political Trust in Amsterdam: Civic Communities and Ethnic Networks"	Journal of Ethnic and Migration Studies	1999	262
C. Uhlaner, B. Cain, and R. Kiewiet	"Political Participation of Ethnic Minorities in the 1980s"	Political Behavior	1989	245
W.T. Cho	"Naturalization, Socialization, Participation: Immigrants and (Non-)Voting"	Journal of Politics	1999	231
B. Cain, R. Kiewiet, and C. Uhlaner	"The Acquisition of Partisanship by Latinos and Asian Americans"	American Journal of Political Science	1991	207
M. Jones-Correa	"Different Paths: Gender, Immigration and Political Participation"	International Migration Review	1998	191
M. Barreto, G. Segura, and N. Woods	"The Mobilizing Effect of Majority-Minority Districts on Latino Turnout"	American Political Science Review	2004	183
A. Pantoja, R. Ramirez, and G. Segura	"Citizens by Choice, Voters by Necessity: Patterns in Political Mobilization by Naturalized Latinos"	Political Research Quarterly	2001	178
D. Shaw, R. de la Garza, and J. Lee	"Examining Latino Turnout in 1996: A Three-State, Validated Survey Approach"	American Journal of Political Science	2000	175

Source: Google Scholar (accessed June 2013).

Table 2. Average Number of Citations per Article by Journal Type

Journal type	Number of articles published	Average number of citations per article
Political science	131	43.5
Immigration and ethnic studies	95	32.3
Other social sciences	62	23.9

Source: Google Scholar (accessed June 2013).

to collect studies focused only on immigrant political behaviours and attitudes, it is perhaps not surprising to observe that more than half of our listed studies (182 of the 288, or 63 per cent) include some quantitative analysis of survey data. Moreover, perhaps as a sign that the field has emerged relatively recently, and because of the high cost of survey research, it is striking and worth mentioning that 83 of these 182 survey-based articles on immigrants (46 per cent) actually rely on studies not specifically designed to study immigrants or ethnic minorities.[7] Rather, these studies rely on samples of immigrants or ethnic minorities derived from more general surveys of the entire population.

This characteristic has important implications for the study of immigrant political integration and for the types of conclusions that have been reached so far. First, these studies rarely make a special effort to reach out to immigrants, either through oversampling or by offering the questionnaire in languages other than the official ones in the country where fieldwork is taking place. Second, in many studies, like those relying on electoral studies in Canada, all immigrant respondents are naturalized citizens. Finally, many of the studies do not contain sets of explanatory variables that may be specific to immigrants and hence critical to understanding the process of immigrant political integration. Questions such as those relating to proficiency in the language of the host country, pre-migration experiences, contact with co-ethnics, or transnational considerations are typically absent from these larger samples of the general populations, and hence they limit the possibilities for investigations by scholars in the field. The consequences are such that many studies have tended to focus on immigrants established in the host country for quite a significant amount of time or those who likely exhibit what we could qualify as a "positive integration bias" – for instance, because of their greater fluency in the language of the host country. As such, they may not always be fully representative of immigrant populations. Fortunately, the field is moving forward, and the question of how best to survey immigrants and ethnic minorities is becoming more salient and is more widely discussed (see Font and Méndez 2013).

In terms of measuring or explaining immigrant political integration – as we will see below – the consequence of this methodological approach is that the field has tended to closely follow mainstream political behaviour research, often neglecting immigrant-specific forms of political engagement or immigrant-specific factors to explain immigrants' political integration. Indeed, given that a significant body of research has been derived from broader political surveys of the entire population and that

Figure 4. How Have Scholars Empirically Measured Immigrant Political Integration?

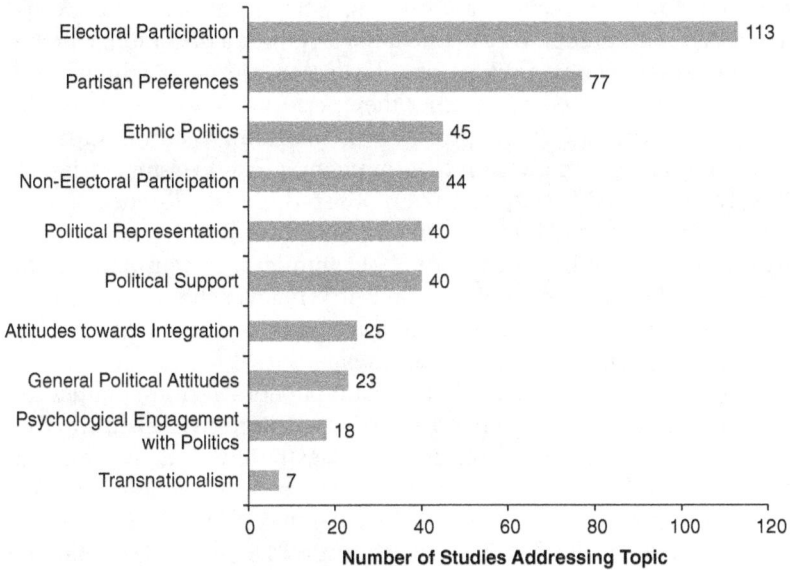

Number of Studies Addressing Topic

elections are the most conventional mode of political participation, it probably comes as no surprise that the predominant focus of immigrant political integration research has been on electoral politics. Do immigrants vote? Do they actively engage in other electoral campaign activities, such as donating money, assisting candidates, or attending political rallies? As seen in Figure 4 above, these are the main questions that have been tackled by more than 113 of all identified peer-reviewed articles on immigrant political integration (39 per cent).[8] In a similar vein, the second most frequent set of questions has concerned immigrants' partisan preferences; 77 articles (27 per cent) asked for which parties immigrants vote and whether they identify with certain parties. Still concerned with elections, we identified 40 studies (14 per cent) of the political representation of immigrants and ethnic minorities. In this spirit, our first three chapters directly address these questions in the context of the Netherlands, Belgium, and the United Kingdom. Moreover, and more specific to the question of political representation, chapters 10 and 11 address the political representation of immigrants and ethnic minorities.

Beyond these three points of focus, the field has been more eclectic. A significant body of research has examined whether immigrants were active in what we could call "ethnic politics." Scholars have been interested in whether immigrants were members of an ethnic association, whether they had attended any political activities organized by an ethnic candidate running for office, or whether they performed what is sometimes called ethnic voting (see Chapter 2). It is interesting that this stream of research has been somewhat more dominant in Anglo-democracies, especially the United States, perhaps motivated by the presence of large communities such as Latinos.[9] One might ask what has motivated this stream of research: is it a concern about immigrant communities' empowerment or a fear of parallel societies? Whatever the roots, the issue of ethnic politics has attracted a significant amount of attention. Our first three chapters will revisit these questions.

Questions about immigrant participation in non-electoral politics follow close behind. Among other questions, scholars have asked whether immigrants were involved in public demonstrations and civic associations and whether they were willing to sign petitions or join boycotts. This set of questions has been more popular in continental Europe than in Anglo-democracies (24.5 per cent versus 14.8 per cent). Obtaining citizenship – and therefore electoral participation such as voting – has been generally more restrictive in continental Europe than in Anglo-democracies. Given these more important legal barriers in Europe, it is perhaps not surprising to observe a stronger interest in political activities that extend beyond voting. With the increasing number of European countries granting voting rights to non-citizens at the municipal level (Seidle 2014), it would also not be surprising to see that immigrant local-level voting has been more often studied in continental Europe than in Anglo-democracies. Unfortunately, however, our review of the field did not codify the level of government for which voting was studied.

Two other streams of research, far less prominent, have focused on forms of political engagement that are specific to immigrants. First, scholars have asked immigrants about their opinions regarding their own integration and that of other immigrants. This stream of research, likely inspired by the debates on immigration policies and integration regimes (Joppke 2010), has examined whether immigrants were interested in acquiring citizenship or had acquired citizenship as well as what their views were with regard to assimilation, acculturation, and integration. Second, only seven studies examined issues relating to transnationalism (from a behavioural perspective). Scholars here have not asked whether immigrants were participating in the host country but rather have examined the types of political linkages they were maintaining with the country of origin: whether they continued to vote or tried to influence politics in the country of origin or the strength with which they identified with the country of origin. Given the increasingly important discussion about transnationalism (Glick Schiller, Basch, and Szanton Blanc 1995) and the post-national citizenship regime (Soysal 1994), it is surprising that this topic has received so little attention.

It is also worth mentioning that we do not observe any obvious cross-time trend in the ways in which scholars have sought to measure immigrant political integration. The only trend we observe is that in the very early years (1955–74), the themes of electoral participation and partisan preferences were predominant, and other themes were quite marginal, but it is worth emphasizing that we identified only nine peer-reviewed articles in this time period.

Let us now turn to what explains immigrant political integration.[10] As seen in Figure 5 below, three broad categories of approach dominate the others in the ways in which scholars have tried to account for variations in immigrant political integration. First, scholars have examined what we call here "acculturation" variables; these include length of residence, proficiency in the language of the host country, naturalization, age at migration, and other variables, such as whether immigrants were educated in the host country and their motivations to stay or aspirations to return. Second, scholars have investigated the role that group characteristics play in the process of immigrant political integration. Under this umbrella, scholars have often asked whether immigrants' race or ethnicity was significantly related to their pattern of political integration; but they have also posed more specific questions, such as the impact of group concentration in a given environment, group socio-economic status, and ethnic group mobilization. Some of these variables also relate to group socialization or identification. In third place, we find that researchers have examined immigrants' individual socio-economic characteristics, such as age, education, and marital status. This category appears as a secondary set of hypotheses, with the rationale behind them often not specific to immigrants. These first three categories of explanation suggest an attempt to understand immigrants from the perspective of their individual and group trajectories in the host country.

We find several other types of explanation far less often examined by immigrant political integration scholars. At the top of this list are "host country characteristics" – examined by 42 studies, or 15 per cent – such

Figure 5. How Have Scholars Explained Immigrant Political Integration?

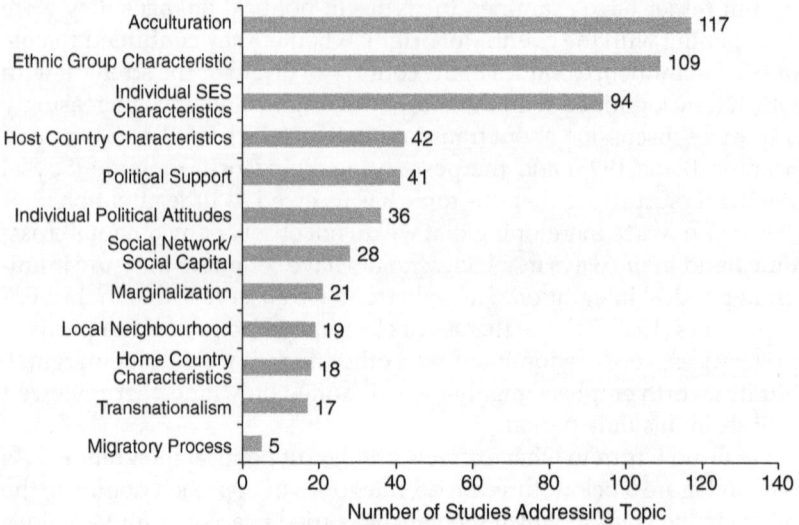

Topic	Number of Studies Addressing Topic
Acculturation	117
Ethnic Group Characteristic	109
Individual SES Characteristics	94
Host Country Characteristics	42
Political Support	41
Individual Political Attitudes	36
Social Network/ Social Capital	28
Marginalization	21
Local Neighbourhood	19
Home Country Characteristics	18
Transnationalism	17
Migratory Process	5

Number of Studies Addressing Topic

as formal regulations (citizenship regimes and laws, diversity and integration regimes) but also contextual variables, such as local hostility towards foreigners, public expenditures, and voter turnout. Here, scholars have tried to understand immigrants' political integration from the perspective of the context in the host country. From a broadly similar perspective, although far less prominent, research has emphasized other characteristics of local neighbourhoods where immigrants live, beyond those relating to the presence of immigrants.

The different emphasis put on individual and group characteristics versus contextual factors is striking, the former being predominant. Part of the explanation for this predominance of individual and group characteristics might actually be linked to the research design of most of the studies over the last decades. Indeed, most studies have actually been case studies, most of the time focused on single host countries, and quite often also focused on single communities. In fact, only eight studies actually employed a design comparing different host countries. Case studies make it difficult to bring in contextual factors as explanatory variables. In this context, the chapter by Helbling et al. appears quite innovative and much needed.

The remaining groups of explanation have been neglected by scholars in trying to understand the factors that structure immigrant political integration. They all share one important characteristic: all four groups refer to realities that are specific to immigrants. First, little has been said about how perceived racial discrimination relates to immigrant political integration. Only 21 studies (or 7 per cent) consider the possibility that in the process of political integration, immigrants react to considerations such as the experience of discrimination and perceived group status in the host country. Yet, as discussed in the chapter by Gidengil and Roy, racial discrimination is not uncommon for immigrants, especially those of visible minority background. It is striking that little attention has been paid to such considerations given the potential they may have in structuring immigrants' political experiences. In the United States, Michelson (2003) has demonstrated the powerful consequences of perceived discrimination on eroding the link of confidence with the host country.

Second, there are few systematic assessments of the impact of where immigrants come from. We tracked 18 studies (6 per cent) investigating the potentially lasting impact of pre-migration experiences. Once again, such a lack of attention appears surprising given the increasing diversity of immigration and the diversity of cultural and political backgrounds that potentially travels with newcomers. Bilodeau (2008) and Bilodeau, McAllister, and Kanji (2010), for instance, highlight how the majority of immigrants settling in Canada and Australia have little experience of democracy and have instead sometimes experienced severe political repression in the country of origin. Jones-Correa and Pietsch and McAllister in this volume follow such an approach.

Third, transnationalism has rarely been studied as a form of political engagement among immigrants; similarly, it has seldom been studied as a potential structuring factor in immigrant political integration. In only 17 studies, scholars have asked what the impact is of holding dual citizenship on immigrant political integration or whether immigrants who maintain strong social, economic, or political ties to the homeland relate differently to political affairs in their host country. This gap in the literature is also somewhat surprising and clearly lags behind the literature that has emphasized the emerging influence of the post-national citizenship regime (Soysal 1994).

Finally, a meagre five studies have focused on the impact of the migratory process itself – that is, the motivation of newcomers for leaving the home country or the administrative migratory status under which newcomers arrived. The lack of attention to this last set of issues is quite striking considering the time and resources that immigrants invest to navigate what could be characterized as the "administrative maze" of immigration admission processes. What might be for the government in the host country just an administrative process is for many immigrants their first real contact with that country. Yet it seems that scholars have never really investigated whether refugees, independent immigrants, or those coming under the family reunification process develop similar relationships with the host country. Scholars have also never investigated whether administrative delays, financial costs, or perceived arbitrary decisions have any short- or long-term effects on the relationship that newcomers develop with the host country.

In summary, the above brief overview reveals a field that has been greatly concerned with issues of mainstream electoral politics. Our review also observed a number of studies asking questions about immigrant-specific situations, such as those relating to what we call ethnic politics, but also more broadly those that examined issues relating to transnationalism and attitudes towards integration. This general focus of the field captures Bloemraad's definition of immigrant political integration, presented earlier, with an emphasis on political participation. The review demonstrated other ways, however, to conceive of immigrant political integration, including a focus on political support. Although far less dominant (only about 40 studies investigated such considerations; see Figure 4 above), this type of questioning is arguably at least as important as the focus on political participation in making sense of the types of relationship that immigrants develop with the host country. The strength of identification with the host political community, the extent of support for core political values, and the level of confidence in the political institutions of the host country are likely to reveal another dimension of the relationship that immigrants develop with the host country and that cannot be revealed when focusing only on newcomers' political participation. The approach is different, however, and might be symptomatic of a greater concern with social cohesion as opposed to immigrants' capacity to articulate a political voice of their own. The field, it seems, would benefit from a stronger emphasis on these dimensions of immigrant political integration as well as on those forms of political engagement that are specific to immigrants.

In terms of explaining immigrant political integration, the field appears to have been heavily dominated by individual-level and group-level characteristics. The explanation for variation in immigrant political integration would likely benefit from a broader approach, one that puts more emphasis on the variety of social, economic, and political experiences that immigrants bring with them and focuses on the context in which immigrants settle. On this latter point, public policy studies in Canada are increasingly devoting attention to documenting and analysing variations in policies relating to diversity at the provincial level (Garcea 2006; Paquet 2013) or municipal level (Good 2009). It is the task of immigrant political integration scholars to investigate whether the types of relationships developed by immigrants with the politics in their host country relate to the context or policies in place where they settle, be it at the local, provincial/regional, or national level.

Of course, it is possible that some of the trends highlighted in this review reflect the biases of the criteria for selecting the studies that were analysed. The studies selected were all published in English and were focused on immigrant political behaviours and attitudes; as a result, they did not include any discussion of immigration policies or integration regimes or a more conceptual discussion of immigrant political integration. In short, the present review offers a behavioural perspective of the field published in the English language. Nevertheless, given these parameters, this Introduction hopes to have set the stage for a better understanding of a significant segment of the field of immigrant political integration and a better understanding of the field about which the 11 chapters that follow were thought of and written, chapters that also purposely adopt a behavioural perspective on immigrant political integration.

NOTES

1   Although the definition of Biles, Burstein, and Frideres addresses the concept of *integration* more generally and not specifically *political integration*.

2   This broader definition is the reason why we prefer the term *integration* rather than *incorporation*, as used by Bloemraad.

3   Not all Anglo-democracies and continental European countries are represented. Including cases such as France, Germany, and Sweden would have made a major contribution. Unfortunately, it was not possible to include them in the volume at the time that it was produced.

4   That is, studies published in English. Given the extensive literature in the United States, Part Two could have focused on that country alone. The predominance of studies focused on the situation of Latinos limits generalizations about other national settings.

5   The term *visible minorities* is an official statistical category of Statistics Canada that refers to whether a person belongs to a visible minority group, as defined by the Employment Equity Act. The act defines visible minorities

as "persons, other than Aboriginal peoples, who are non-Caucasian in race or non-white in colour." The visible minority population consists mainly of the following groups: Chinese, South Asian, black, Arab, West Asian, Filipino, Southeast Asian, Latin American, Japanese, and Korean.

6 This database is limited to peer-reviewed journal articles published on the behavioural or attitudinal integration of immigrants with regard to politics. Accordingly, this list does not include any publications in the form of books, book chapters, doctoral dissertations, or conference papers. The compilation is also limited to journals published in English. Accordingly, the reader should keep in mind any possible bias that such limitation in our coverage may entail. See Appendix A in this volume for more information on our methodology.

7 Beyond the use of quantitative survey data, about 15 per cent of the studies used qualitative analysis, and 32.6 per cent included some sort of quantitative analysis of non-survey data. (These categories are not mutually exclusive.) This includes lists of registered voters, voter data, lists of MPs, official census data, naturalization rates, ecological inferences, voting records of political representatives, a database of campaign contributions by surname, and field experiments using mailings.

8 Each study can have multiple dimensions for measuring immigrant political integration.

9 Results not shown.

10 It should be noted that only those variables were coded for which explicit hypotheses were mentioned.

PART ONE

Immigrant Political Integration in Western Democracies

1 New Voters, Different Votes? A Look at the Political Participation of Immigrants in Amsterdam and Rotterdam

ANJA VAN HEELSUM, LAURE MICHON, AND JEAN TILLIE

Whereas civil and social rights have been granted to foreigners over time, political rights have often been seen as one of the last privileges of a nation's citizens. Currently, however, a majority of European Union (EU) member states offer the possibility to non-nationals to vote: 14 out of the 25 member states have enfranchised foreigners, although often only at the local level (Bauböck 2006, 121). In the Netherlands, this right was granted in 1985 to all non-nationals who had lawfully lived in the country for at least five years. One of the main reasons for granting this right was to promote the integration of immigrants. The argument went that once immigrants had the right to vote, their interest in the Dutch political system would increase. This was seen as beneficial for their integration into Dutch society (Jacobs 1998, 114; Tillie 2000, 12). Of course, not everyone supported the extension of political rights to non-nationals; some feared that immigrants would set up their "own" political parties (on an ethnic or religious basis), a situation that would lead to segregation (see Jacobs 1998, 119).

Were these fears justified? Did local enfranchisement for all non-nationals in the Netherlands lead to political segregation? Or did it contribute to better integration into Dutch society? This chapter examines how immigrants have used their newly acquired political rights in the Netherlands. Three dimensions are examined. First, do immigrants vote in local elections? Second, which party do they support? And third, do they run for office? Most of the findings presented in this chapter have been published in Dutch in various books and articles. With this chapter, we hope to make these results available to a larger scientific audience. The main focus of the chapter is on two immigrant-rich Dutch cities, Amsterdam and Rotterdam. When speaking about turnout and party choice, we will mostly rely on data collected during the last five municipal elections (between 1994 and 2010). To complement our investigations, we also present some evidence about trends observed in national politics.[1]

Four large groups of immigrants are examined: Surinamese, Turks, Moroccans, and Antilleans. We will begin with the Surinamese. A relatively small number of immigrants from the former colony of Suriname arrived in the Netherlands between 1945 and 1960; and a much bigger group came immediately after the independence of Suriname in 1975, but still with Dutch passports. In the 1980s, the community continued to grow, bolstered by immigration, and showed high rates of intermarriage with the native Dutch.

In contrast, it was the booming economy and the need for (cheap) labour in the 1960s that induced the movement of immigrants from Turkey and Morocco. At first, both the government and the immigrants thought their stay would be temporary, but their immigration became permanent as their wives and children also arrived during the 1970s and 1980s. The Turkish and Moroccan communities still grow because of marriage with partners from the country of origin and a relatively high birth rate.

The fourth and smallest group of immigrants examined (see Figure 1.1 below), from the former Dutch Antilles, came a bit later. A change in the status of one of the Antillean islands, Aruba, in 1986 provoked a significant influx.[2] Most immigrants from the former colonies (Suriname and the Dutch Antilles) had Dutch nationality when they arrived in the Netherlands and, hence, immediately had the right to vote and stand as a candidate in national, provincial, and local elections. As for immigrants from Turkey and Morocco, most of them have acquired Dutch nationality by naturalization (or birth), while retaining the nationality of their country of origin (or that of their parents).

Electoral Turnout of Immigrants in Amsterdam and Rotterdam

To begin our investigation, we examine immigrants' turnout in local elections in Amsterdam and Rotterdam. Whether immigrants voted is a helpful indicator of their level of political integration. By voting, immigrants not only indicate a certain level of engagement in Dutch society but also contribute to the legitimacy of the governing authorities. These are critical issues, especially in cities like Amsterdam and Rotterdam, where almost half of the population is of non-Dutch origin. The legitimacy of the governing authorities depends not only on an acceptable

Figure 1.1. Main Groups of Immigrants from Non-EU Countries
in the Netherlands, 2010

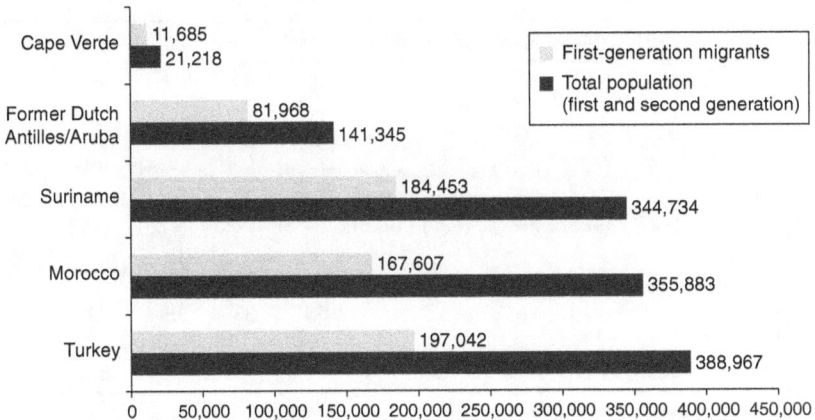

Source: CBS (2010).

level of participation but also on the proportional participation of different groups within society (Kymlicka 1995; Young 2000). Thus, a low turnout of immigrants in Amsterdam and Rotterdam would mean that the governing authorities may not be aware of the preferences of this segment of the population, and such a government would therefore not represent immigrants (Tillie 2000, 83).

Table 1.1 below presents turnout figures for five municipal elections (1994, 1998, 2002, 2006, and 2010) for Amsterdam and Rotterdam. While the table shows some changes in overall turnout in local elections, the changes in immigrant turnout are much more noteworthy. Important, too, are the differences in immigrant turnout between the two cities and among immigrant groups. In both cities overall, there was somewhat of a decline in voter turnout between 1994 and 2010, but it is interesting to note that not all groups were affected equally. The most important trend for the focus of this chapter likely concerns the shrinking gaps in voter turnout between the local population and two immigrant groups. It is worth emphasizing that during the 1994–2010 period, the gaps in turnout between the local population and immigrants from Turkey and Morocco decreased considerably. In Rotterdam, the participation of Moroccan and Turkish immigrants in 1994 lagged behind that of the local population by about 29 and 34 points, respectively, but in 2010,

Table 1.1. Turnout of Immigrant Voters in Amsterdam and Rotterdam, 1994–2010 (%)

Country of origin of voter	Amsterdam					Rotterdam				
	1994	1998	2002	2006	2010	1994	1998	2002[a]	2006	2010[a]
Turkey	67	39	30	51	44	28	42	54	56	46
	(+10)	(−7)	(−18)	(0)	(−7)	(−29)	(−6)	(−1)	(−2)	(−1)
Morocco	49	23	22	37	38	23	33	40	58	47
	(−7)	(−23)	(−26)	(−14)	(−13)	(−34)	(−15)	(−15)	(0)	(−1)
Suriname/ Dutch Antilles	30	21	26	26	26	24	25	31	41	26
	(−27)	(−25)	(−22)	(−25)	(−25)	(−33)	(−23)	(−24)/ 19 (−36)[b]	(−17)	(−22)/ 18 (−20)[b]
Cape Verde	–	–	–	–	–	34	33	25	39	22
						(−23)	(−15)	(−30)	(−18)	(−26)
Overall turnout	56.8	45.7	47.8	50.8	51.3	56.9	48.4	55	57.8	47.6

Sources: Tillie (2000); van Rhee (2002); Michon and Tillie (2003a); van Heelsum and Tillie (2006); van der Heijden and van Heelsum (2010).
a From Centrum Onderzoek en Statistiek, using another research method.
b In 2002 and 2010, these two groups were identified separately.

the observed gaps were only approximately 1 point. This reveals a major convergence of participation. In Amsterdam, the situation is a bit more complicated, but the participation of immigrants from Turkey and Morocco trends towards that of the local population. It is interesting to note that while convergence in levels of participation seems to be occurring for Turkish and Moroccan immigrants in both Rotterdam and Amsterdam, immigrants from Suriname and the Antilles, and also those from Cape Verde, continue to lag significantly behind the rest of the population, by margins of about 20 to 25 points.

The questions thus arise: Why are these changes taking place? Why do they affect two groups more than the others? And why are the changes more evident in Rotterdam than Amsterdam? It is difficult to answer these questions in the context of this study, but we present below some possibilities that would be worth exploring in the future.

First, one might think that the effect of local enfranchisement rights is taking time to materialize; the shrinking gaps over time between the local population and immigrants from Turkey and Morocco would be a reflection of this progressive effect. Similarly, one might reason that given the timing of immigration of both groups of immigrants, by 1994 most had not yet acquired Dutch citizenship, while, in comparison, by 2010 many voters from these groups had likely become Dutch citizens and hence would have a greater tendency to participate. Although these explanations might offer some potential for understanding the cross-time changes observed in Table 1.1, they do not explain why a similar convergence was not observed for immigrants from Suriname, the Dutch Antilles, or Cape Verde.

Another explanation would point to the varying strength and richness of the ethnic network of each group of immigrants. Fennema and Tillie (1999) observed that the stronger the network of immigrant ethnic associations, the greater the political participation of individuals in this group. More specifically, they observed that the Turkish community in Amsterdam had the strongest ethnic network, followed by the Moroccan, the Surinamese, and the Antillean communities (ibid., 721) and that this rank order was the same as that in election turnout, as also demonstrated in this chapter.

This still leaves us with the marked differences between Amsterdam and Rotterdam. In line with the ethnic-network argument, it is important to note (without going into the details of the municipalities' policies) that before 2002, ethnic organizations received less support (through funding, for instance) from Amsterdam than from Rotterdam. The trend in Amsterdam was to develop a broad "diversity policy" that addressed women, youngsters, the elderly, and ethnic groups equally and did not focus specifically on the role of ethnic organizations. Rotterdam, on the other hand, chose up until 2002[3] to actively support immigrant organizations through specific policies and to promote turnout through ethnic organizations. This policy of favouring and supporting local ethnic organizations seems to have had the effect of bolstering immigrant participation in comparison to Amsterdam.

Immigrants' Electoral Choice in Amsterdam and Rotterdam

When they vote, where do immigrants in Amsterdam and Rotterdam place their vote? We will see in chapters 2 and 3 that in Brussels and the United Kingdom, immigrants tend to vote for the Labour Party, and we also know that in Canada, immigrants for a few decades showed a strong preference for the Liberal Party (Bilodeau and Kanji 2010). What do we observe in the Netherlands? Are immigrants also supporting large centre-left parties? To answer this question, the analysis that

Table 1.2. Results for the PvdA in Amsterdam Municipal Elections, 1994–2010 (%)

	Overall	Turks	Moroccans	Surinamese	Antilleans
1994	26	35 (+9)	39 (+13)	48 (+22)	40 (+14)
1998	28	47 (+19)	55 (+27)	56 (+28)	57 (+29)
2002	29	44 (+15)	57 (+32)	62 (+33)	53 (+24)
2006	39	87 (+48)	77 (+38)	81 (+42)	54 (+15)
2010	29	57 (+28)	73 (+44)	54 (+25)	43 (+14)

Note: Numbers in parentheses report the difference in PvdA support compared to overall city results.

follows reports the proportion of support for the large centre-left Partij van de Arbeid (PvdA) among the four immigrant groups and the local population for the 1994–2010 period in both Amsterdam and Rotterdam.

In Amsterdam, as reported in Table 1.2 above – although a close examination of the reported vote reveals multiple and complex movements across elections – a major constant factor in the party choice of immigrant voters is the hegemonic position of the PvdA. All four groups, in all five elections between 1994 and 2010, expressed a strong support for the PvdA; in effect, the PvdA was the first choice of immigrant voters in Amsterdam in all five elections and among all four immigrant groups. The only exception is 1994, when the Turks showed a strong preference for the Christen Democratisch Appel (CDA) and the Moroccans for GroenLinks. The PvdA did not always receive the majority of the vote from each community, but the comparison with the local population in Amsterdam is striking. All four groups of immigrants voted for the PvdA in substantively larger proportions than the local population. For Turks and Moroccans, this greater propensity even increased significantly during the 1994–2010 period from 9 to 28 points and from 13 to 44 points, respectively. For immigrants from Suriname and the Dutch Antilles, although support fluctuated across the five elections examined, their greater propensity overall to vote for the PvdA did not increase as much as it did among the other immigrant groups.[4]

In Rotterdam, the data reported in Table 1.3 below present somewhat similar trends to those of Amsterdam, but also marked differences. They show that during the period covered, the PvdA benefited almost systematically from greater support from the immigrant population than the local population, but it was not always the preferred choice. Indeed, it is not reported in Table 1.3, but a close look at immigrants' preferences

Table 1.3. Results for the PvdA in Rotterdam Municipal Elections, 1994–2006 (%)

	Overall	Turks	Moroccans	Surinamese	Antilleans
1994	25	32 (+7)	27 (+2)	59 (+44)	60 (+35)
1998	30	30 (0)	38 (+8)	71 (+41)	56 (+26)
2006	37	83 (+46)	87 (+50)	86 (+49)	75 (+38)

Note: Numbers in parentheses report the difference in PvdA support compared to overall city results.

indicates that in both 1994 and 1998, the PvdA was not the preferred choice of either Turks or Moroccans. For example, in 1994, the plurality of votes among Turks and Moroccans went to the CDA (36 per cent) and GroenLinks (54 per cent), respectively. This seems, however, to have been a one-time breakthrough for these parties because while it is not shown in the data presented here, Turks and Moroccans were voting in massive numbers for the PvdA before 1994 (Pennings 1987; Rath 1990) and were back to supporting the PvdA in 2006, giving it a huge lead over the other parties. In comparison, voters from Suriname and the Antilles strongly favoured the PvdA in all election years, with very little diversification of party choice.

There seem to be marked differences between Turks and Moroccans on the one hand and Surinamese and Antilleans on the other. While the latter two communities seem to be characterized by stability during the 1994–2010 period, the former two seem to be characterized by significant movement. First, this is true for electoral turnout. Between 1994 and 2010, the participation of Turks and Moroccans converged with that of the local population in both Amsterdam and Rotterdam, while immigrants from Suriname and the Antilles continued to lag behind the local population by significant margins. Second, this is also true for electoral choice. Between 1994 and 2010, Turks and Moroccans voted for the PvdA in increasing numbers, while little movement was observed among immigrants from Suriname and the Antilles. Why? Once again, it is difficult to answer with confidence, but it is worth emphasizing once more that particularly Turks possess much stronger and richer ethnic networks than immigrants from Suriname and the Antilles, and such networks are known to strengthen immigrant participation (Fennema and Tillie 1999). Arguably, the variation across elections in the choice of Turks and Moroccans, as well as their greater participation, might be the result of stronger ethnic mobilization.

Table 1.4. Number of Councillors of Foreign Origin Elected in Local Dutch Elections, 1994–2010 (%)

Country of origin	1994	1998	2002	2006	2010
Turkey	32 (44%)	74 (49%)	113 (55%)	157 (52%)	163 (54%)
Morocco	7 (10%)	21 (14%)	26 (13%)	66 (22%)	66 (22%)
Suriname	21 (29%)	33 (22%)	36 (18%)	38 (13%)	32 (11%)
Dutch Antilles	1 (1%)	8 (5%)	5 (2%)	6 (2%)	7 (2%)
Other	12 (16%)	14 (9%)	24 (12%)	35 (12%)	35 (12%)
N (100%)	73	150	204	302	303

Sources: IPP (2006, 8); Dekker (2010).

Running for Office in Amsterdam and Rotterdam

Expressing a voice by voting is certainly one step in the process of political integration; running for office is another. Table 1.4 above shows the number of immigrant candidates who were successfully elected to public office in the Netherlands between 1994 and 2010. It does not show how many ethnic candidates ran compared to those who were elected, but it nevertheless provides a useful benchmark for assessing immigrants' penetration of elected office.

Table 1.4 shows that significant changes took place in the Netherlands between 1994 and 2010, when the number of immigrant local councillors actually quadrupled. However, we should not overlook the fact that 303 immigrant councillors elected in 2010 still represent only about 3 per cent of the total number of local councillors, substantively below their overall representation in the population. The number of local councillors of Turkish origin, in particular, increased, representing by 2010 more than half of all immigrant local councillors in the country. Not surprisingly, there is an important variation between the countryside and the cities: the bigger the city, the more immigrant councillors were elected to the local assembly (IPP 2006, 8). It is also not surprising that in 2002 and 2006, most immigrant local councillors were elected for the PvdA (in both years, more than 80), something that reflects the strong position of the PvdA described earlier. In both of these years, about 40 councillors were elected for the CDA and 33 for GroenLinks (IPP 2006, 9; ISP 2002).

Looking more specifically at Amsterdam and Rotterdam in Table 1.5 below, it is apparent that the number of immigrants on municipal councils has been growing steadily over time as well.

Table 1.5. Number of Councillors of Immigrant Background Elected in Amsterdam and Rotterdam, 1986–2010 (% of total seats)

	1986–90	1990–4	1994–8	1998–2002	2002–6	2006–10	2010	Number of seats in 2010
Amsterdam	3	4	8	11	7	10	6 (13)	45
Rotterdam	1[a]	2[a]	2	8	9	10	10 (22)	45

Source: For 1986–2002: Berger et al. (2001).
Note: Numbers include councillors who stepped down prematurely and joined a council during a session.
a Estimate only; precise information was not available.

Why are there not more councillors of foreign origin? In contrast to the situation presented by Karen Bird in Chapter 10 regarding visible minorities in local politics in Ontario (Canada), it seems that institutional factors play a crucial role here. Indeed, the answer may lie in part in the selection mechanism of candidates. In their study of the recruitment of municipal candidates for the 1998 elections in the Netherlands, Leijenaar, Niemöller, and van der Kooij (1999, 105) argue that the small number of women and immigrants on the selection commissions explains why few women and immigrants are selected to become candidates. Berger and her colleagues come to a similar conclusion in their study of the political participation of immigrants in four Dutch cities. They examined 14 local selections, and 10 of them had no immigrants on the nomination committees (Berger et al. 2001, 52–3), which were dominated by white and highly educated men aged 50 years or older. Moreover, nomination committees used very traditional means of scouting potential candidates, thereby showing little initiative to look for immigrant candidates (ibid., 53–4).

The key role of immigrant councillors in reaching out to immigrant communities – especially during elections – could mean that the number of immigrant councillors will likely increase in the future. In addition to reporting on recruitment, Berger et al. (2001) documented the experiences of immigrants as local councillors. They observed that immigrant politicians were keenly aware of their position as *immigrant* councillors – and thus capable of attracting votes – and that parties therefore had a rationale to put them forward as candidates (ibid., 69). It was clear, though, that these immigrant councillors did not wish to be seen as representing only immigrants; this has been confirmed by later studies (IPP 2006, 19; Michon 2011, 134–5).[5] But how do immigrant voters view ethnic candidates? And do they vote for them?

"Ethnic Voting" among Immigrant Voters?

The data on immigrant representation in Amsterdam and Rotterdam indicate that significant improvement was made between 1994 and 2010. But is the success of immigrant representatives linked to ethnic mobilization? Are immigrant representatives elected because other immigrants vote overwhelmingly for them? Are these "ethnic votes" – i.e., immigrants voting for a person of the same ethnicity (Lawrence 1974; Rath 1988) – more common among certain immigrant groups? Karen Bird in Chapter 10 presents some evidence pointing to more positive evaluations of candidates when voters and candidates share a common ethnic background. Do we observe the same in local politics in the Netherlands?

As noted at the beginning of this chapter, at the time that voting rights were granted to non-nationals, some observers feared that immigrants would set up their "own" political parties, a situation that would lead to segregation (Jacobs 1998, 119). The Dutch political system allows us to investigate this using a different methodology than Bird because voters can express two types of preferences on their ballot: first, they must choose a party; and second, they can either choose which candidate they prefer from the list of candidates for their preferred party or simply pick the first candidate on the list. Dutch voters often vote for the first candidate on a list. However, voting for a candidate other than the first one on the list can be seen as a more "conscious" vote: the voter chooses not only a party but also the candidate who he or she thinks will best represent him or her. It may be someone the voter knows, or someone chosen because of his or her political ideas, because he is a man or she is woman, or because he or she has the same ethnicity as the voter, and so on. Accordingly, knowing that the Dutch electoral system allows voting for a specific candidate on a list rather than simply for a party, we can investigate the questions posed above by examining the preferences expressed for specific candidates. In this section, we examine whether such ethnic voting has been happening in Amsterdam and Rotterdam.

A simple look at party preferences would lead to the conclusion that immigrants have engaged very marginally in the practice of ethnic voting. There have been ethnic parties (for instance, voters could vote for the Arab Democratic League during the 2006 local elections in Amsterdam), but they have remained very marginal and never able to win a seat on

Table 1.6. Votes for Candidate of Same Ethnicity in Amsterdam and Rotterdam, 1998–2010 (%)

Country of origin of voter	Amsterdam				Rotterdam	
	1998	2002	2006	2010	1998	2006
Turkey	67	75	50	25	82	48
Morocco	40	65	40	19	53	35
Suriname	26	55	11	12	42	40
Dutch Antilles	a	2	2	a	5	2

Sources: Michon and Tillie (2003a); van Heelsum and Tillie (2006); van der Heijden and van Heelsum (2010).
a In 1998 and 2010, there were no Antillean candidates in the Amsterdam elections.

municipal council. As mentioned, the PvdA and GroenLinks have been the most successful in attracting immigrants. When voting for these mainstream parties, however, do immigrants seize the opportunity to vote for a candidate of the same ethnic background?

Table 1.6 above summarizes the figures for ethnic voting for Amsterdam and Rotterdam since 1998. One thing of note is that the proportion of immigrants voting for a candidate of the same ethnic background varies from one election to the other. This may not come as a big surprise because the number of candidates from each group of immigrants may vary significantly from one election to the other. Despite this variation across elections, however, one striking finding emerges from Table 1.6: Turkish voters are systematically the most keen to vote for a candidate of the same ethnic group, followed by immigrants from Morocco and then immigrants from Suriname. The proportion of ethnic votes expressed by immigrants from the Dutch Antilles is very marginal and can likely be explained by the very limited presence of candidates of Antillean origin. Once again, the order from high to low ethnic voting among the different ethnic groups is broadly the same as the order observed for the other dimensions examined in previous sections of this chapter.

Thus, these data provide some evidence of ethnic voting, but some caution is also necessary. The fact that immigrants choose a candidate of the same origin as them from the list of candidates of mainstream parties does not necessarily indicate that the ethnicity of this candidate was a strong motivation for voting this way; in fact, immigrant voters may simply be responding to an opportunity that is offered to them. We do not know how they would have voted had this candidate not been present on the list.

Political Participation in Dutch National Elections

This chapter on the political participation of immigrants in Amsterdam and Rotterdam cannot end without taking a brief look at the
situation in national Dutch elections. Are similar trends observed?
Research into turnout and party choice of immigrants in the Netherlands at any level other than the local level is rare. There is an important difference in who is entitled to vote: only Dutch citizens can participate in national elections. This means that only naturalized Dutch
citizens are enfranchised at the national level. The number of immigrants allowed to cast a vote at the national level has increased every
year since the arrival of the first Turks and Moroccans because the
numbers who acquire Dutch citizenship are increasing. In 2002, about
725,000 Dutch citizens of foreign descent (of all origins) had the right
to vote in parliamentary elections, representing about 6 per cent of the
total electorate (Michon and Tillie 2003b, 128). In 2006, 1.2 million persons originating from the main immigrant countries – approximately
10 per cent of the total electorate – had the right to vote; 235,000 of them
were of Turkish origin, 235,000 of Surinamese origin, 195,000 of Moroccan descent, and 85,000 from the Dutch Antilles (Dekker 2006).

The figures shown in Table 1.7 below on the participation of immigrant voters in Dutch national elections are drawn from the data on the
2006 elections gathered in the streets by marketing research institute
Foquz EtnoMarketing. The table summarizes both the turnout and
the party choice of the different immigrant groups, and the data indicate that 69.7 per cent of voters of foreign origin cast their vote (Foquz
EtnoMarketing 2006). This is higher than the turnout at the local level, but lower than the turnout of the electorate as a whole. Moreover,
there are important differences among immigrant groups: more voters
of Turkish, Surinamese, and Moroccan origin cast their vote than voters of Antillean origin.

As observed for the local elections in Amsterdam and Rotterdam, the
PvdA benefited from the support of immigrants in these elections: it
did better among all groups of immigrants than among the local population and even won the plurality of votes cast by all immigrant groups
examined. In comparison, the CDA received the plurality of votes cast
at the national level. It is interesting that the left-wing SP was also very
successful among all immigrant groups in that year, much more than
among the electorate as a whole, a finding that further supports immigrants' left-leaning orientation. On the other hand, the CDA and

Table 1.7. Party Choice of Immigrant Voters in Dutch Parliamentary Elections, 2006 (%)

Country of origin of voter	Socialist Party (SP)	GroenLinks	PvdA	Social Liberal Party (D66)	CDA	People's Party for Freedom and Democracy (VVD)	Other parties	Turnout	N
Turkey	22	21	36	12	7	3	–	71.5	227
Morocco	18	5	69	2	3	1	3	69.1	187
Suriname	21	8	43	6	13	7	3	74.0	195
Dutch Antilles	24	11	35	7	10	7	8	61.6	153
Election results	16.6	4.6	21.2	2.0	26.5	14.7	14.5	80.35	

Sources: Foquz EtnoMarketing (2006); CBS (2010).
Note: Parties are ordered on a left-right continuum.

right-wing VVD were relatively unpopular among immigrant voters. The different eligible electoral populations in local and national elections, and our limited data for the 2006 elections, cannot make a valid comparison between results at the local level (see previous sections) and the national level. Nevertheless, it seems clear that left-wing preferences (and mainly for the PvdA) among immigrant voters are equally present at both levels.

Despite the greater barriers to immigrant participation at the national level than at the local level, it is worth observing that immigrants have been more successful in being elected to the Dutch Parliament than to the local councils, as reported in Table 1.8 below. It took time, however, to obtain some immigrant representation in Parliament. Some consider that the first member of Parliament (MP) of foreign origin was elected in 1933, an Indonesian Communist representative (Rath 1985, 53). But, at the time, Indonesia was still a colony of the Netherlands. Therefore, others claim that the first "real" immigrant MP was John Lilipaly, a PvdA politician of Moluccan origin elected in 1986. In either case, Lilipaly remained the only MP of foreign origin in the Second Chamber of the Dutch Parliament until 1994. Things changed significantly after the elections that year, when seven MPs of foreign origin were elected: Dutch citizens of Moroccan, Surinamese, and Moroccan origin who ran for Parliament for the PvdA, GroenLinks, D66, and the right-wing VVD. Since then, the number of MPs of foreign descent has

Table 1.8. MPs of Non-Western Origin in the Second Chamber of the Dutch Parliament, According to Origin and Party, 1986–Present

Period of office	Turkish	Moroccan	Surinamese	Antillean	Other	N	%
1986–90					PvdA	1	< 1
1990–4					PvdA	1	< 1
1994–8		GrL, PvdA, VVD	GrL, PvdA	D66	PvdA	7	5
1998–2002	PvdA, CDA, VVD	GrL, PvdA, VVD	GrL, PvdA, VVD		PvdA, GrL	11	7
2002–3	PvdA, CDA (2)	SP, GrL, PvdA, LPF	CDA (2), LPF		GrL, LPF	12	8
2003–6	GrL, PvdA, D66, CDA (2), VVD	SP, GrL, PvdA	PvdA, CDA (2), VVD	PvdA	GrL, VVD, LPF	17	11
2006–10	SP, D66, CDA	GrL (2), PvdA (2)	PvdA, CDA, VVD	PvdA, ChU	PvdA, SP, GrL	15	10
2010–present	SP, GrL, PvdA (2), D66, CDA	GrL, PvdA (2), D66, VVD	PvdA, CDA	PVV, ChU	SP, GrL	17	11

Notes:
Numbers include MPs who stepped down prematurely and those who came in during the period of office.
The number of seats in Parliament is 150.
Abbreviations: ChU: ChristianUnion; GrL: GroenLinks; LPF: Pim Fortuyn List, disbanded in 2007; PVV: Party for Freedom.

been steadily increasing, reaching a proportion of more than 10 per cent of the 150 seats in the Second Chamber in 2010. It is interesting to note that although the PvdA has been a pioneer in putting forward candidates of immigrant background, and immigrants tend to express a strong preference for it, we can see a large diversity of political affiliation in immigrant representatives.

We do not have information on the propensity for "ethnic voting" in national elections, but one case illustrates the potential of such a practice. In the 2006 elections, for the first time, a Turkish D66 candidate managed to obtain a seat in the Second Chamber because of the high number of preferential votes – 34,564 (Dekker 2006). Turkish organizations had called on voters to support this candidate after the debate on "the Armenian issue." (In September 2006, following a discussion on Turkey's denial of the Armenian genocide, candidates of Turkish origin were asked for their position: was it genocide or not? Two candidates from the CDA and one from the PvdA who refused to use the word *genocide* were removed from the electoral lists. D66 refused to position itself in this debate and also refused to ask its candidate of Turkish origin to do so.) The support activities of the Turkish associations were apparently successful.

Conclusion

Since the Netherlands granted voting rights to non-nationals in 1985, immigrant turnout and party choice have been the subject of electoral research. This chapter has presented some of the key trends observed in the cities of Amsterdam and Rotterdam. First, although there have been some cross-time changes as well as differences across groups and between the two cities, it appears that immigrants tend to vote less often than the rest of the Dutch population. Second, immigrants in the Netherlands tend to vote for left parties, mainly the PvdA. Similar analyses exist for Belgium and the United Kingdom (see chapters 2 and 3 in this volume) and for Canada and Australia (Bilodeau and White 2014). We could not examine in detail in this chapter the roots of such preferences, but it seems that their ideology draws immigrants to left-wing parties. (See Chapter 3 on this issue in the context of the United Kingdom.) Third, and linked to the previous point, immigrant candidates seem to significantly attract immigrant voters.

This chapter has presented trends that suggest a certain level of ethnic voting, thus supporting some of the findings observed in Chapter 10 in this volume. Although compelling, the ethnic-voting hypothesis does not really explain why immigrant candidates run in greater numbers for the PvdA than any other party. Is it ideological affinity or a more open selection mechanism? This remains to be seen. Fourth, some significant changes are taking place in the representation of immigrants in Dutch political institutions: the data presented indicate a steady increase in the number of representatives of foreign origin in Dutch assemblies until 2010, both at the local and at the national levels.

The fifth and final important finding concerns the marked differences between the groups of immigrants examined. On all dimensions examined (turnout, electoral choice, candidates, and ethnic voting), immigrants from Turkey and to some extent Morocco appear to have a more distinct profile of integration than immigrants from Suriname and the Dutch Antilles. During the period examined, their level of participation aligned more with that of the rest of the population, their level of mobilization to vote for the PvdA increased, they rallied behind candidates of their communities in greater numbers, and, perhaps not surprisingly, have managed to become better represented in Dutch political institutions. The question is why.

A likely explanation points to ethnic mobilization, and it can be argued that the information presented in this chapter points in this direction. Immigrants from Turkey and Morocco, mobilized in greater numbers through ethnic networks, are voting more often, more homogeneously (for left-wing parties), and for candidates from their communities, and hence they successfully elect more representatives from their communities. We did not demonstrate such processes formally, but the evidence points in that direction. This hypothesis is consistent with other research that has been carried out in the Netherlands by one of the authors, which has shown that there are stronger ethnic networks and ethnic organizations in the Turkish and Moroccan communities than in the others and that they are associated with greater participation and political trust (Fennema and Tillie 1999).

NOTES

1 Earlier research does not allow for comparison because of different research methods and, especially, different definitions of research populations (Pennings 1987; Rath 1990). However, from 1994 on, ethnicity was defined using the same criteria as in the registers of the municipality; thus, it was also possible to measure turnout. Surveys conducted during each election since 1994 followed the same procedure: on the day of the municipal elections, voters leaving pre-selected polling stations were asked to fill out a questionnaire about their party choice and party preferences. To measure turnout, non-response was also registered (see Tillie 2000). The municipality provided the number of (potential) registered voters for each immigrant group in advance.

2 Since then, a growing number of asylum-seekers have arrived, mainly from areas in developing countries (experiencing civil war): Sri Lanka, Iraq, Iran, Afghanistan, Somalia, etc. Since 2000, the number of Chinese and Polish immigrants has increased considerably, as has the number of registered Polish immigrants since the accession of 10 new member states to the EU in 2004. We do not provide evidence for these communities because they are not well represented in the survey instruments used for our

investigation. The term *immigrants* refers to both first- and second-generation immigrants, irrespective of nationality.

3 In March 2002, *Leefbaar Rotterdam* ("Liveable Rotterdam") became the main party on Rotterdam's municipal council. Rotterdam had thus consciously broken with previous policy, particularly regarding integration and the funding of ethnic and/or immigrant organizations.

4 In 2002, the choice of Surinamese voters for local parties (included in "other parties") greatly increased. This was particularly due to the success of Toekomst 21, a local party led by a Surinamese politician that includes other Surinamese as well as Antillean and Dutch politicians. The party was supported by 9 per cent of voters from Suriname.

5 If they encountered specific obstacles in their political careers (half of the respondents said they did), they were in the party, not in the council. Existing networks and specific habits (such as the many meetings and discussion sessions that the Dutch are so keen on) were difficult to cope with (Tillie 2000, 67). However, a large majority of the respondents stated that they had not experienced discrimination (ibid., 68).

2 Is It Really Ethnic Voting? Ethnic Minorities in Local Elections in Brussels[1]

DIRK JACOBS, CELINE TENEY, ANDREA REA,
AND PASCAL DELWIT

Given the important numbers of non–European Union (EU) foreigners who have acquired Belgian citizenship over the last two decades, combined with demographic developments in the major cities, ethnic minorities have become a significant electoral group. This is especially the case in Brussels, the capital of Belgium and of the EU. In the Brussels–Capital Region, 26 per cent of the population is non-Belgian. According to our estimates, about 42 per cent of the population (of 1.1 million inhabitants) is of foreign descent.[2] It is interesting that newcomers of EU origin (who make up half of the foreign population of Brussels) are almost invisible in local politics, whereas immigrants of non-EU origin have recently acquired considerable political clout.

Numerous studies have been undertaken during the last couple of years in Belgium on the link between immigrant associational life and political participation (Jacobs, Phalet, and Swyngedouw 2004; Bousetta, Gsir, and Jacobs 2005) and on the profiles of politicians of immigrant origin (Jacobs et al. 2006), but not yet on party choice or voting patterns among ethnic-minority groups. In this chapter, we present an analysis of voting patterns of ethnic-minority groups in Belgium, making use of exit poll data from the local elections for three municipalities in the Brussels–Capital Region. It investigates whether voters of non-EU immigrant origin have a particular voting pattern. It also examines the issue of ethnic voting. It thus evaluates whether the same patterns can be found in Belgium as those that have been observed in the neighbouring country, the Netherlands (see Chapter 1). This has often been assumed based on scant comparisons, but they can now be empirically assessed for the first time. The comparison with the Netherlands is interesting because that country has a comparable immigration history, political structure, and electoral system.

The broader relevance of the outcome of this Belgian case study for political science theory is situated at the intersection of two debates. First, it contributes to the debate on the voting behaviour of immigrant populations. We know that socio-economic status (SES) is a primary determinant of individual political participation (Verba, Schlozman, and Brady 1995), and it is readily assumed that this applies equally to ethnic-minority group members. Leighley (2001), however, stressed that contextual characteristics such as candidate and group mobilization are equally important in understanding ethnic-minority political participation. Indeed, individuals of lower social status rely on collective mobilization more heavily than individuals of higher social status. Mobilization by immigrants around their ethnicity as a group characteristic is therefore to be expected as a cost-reduction strategy (Verba, Nie, and Kim 1978).

Second, this case study contributes to the debate about the impact of political-opportunity structure on immigrant mobilization. Koopmans et al. (2005) have shown that political-opportunity structures – including discursive-opportunity structures stemming from citizenship models and immigration regimes – shape claims of immigrants, their public representations, and even their mobilization strategies. Given the dominance of the French-inspired republican-assimilationist model in Brussels (Bousetta, Gsir, and Jacobs 2005), in which political mobilization along ethnic lines is largely criticized as leading to segregation and posing a threat to social cohesion, ethnic electoral mobilization is not actively stimulated, but at best condoned. The situation is quite different in urban areas of the Netherlands, where, as discussed in the preceding chapter, immigrant political mobilization has – at least until the end of the 1990s – been actively applauded and stimulated. In line with the literature on discursive- and political-opportunity structures, one can expect that ethnic voting and ethnic mobilization, over and beyond class mobilization, will be less important in the Brussels case than in the Dutch case.

The Advance of Immigrant-Origin Politicians

As a result of their demographic weight, the increased attention focused on the immigrant-origin electorate, and the preferential voting system used in Belgian elections, immigrant politicians of non-EU origin are becoming more and more successful. Since the mid-1990s, the immigrant-origin population (that is, coming from outside the current EU) has been rapidly acquiring Belgian state citizenship (and thus voting rights on all levels) and has been paid increasing attention by political parties in

Figure 2.1. Elected Politicians of Non-EU Origin in Local and Regional Elections in the Brussels–Capital Region

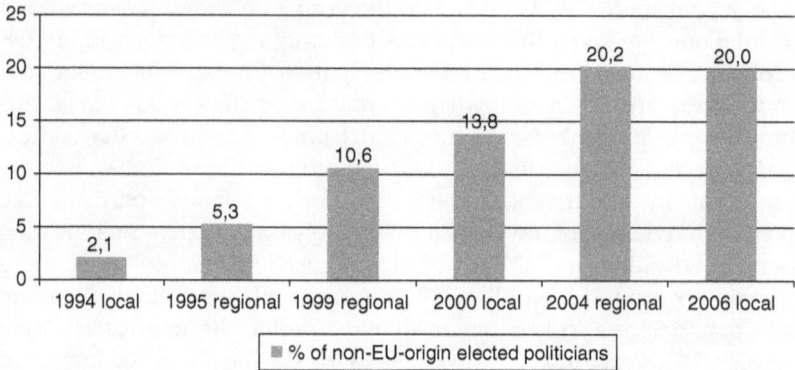

% of non-EU-origin elected politicians

Brussels. In neighbourhoods with high concentrations of immigrants – which tend to overlap with the less desirable parts of the city – parties have waged very lively and intense campaigns. It is interesting that the processes of co-opting immigrant-origin politicians and targeting immigrant voters have taken place in a discursive context, which have, at the same time, condemned *le communautarisme*[3] and depicted ethnic voting as a phenomenon to be avoided (Bousetta, Gsir, and Jacobs 2005).

Figure 2.1 above depicts the steady increase in the percentage of elected politicians of non-EU origin in the local and regional assemblies in the Brussels–Capital Region from 1994 to 2006. The October 2000 elections constituted a landmark in the political participation of immigrant-origin citizens, at least in the Brussels–Capital Region, and there was a remarkable increase in elected Belgian politicians of non-EU origin (Jacobs, Martiniello, and Rea 2002). In the 1994 local elections, of 650 elected councillors, a relatively small number (14) were of non-EU origin (or 2.1 per cent). In the 2000 local elections, however, that number rose to 90 (of 653 elected councillors); most were of Maghreb origin (Jacobs, Martiniello, and Rea 2002). This amounts to a representation rate of 13.8 per cent.

Although the 2000 elections were a landmark in the political participation of immigrant-origin citizens, the results of the regional elections in Brussels in the second half of the 1990s had already signalled the growing importance of immigrant-origin politicians at the local level. Regional elections are now held every five years, but they used to coincide with federal elections, which are held every four years. In the regional elections of 1995, four of the 75 candidates elected to Parliament (or 5.3 per cent) were of foreign origin (three from Morocco and one from Tunisia). After the 1999 regional elections, no less than eight members of Parliament (MPs) were of foreign origin (or 10.6 per cent). All were actually of Belgian-Maghreb origin (seven from Morocco and one from Tunisia).

In the 2004 regional elections, Belgians of non-EU immigrant background once again played a prominent role in electoral campaigns and had some considerable electoral success. Of the 72 francophones elected to the Brussels Parliament, 17 were of non-EU origin. Among them, 12 were of Moroccan origin, two of Turkish origin, one of Tunisian origin, one of Congolese origin, and one of Guinean origin. Of the 17 Flemish members elected, one was of Moroccan origin. In total, 20.2 per cent of the 89 MPs were of non-EU immigrant origin.

In addition, the growing success of politicians of immigrant origin translated into executive power. On the local level, following the 2000 local elections, 12 politicians of immigrant origin (Moroccan, Turkish, and Congolese) became councillors. In 2004, a francophone politician of Turkish origin (Mr Emir Kir) was appointed secretary of state in the Brussels government. At the same time, a woman from Brussels of Moroccan origin (Mrs Fadila Laanan) was appointed minister of French culture, youth and public broadcasting in the government of the French Community of Belgium, while a Brussels politician of Congolese origin was appointed secretary of state for family affairs at the federal level (Mrs Gisèle Mandaila).[4]

In the October 2006 municipal elections, the remarkable success of immigrant-origin politicians – mainly Moroccan – was confirmed in Brussels. Of the 663 local councillors elected, 138 (20 per cent) were of foreign origin, most of whom were of Moroccan descent, followed by politicians of Turkish and Congolese origin. These elections introduced a change in the electoral law, allowing non-Belgians of non-EU origin to cast their vote for the first time (although they could not stand as a candidate). However, we assume that this enfranchisement of non-Belgians was not the main explanatory factor in the ongoing success of immigrant-origin politicians. Of the 42,298 potential voters among "third-country nationals" (i.e., foreigners who were not EU citizens), only 6,622 registered as voters, thus representing only 1.12 per cent of the total electorate.

Ethnic Minorities as a New Electoral Force?

During the debates about the local enfranchisement of non-nationals in Belgium, one recurring topic was which political parties would reap the greatest benefit. It was widely assumed that these would be the left-wing parties, mainly the Socialist Party (PS) and Ecolo (*écologiste*, or environmentalist). Given the increasing demographic – and hence electoral – importance of Belgians of foreign origin in the major cities, almost all parties were already vying for candidates of immigrant background long before third-country nationals were enfranchised. They had apparently all – at least on the francophone side – made the assessment that they could gain from the increase in immigrant-origin voters. For example, by examining the profiles of candidates running in the 2004 regional elections and 2006 local elections in Brussels, one can see a pattern emerging: political parties were carving out a particular ethnic niche for themselves (Jacobs et al. 2006).

Today, the PS clearly has the greatest diversity, even outperforming the environmentalist party, which was the first to put immigrant-origin politicians into prominent positions; the Christian Democratic Party (CDH) is trying to play catch-up and seems to be increasingly focusing on the sub–Saharan African community. The Mouvement réformateur (MR), a francophone right-liberal party, has invested less in attracting immigrant-origin candidates, but it too has competed for immigrant voters. Undoubtedly, this competition explains some of the remarkable success – in terms of descriptive representation – of ethnic-minority politicians in Brussels. The reader needs to keep in mind that this inclusion of immigrant-origin politicians has taken place in a discursive context, one in which all political parties have – rather hypocritically – presented political mobilization on an ethnic ticket as something undesirable. Ethnic-minority voters are supposedly just ordinary voters, just as there is nothing particular about ethnic-minority candidates.

In the remainder of this chapter, we focus on the voting behaviour of voters of non-EU immigrant origin in three municipalities in Brussels during the October 2006 local elections. We want to assess whether ethnic minorities vote for a particular party, but, what is more important, we want to verify to what extent ethnic origin as such is an explanatory variable for voting behaviour. Indeed, voters of immigrant origin might very well be just ordinary voters. Perhaps ethnic origin or migration history has no particular, additional explanatory importance once we take into account structural socio-demographic factors in party choice, such as gender, level of education, and SES. Furthermore, we want to assess to what extent ethnic voting takes place – by which we mean preferential voting for immigrant candidates of the same ethnic origin. To answer these questions, we will make use of exit poll data gathered by the Centre d'étude de la vie politique (CEVIPOL) of the Université libre de Bruxelles (ULB) during these elections.

The CEVIPOL Exit Polls in the 2006 Local Elections

On 8 October 2006, local election day in Belgium, CEVIPOL-ULB organized exit polls in three municipalities of the Brussels–Capital Region: Forest, Schaerbeek, and Molenbeek. During the entire day, voters were polled at random at several polling stations after casting their vote. In a short questionnaire, the CEVIPOL team asked voters about their voting behaviour, a limited number of socio-demographic questions, and a small set of questions on political topics. In total, 533 voters participated in Forest, 427 in Molenbeek, and 592 in Schaerbeek.[5]

Schaerbeek is a municipality with a large, visible Turkish and Moroccan community, whereas Molenbeek is a municipality with a large, visible Moroccan community. Forest has a more mixed ethnic composition (although with an important Moroccan presence) and a larger Belgian population without immigrant background. Taken together, these three municipalities are representative of the northwestern part of the Brussels–Capital Region (often called the Lower Town as it is situated mainly down the slope from the city centre), in which mainly working-class and middle-class neighbourhoods are located and where most non-EU-origin immigrants live.[6] It cannot be claimed that our three municipalities are representative of the entire Brussels–Capital Region, but they do give a good assessment of the electoral patterns in the Lower Town.

We cannot pool the data for the three municipalities to analyse party choice because the main francophone political parties did not participate independently, or in the same combinations, in the three local elections. In Forest, for example, both the MR and the CDH presented a joint list of candidates headed by the incumbent mayor, while they participated separately in Schaerbeek. Moreover, in Molenbeek, the CDH presented a joint list of candidates headed by the incumbent mayor (a member of the PS).

However, our analysis does focus attention on parties linked to one of the four main political positions in the francophone political landscape: the environmentalists, the PS, the MR, and the CDH. Their lists of candidates often (but not always) included politicians from "sister" Flemish parties. After explaining patterns in voting behaviour, we will group all other – often small – parties together for each municipality.

Party Choice by Ethnic Minority

In each of the municipalities, over 90 per cent of the polled individuals have Belgian citizenship (which corresponds to their representation in the overall electorate). Given the small absolute numbers of non-Belgians who were polled, we refrain from discussing in detail the party preferences of non-Belgian voters compared to those of Belgians. We simply note that there is no statistically significant relationship between citizenship type (EU, non-EU, or Belgian) and party preference.

We can, however, examine the voting behaviour of people of foreign origin (but often holding Belgian citizenship) as their numbers are sufficiently large in our samples. This fact in itself attests to the importance of ethnic diversity in the electorate in the three Brussels municipalities under study. We used the citizenship of the mother (at her time of birth) as a proxy for the foreign origin of the voters. Using this indicator, we can identify both the first generation and the second generation of immigrants in our sample.[7]

In the Schaerbeek sample, 56.2 per cent of voters had a Belgian mother, 12.6 per cent had a Moroccan mother (74 cases), and 10.7 per cent had a Turkish mother (63 cases). In the Forest sample, 62.6 per cent of voters had a Belgian mother, 14.7 per cent had a Moroccan mother (78 cases), 3.4 per cent had a French mother (18 cases), and 3 per cent had a Congolese mother (16 cases). In the Molenbeek sample, 51.8 per cent had a Belgian mother, 21.9 per cent had a Moroccan mother (93 cases), and 5.4 per cent had a Congolese mother (23 cases). In the three municipalities, no other origins among the electorate passed the 3 per cent mark. In the discussion that follows, we opt to look at the results only for those groups that have at least 30 cases, and we group the results for the rest into two generic categories (EU origin and non-EU origin).

We see in Table 2.1 below for Schaerbeek that among Belgian voters without immigrant background, the mayoral list (fielded by the MR) was the most popular, followed by the environmentalist party. The MR scores far lower among voters of EU origin, but still achieves the best score. Strikingly, the PS is the leading party among voters of Moroccan origin, while the MR comes a close second. The PS scores equally well among those of Turkish origin, but the MR scores even higher. Among voters of other non-EU origins, the MR is still the largest party, followed closely by the PS. The overall conclusion for Schaerbeek is that ethnic-majority and ethnic-minority groups have somewhat different voting patterns. Ethnic-minority groups tend to support the PS far more than the ethnic-majority group does. The mayoral list scores well in all ethnic groups but highest among Belgians without a migration history and among Turks. Clearly, voters in Schaerbeek of immigrant origin do not vote overwhelmingly for the left.

Table 2.1. Party Preferences According to Origin in Schaerbeek (%)

	Belgian (N = 327)	EU (N = 72)	Moroccan (N = 73)	Turkish (N = 61)	Other non-EU (N = 48)
PS	11.6	15.3	38.4	36.1	29.2
Ecolo	25.1	30.6	5.5	3.3	14.6
CDH	8.0	15.3	17.8	9.8	14.6
Mayoral list (MR)	46.2	34.7	35.6	47.5	31.2
Other parties or void	9.2	4.2	2.7	3.3	10.4
Total	100	100	100	100	100

Chi-square: 79,461; df = 16; p < 0.001; Cramer's V: 0.185 (N = 581 valid cases)

Table 2.2. Party Preferences According to Origin in Forest (%)

	Belgian (N = 324)	EU (N = 87)	Moroccan (N = 78)	Other non-EU (N = 32)
PS	25	26.4	42.3	43.8
Ecolo	28.7	25.3	6.4	15.6
Mayoral list (MR-CDH)	36.4	39.1	33.3	31.2
Other parties or void	9.9	9.2	17.9	9.4
Total	100	100	100	100

Chi-square: 30,376; df = 12; p < 0.001; Cramer's V: 0.139 (N = 522 valid cases)

Table 2.2 above gives the results for Forest. We observe that the mayoral list (a coalition between the MR and the CDH) scores well in all groups. The PS achieves better scores among voters of Moroccan origin and voters of non-EU origin than among voters of the ethnic-majority group and voters of EU origin. We can once again conclude that different ethnic groups have somewhat different voting behaviour. Voters of immigrant origin do not vote solely for the left; an important proportion supports the centre-right list of the incumbent mayor. Compared to the situation in Schaerbeek, the PS needs to lean less heavily on the support of ethnic-minority voters for its overall score, although that support remains crucial.

Table 2.3 below presents the results for Molenbeek, where there seems to be a rather large variation in voting patterns across groups. The mayoral list (the PS in coalition with the CDH) receives overwhelming support from non-EU-origin voters, notably those of Moroccan origin. Support is much weaker among Belgians without a migration background, who tend to support the MR; our exit poll finds that all

Table 2.3. Party Preferences According to Origin in Molenbeek (%)

	Belgian (N = 220)	EU (N = 65)	Moroccan (N = 93)	Other non-EU (N = 47)
MR	45.9	36.9	8.6	10.6
Ecolo	11.4	9.2	7.5	12.8
Mayoral list (PS-CDH)	22.7	38.5	75.3	59.6
Other parties or void	20.0	15.4	8.6	17.0
Total	100	100	100	100

Chi-square: 91,295; df = 9; p < 0.001; Cramer's V: 0.268 (N = 425 valid cases)

support for the far-right party, Vlaams Belang (FN), comes from this "autochthonous" group. One could argue that ethnic-minority groups in Molenbeek vote predominantly and overwhelming for the left.

To sum up, the data for Schaerbeek, Forest, and Molenbeek suggest that there is quite a lot of variation in party preference by different ethnic groups from one municipality to the other. Voters of immigrant origin do not necessarily vote for the left, but the PS often has to rely heavily on them to achieve its overall result. Having an incumbent candidate seems to enable parties to attract the support of some voters of immigrant origin.

Does Ethnicity Really Play a Role in Party Preference?

We have established thus far that there is an association between ethnic background and party preference. Does this also mean that ethnic origin is really a relevant explanatory variable for voting behaviour? Studies of immigrant voting patterns often stop the analysis here, after having done some bivariate test establishing the voting preferences of particular immigrant groups (see Chapter 1 on the Netherlands; also Tillie 2000; van Heelsum and Tillie 2006), but we want to go a step further. Perhaps ethnic origin or migration history has no particular additional explanatory importance once we take into account structural socio-demographic factors for party choice such as gender, education, and SES. Indeed, immigrant voters might have a particular voting pattern that could, for instance, be totally attributed to their educational level or SES. If working-class people are more represented among ethnic-minority groups than among the ethnic-majority group, it should come as no surprise that the PS is able to attract more voters from immigrant-origin groups.

To estimate the impact of several structural characteristics on the vote for a particular party, we made use of multinomial logistic regression. The results were interpreted using deviations (expressed in percentage points) from the overall percentage for each category using LEM software (Vermunt 1997) and following the procedure suggested by Kaufman and Schervish (1986). Table 2.4 below provides an overview of the strength of the effect of each of the structural determinants of voting behaviour. Strength can be assessed through the L^2/df ratio: the larger this number is, the stronger the effect. For Schaerbeek, it is clear that origin has an important impact, one that is even stronger than the effects of education and SES. For Forest, origin has an important impact, comparable to that of education and SES. Finally, for Molenbeek, the effect of ethnic origin dominates all other effects. Thus, it seems that ethnic groups in all three cities do have their own voting patterns independent of educational level and SES.

To gain a better insight into the effect of each of the structural characteristics, we examined the effects of all categories of the different variables on voting behaviour for all three cities in the 2006 local elections. Presented in the tables below, these effects are expressed as percentage-point differences to the overall percentage obtained by each party. In reading these tables, one has to bear in mind that net effects for each predictor are indicated and controlled for the impact of all other predictors in the model. In addition, a difference in the overall percentage of a party should be interpreted in light of the importance of that overall percentage; for example, a difference of 5 per cent for a particular category is of much greater importance for a small party than for a large one.

Without going into detail about all of the results, we can observe that in Schaerbeek (see Table 2.5 below), being of Moroccan or non-EU origin significantly increases the probability of a PS vote. When educational level and SES are kept constant, voters with a Moroccan background are 14 per cent more likely to support the PS. Controlling for all other effects, 34 per cent of voters of Moroccan origin vote for the PS. It was, however, the MR that won the elections among voters of Moroccan origin: controlling for educational level and SES, 40 per cent of voters of Moroccan origin voted for the MR's list of the incumbent mayor. Voters of Turkish origin voted up to 54 per cent (42 per cent average plus 12 percentage points for the "Turkish" effect) for the MR's list, whereas 28 per cent of them voted for the PS.

The evidence for Schaerbeek is quite clear: voters of immigrant origin have a particular voting behaviour, independent of their level of

Table 2.4. Multinomial Logistic Model for Voting Behaviour during the 2006 Local Elections

	L^2	Df	Significance	L^2/df
Schaerbeek				
Gender	3.64	4	0.46	0.90
Education	37.01	12	< 0.001	3.08
SES	39.54	20	0.01	1.98
Origin (nationality of mother)	67.19	16	< 0.001	4.20
	Likelihood ratio chi-square (L^2) = 169,007; df = 52; p < 0.001			
Forest				
Gender	1.90	3	0.59	0.63
Education	19.48	9	0.02	2.16
SES	29.91	15	0.01	1.99
Origin (nationality of mother)	20.32	9	0.02	2.26
	Likelihood ratio chi-square (L^2) = 85,490; df = 36; p < 0.001			
Molenbeek				
Gender	2.57	3	0.46	0.86
Education	8.97	9	0.44	1.00
SES	14.29	15	0.50	0.95
Origin (nationality of mother)	70.44	9	< 0.001	7.83
	Likelihood ratio chi-square (L^2) = 122,915; df = 36; p < 0.001			

Table 2.5. Net Effects of Socio-demographic Variables on Voting Behaviour in Schaerbeek

	PS	Ecolo	CDH	Mayoral List (MR)	Other or void
Average score (%)	19.6	20.1	10.9	42.1	7.3
Origin (significant)					
Belgian mother	−6.21	+5.03	−2.57	+1.11	+2.64
EU mother	−3.58	+12.76	−4.97	−3.98	−0.23
Non-EU mother	+10.66	−5.26	+8.69	−12.14	−1.94
Moroccan mother	+14.51	−15.28	+7.96	−1.48	−5.72
Turkish mother	+9.08	−16.82	+0.99	+12.18	−5.43
N = 577					

Note: Multinomial logistic regression analyses controlled for gender, level of education, and employment and professional status.

Table 2.6. Net Effects of Socio-demographic Variables on Voting Behaviour in Forest

	PS	Ecolo	Mayoral List (MR-CDH)	Other or void
Average score (%)	28.6	24.1	36.4	10.9
Origin (significant)				
Belgian mother	−3.21	+4.25	−0.68	−0.40
EU mother	−1.64	+2.00	+1.50	−1.86
Non-EU mother	+14.38	−6.44	−5.58	−2.36
Moroccan mother	+9.31	−17.28	+3.21	+4.76
N = 514				

Note: Multinomial logistic regression analyses controlled for gender, level of education, and employment and professional status.

education or SES. They do not, however, vote overwhelmingly for the left. The MR's list is able to attract significant support from voters of non-EU origin (as it does from Belgian voters with no immigrant background). In contrast, the PS is heavily dependent on the immigrant vote. The environmentalists seem to be unable to be an attractive option for the non-EU-immigrant voter, although it was one of the first parties to open up its lists to candidates of foreign origin. Compared to the environmentalists, the CDH has more appeal among immigrant voters.

The existence of a typical immigrant vote is confirmed in the data for Forest (see Table 2.6 above). Once again, controlling for level of education and SES, ethnic origin has a significant effect on party preference. The PS profits most from the non-EU-origin immigrant vote, while the environmentalists once again fail to attract the immigrant vote. The list of the incumbent mayor, fielded by both the MR and the CDH, holds its ground among Moroccan-origin voters (gaining 39 per cent of the votes in that category). It is noteworthy that the number of candidates of Maghreb origin was significantly higher on the list of the incumbent mayor (six candidates) than on the environmentalists' list (two candidates), a fact that might have had some impact.

The importance of the ethnic vote is, however, most remarkable in Molenbeek (see Table 2.7 below), where it takes on an entirely different form. The list of the incumbent mayor (PS and CDH) receives overwhelming support from non-EU-origin voters, particularly those of Moroccan origin (33 per cent, on top of an average of 40 per cent), when controlling for level of education and SES. In contrast, the MR has

Table 2.7. Net Effects of Socio-demographic Variables on Voting Behaviour in Molenbeek

	MR	Ecolo	Mayoral List (PS-CDH)	Other or void
Average score (%)	32.5	10.4	40.8	16.3
Origin (significant)				
Belgian mother	+12.47	+0.90	−17.27	+3.90
EU mother	+3.70	−1.15	−1.77	−0.79
Non-EU mother	−18.75	+3.42	+16.34	−1.00
Moroccan mother	−22.75	−2.95	+33.63	−7.93
N = 422				

Note: Multinomial logistic regression analyses controlled for gender, level of education, and employment and professional status.

severe difficulty in appealing to immigrant-origin voters (receiving a mere 10 per cent score). However, it scores quite well among voters with no immigrant background (44 per cent compared to "only" 23 per cent for the PS). The environmentalist party is able to hold ground in all groups, but has to settle for a low overall result.

In all three municipalities, immigrant origin has a significant explanatory importance over and above other socio-demographic factors such as level of education and SES. Although ethnic-minority voters display diversified voting behaviour (they potentially support all parties), they seem to be systematically over-represented among the supporters of some parties (mainly the PS) and under-represented among the supporters of others (mainly the environmentalist party). Therefore, it is clear that particular patterns of ethnic-minority voting are just as present in the Belgian case as in the Dutch case (Tillie 2000; van Heelsum and Tillie 2006), despite the unfavourable discursive-opportunity structures for ethnic mobilization in Brussels.

Another striking finding is the fact that the local context can result in quite divergent patterns. In our three municipalities, the incumbent coalition (or at least the list of the incumbent mayor) does particularly well among voters of immigrant origin. Given that we have carried out the analysis for only three municipalities, we cannot claim that this is a general effect, one that is typical of the immigrant vote. Further research that includes more municipalities (or, if the analysis were to be done for elections other than local elections, more electoral districts) would have to investigate this more closely. What we can safely conclude from our

Table 2.8. Votes for a Candidate of Foreign Origin by Birthplace of Mother (%)

	Belgium (N = 859)	EU (N = 213)	Turkey (N = 71)	Morocco (N = 240)	Other non-EU (N = 124)	Total (N = 1,507)
No	75.7	64.8	21.1	41.7	54.0	64.4
Yes	24.3	35.2	78.9	58.3	46.0	35.6

analysis, however, is that there is indeed a phenomenon of ethnic voting to be observed in the Brussels–Capital Region.

Who Votes for Ethnic-Minority Candidates?

Of all of the participants in our exit polls in all three municipalities, 35.6 per cent cast a preferential vote for an ethnic-minority candidate. As we can see in Table 2.8 above, voters both with and without an immigrant background vote for candidates of foreign origin. It would therefore be a mistake to assume that candidates with a foreign background are only or mainly elected owing to the support of voters who are equally of foreign descent. Of the 537 voters who reported casting a preferential vote for an immigrant-origin candidate, 209 have no immigrant background (38.9 per cent) themselves. Nevertheless, it is true that voters who are of immigrant origin vote significantly more often for a candidate of foreign origin than voters with no immigrant background.[8]

In Table 2.9 below, we present the results of a logistic regression model in which we try to predict who votes for a candidate of foreign origin. Level of education has no significant effect; neither has SES. Younger-generation (18 to 34 years old) and middle-aged (34 to 54) voters are more than twice as likely to cast a preferential vote for a candidate of foreign origin compared to the older generation (55 and older). Controlling for the effect of other variables, those who cast a preferential vote for a female candidate are almost four times as likely to vote equally for a candidate of foreign origin compared to someone who did not vote for a woman. This seems to show that there is a group of voters who deliberately cast a "symbolic" vote with which they want to show that diversity in elected bodies is important (Swyngedouw and Jacobs 2006). Controlling for the other variables in the model, people of foreign origin are still significantly more likely to cast a preferential vote for a candidate of foreign origin than people with no immigrant background. People with a Moroccan mother are 4.4 times more likely, and

Table 2.9. Preferential Vote for Candidate of Foreign Origin in Schaerbeek, Molenbeek, and Forest

	B	SE	Significance	Exp (B)
Origin (ref: Belgian)	–	–	.00	–
EU origin	.46	.18	.01	1.58
Non-EU origin	1.05	.22	.00	2.86
Moroccan origin	1.50	.17	.00	4.46
Turkish origin	2.58	.33	.00	13.22
Age (ref: 55 years and over)	–	–	.00	–
18–34 years	.86	.18	.00	2.35
35–54 years	.88	.17	.00	2.41
Education (ref: university)	–	–	.88	–
Low level	–.15	.18	.42	.86
Intermediate level	–.09	.17	.59	.91
High level (no university)	–.07	.18	.71	.94
Preferential vote woman	1.35	.14	.00	3.87
Gender (ref: man)	–.33	.12	.01	.72
Constant	–2.49	.22	.00	.08

Note: Logistic regression.
R^2 = 0.189 (Cox & Snell); 0.259 (Nagelkerke); Model chi-square = 307,888; df = 11; p < 0.001; N = 1,507

people with a Turkish mother are 13 times more likely, to vote for a candidate with a foreign background than voters with a Belgian mother. Just as in the Dutch case (see Chapter 1; Tillie 2000), ethnic preferential voting is thus an important phenomenon in Belgian elections.

Conclusion

In recent years, immigrant-origin ethnic minorities have become a significant electoral group in Belgian cities. The voting preferences of immigrant groups, however, remained uncharted terrain, leading to all kinds of speculation. In this chapter, we presented the first analysis of voting patterns of ethnic-minority groups in Belgium, making use of exit poll data for the October 2006 local elections for three municipalities in the Brussels–Capital Region. We investigated whether voters of non-EU immigrant origin have a particular party preference, something that cannot be explained by other background variables such as level of education or SES. Our data clearly suggest that ethnic origin has a significant impact on party preferences, over and beyond other socio-structural determinants. Overall, voters of Moroccan origin have a strong tendency to support the PS, but voters of non-EU origin do not systematically vote for the left. Indeed, the environmentalist party seems to have a difficult time winning support from non-EU-origin immigrant groups; it fails where centrist and right-wing parties succeed (for instance, with the Turks in Schaerbeek). Our data seem to suggest that political parties can conquer local ethnic electoral niches. The results also seem to suggest that having an incumbent candidate enables parties to attract a certain amount of support from ethnic-minority voters.

We also investigated the issue of preferential voting for candidates of immigrant origin. People both with and without an immigrant background appear to deliberately vote for candidates of foreign origin. It would therefore be a mistake to assume – as is often the case in Belgian political debate and the Belgian media – that candidates with a foreign background are elected only or mainly because they have the support of voters who are equally of foreign descent. It is, however, correct that immigrant voters are more likely to vote for politicians of foreign descent than majority-group voters are.

In future research, we hope to be able to compare our results with insights into, and empirical results for, the political participation of immigrants in other continental European countries, which have seen an equally substantial increase in the electoral potential of ethnic-minority groups in their urban areas. A preliminary comparison of the Belgian data with the insights from the Netherlands presented in Chapter 1 seems to suggest that ethnic-minority electoral mobilization is a constant phenomenon, regardless of the political-opportunity structure. However, before formulating a final conclusion on this issue, more data needs to be gathered in other European countries. Such data are still relatively rare (limited to the Netherlands, the Scandinavian countries, the United Kingdom, and Germany) and of varying quality, and it sometimes stops short of undertaking a multivariate analysis. While race and ethnicity are common variables to be taken into account in the Anglo-Saxon electoral context (as described in chapters 3 and 8), sociologists and political scientists in continental Europe are only now starting to seriously study the voting behaviour of immigrant ethnic-minority groups.

NOTES

1 This chapter is a modified version of an article published in *Acta Politica* 45, no. 3 (2010): 273–97. We thank the Faculté des Sciences sociales et politiques/Solvay Business School of the Université libre de Bruxelles for

financial assistance in organizing the exit polls. We also thank *Acta Politica* for permission to reprint.

2 There are currently no official ethnic statistics available in Belgium, only figures distinguishing nationals and non-nationals (see Jacobs and Rea 2009).

3 In French public discourse, *le communautarisme* refers to the valorization of cultural difference and the process of mobilizing around an ethnic identity. It has a negative connotation among French political elites.

4 We will not discuss the presence of immigrant-origin politicians at the federal level, but it is worth mentioning that several MPs of Moroccan and Turkish origin have sat in both the federal and the European parliaments since 1999.

5 The results of the exit polls corresponded fairly well to the official voting results. These results are not presented; see the original article for more information (referred to in note 1 above). Nevertheless, the exit poll results do contain a bias in that voters for extreme-right-wing parties are under-represented, whereas environmentalist voters are over-represented. Voters for small Flemish parties also tend to be under-represented. It is impossible to assess to what extent our samples correspond to the actual ethnic composition of the three municipalities as no census or other official population data on ethnicity is publicly available in Belgium (see Jacobs and Rea 2009). However, the characteristics of our samples correspond to what we might expect based on local knowledge.

6 We did not organize an exit poll in the southeastern part of the Brussels–Capital Region (often called the Upper Town as it is situated mainly up the slope from the city centre), where mostly upper-class neighbourhoods are located and non-EU-origin immigrants are under-represented.

7 There is a large overlap between the citizenship of the mother and the citizenship of the father, and we therefore opted to limit our attention to the citizenship of the mother. Cramer's V for Schaerbeek: 0.800 ($p < 0.001$), for Forest 0.831 ($p < 0.001$), and for Molenbeek 0.869 ($p < 0.001$).

8 Cramer's V: 0.331 ($p < 0.001$).

3 British Citizens like Any Others? Ethnic Minorities and Elections in the United Kingdom

SHAMIT SAGGAR

The United Kingdom, in common with many other Western democracies, has witnessed significant immigration during the past half-century. The bulk of this migration was linked to post-war reconstruction and economic labour shortages, attracting a swell of former Commonwealth workers from South Asian, African, and Caribbean sources, in particular. Further chain migration and family reunification, and significant internal demographic growth, have had a significant impact on the ethnic, religious, and cultural diversity of the United Kingdom. Whereas countries such as Canada have followed a model that focuses on *visible minorities* (see Chapter 8), in the United Kingdom the nearest equivalent has been a long-standing policy, media, and political concentration on *ethnic minorities*. Broadly speaking, this refers to immigrants and their offspring from New Commonwealth sources; and from the perspective of data enumeration, the term is an umbrella descriptor of five key, self-defined ethnic categories: Indian, Pakistani, Bangladeshi, black African, and black Caribbean.[1] These ethnic minorities have, in turn, been the subject of considerable debate over race and racialization of British society in a manner comparable to familiar racialization arguments in the United States. Table 3.1 below effectively tracks population change among these ethnic-minority groups going back two decades. The proportion of ethnic minorities in the United Kingdom increased from 8.8 per cent to 14.1 per cent in 10 years, a 60 per cent increase.

These ethnic minorities are, on average, more likely to experience social and economic disadvantage. Their educational qualifications and skills tend to deliver fewer outcomes in labour markets; their residential housing patterns tend to be in less affluent places associated with poorer public services and economic infrastructure; their health experiences

Table 3.1. Ethnic Minorities in the United Kingdom, 2001 and 2011 Census for England and Wales (%)

		2001	2011
Asian	Indian	2.0	2.5
	Pakistani	1.4	2.0
	Bangladeshi	0.5	0.8
	Chinese[a]	0.4	0.7
	Other Asian	0.5	1.5
	Total	*4.8*	*7.5*
Black	African	0.9	1.8
	Caribbean	1.1	1.1
	Other black	0.2	0.5
	Total	*2.2*	*3.4*
Mixed/multiple ethnic groups		1.4	2.2
Other ethnic groups		0.4	1.0
Total		8.8	14.1

Source: UK ONS (2001, 2011).
[a] Comparability issues exist among these ethnic groups for the 2001 and 2011 census.

and outcomes remain below those of their white peers; and, of course, they also continue to be affected by discrimination and prejudice, which separates them in another way from whites (Speaker's Conference 2009). But, as ever, these "on average" pictures can and do mislead, with some minorities far more likely to experience social exclusion, weak progression, and discrimination than others.

The assumption remains that these differences signify important distinctions about the long-term political integration of ethnic minorities into the democratic system. At the very least, the distinctiveness of minorities in social, economic, and cultural realms is thought to affect the way that they think about politics, elections, and democracy. More specifically, it is often thought that ethnic minorities are not characterized by the same kinds of political participation and representation as the white majority. This chapter presents some basic evidence and discussion regarding three dimensions of ethnic minorities' political integration in the United Kingdom. First, are they registered to vote, and do they vote? Second, of those who participate in national elections, for whom do they vote and why? And third, do ethnic minorities tend to run for office and become elected, for which parties, and why are they not more numerous?

Voter Registration and Turnout among Ethnic Minorities
in the United Kingdom

The place to begin the investigation is with ethnic minorities' registration to vote and actual turnout level. Traditionally speaking, there have been basic questions concerning their involvement in the democratic process, which begin with legal eligibility. The United Kingdom remains something of an outlier in that it has granted full political rights to postwar New Commonwealth immigrants because many held British citizenship at the point of settlement and thus the accompanying privileges – i.e., political rights. As a result, political participation and integration debates between the 1950s and 2000s have been mostly devoid of concerns about such rights. Moreover, potential voter registration and turnout among these groups have been closely monitored, chiefly because regular and vocal claims have been made about the electoral influence of ethnic-minority groups. In essence, political parties have largely internalized the suggestion that an "ethnic vote" can be identified and courted, as seems to be also the case in the Netherlands (Chapter 1) and Belgium (Chapter 2). This suggestion stands up only to the extent that such ethnic-minority voting groups exhibit registration and turnout rates that compare favourably with their white counterparts. Finally, early empirical studies of ethnic-minority voting pointed to quite considerable variations in registration and turnout among and within ethnic minorities; such variance, inevitably, affected calculations about their electoral influence (Saggar 2000).

Table 3.2 below sets out the picture from the general election in May 2010. Using the ethnic-minority survey over-sample, and using data from the British Election Study (BES) and Ethnic Minority British Election Study (EMBES), a picture of electoral participation can be drawn that enables formal comparison across ethnic lines. Two observations stand out with regard to electoral registration. First, overall, ethnic minorities tend to have fairly high levels of electoral registration. Given the disadvantaged socio-economic profiles of ethnic-minority groups, we could have expected much larger gaps in registration levels compared with the white population. Second, variation among ethnic-minority groups is evident from these data, confirming earlier studies and suggesting the need for parties to mobilize each ethnic-minority group using a unique strategy. More specifically, we observe that black Africans are by far the least likely to be registered for voting; for example, only

Table 3.2. Validated Registration and Validated Turnout, 2010 General Election, United Kingdom (%)

	Registered at current address[a]	Voted[b]
Indian	78	78
Pakistani	78	78
Bangladeshi	73	78
Black Caribbean	72	75
Black African	59	73
White	90	78

Sources: BES (2010); EMBES (2010).

[a] Other remaining survey responses were as follows: Reported being registered at another address/Not registered at current address/Other (unable to verify data).

[b] Weighted percentages (using separate weights for the BES and EMBES), unweighted numbers, and respondents who were not registered at the address have been excluded from the base.

about 59 per cent were registered for the 2010 elections. In comparison, all other ethnic-minority groups (Indian, Pakistani, Bangladeshi, and black Caribbean) present levels of registration in the low and high 70s. Registration is about 90 per cent for white people.

While we observe significantly lower registration levels among ethnic minorities and also significant variation across ethnic-minority groups, we observe little variations in voter turnout among whites and all ethnic minorities. Of the five ethnic-minority groups analysed in respect of self-reported turnout rates, the differential is just 5 per cent (73 to 78). Three ethnic-minority groups (Indian, Pakistani, and Bangladeshi) actually report turnout levels similar to the white population. Only blacks (African and Caribbean) report levels marginally lower than for the white population.

Of course, sitting behind formal electoral participation is the murkier question of political awareness, interest, and civic-mindedness. Many social capital theorists have emphasized these underlying building blocks of formal participation (Krishna 2002; Putnam 1995), and, in the case of some ethnic minorities, there has been a long-standing suggestion that patchy registration and turnout might reflect a degree of political disengagement (Letki 2008).

Table 3.3 below sketches some evidence regarding general levels of support for democracy alongside a range of civic values held by ethnic-minority groups from a study by Heath and Khan using the 2010 EMBES (2012). Their findings reveal significant variations among ethnic-minority groups in levels of satisfaction with democracy and political trust. On the

Table 3.3. Satisfaction with Democracy and Political Trust[a] (%)

	Very or fairly dissatisfied with democracy	Agree that parties are interested only in votes	Distrust Parliament	Distrust politicians	Distrust police	N
Mixed	52	46	54	58	32	93
Black Caribbean	49	53	51	61	38	594
Indian	25	37	29	36	18	586
Pakistani	23	41	29	38	17	667
Bangladeshi	20	39	23	31	17	270
Black African	24	49	28	36	23	524
All minorities	30	44	34	42	23	2,782
White British	37	n/a	44	54	18	2,761

Sources: For table: Heath and Khan (2012); for statistics: BES (2010); EMBES (2010), currently unweighted.
[a] Trust questions were rated on a scale of between 0 (no trust) and 10 (a great deal of trust); higher percentages reflect those reporting less trust than the midpoint – i.e., scoring lower than 5.

one hand, most ethnic-minority groups actually display less dissatisfaction with democracy than their white counterparts, by margins of 12 to 17 percentage points. On the other hand, black Caribbean and those of mixed ethnic backgrounds are substantively more dissatisfied – sometimes twice as much – than whites and other ethnic-minority groups. On trust in politicians and Parliament, these same intra-minority variations are quite startling. The findings reported in Table 3.3 are important as they suggest that although voter registration may be lower among many ethnic-minority groups – especially black Africans – this does not seem to reflect dissatisfaction or cynicism with the political system. One could argue that this greater satisfaction with democracy helps compensate for the negative impact that these groups' disadvantaged socio-economic profile might have on their political engagement. This raises the question of where such positive evaluations of the political system come from, a question that Pietsch and McAllister attempt to answer in the Australian context (see Chapter 5).

The "Iron Law": Ethnic Minorities' Long-Standing Support for the Labour Party

Once registered and able to vote, for whom do ethnic minorities vote? The evidence accumulated over the years has shown that ethnic minorities and white voters are significantly different from one another in

Figure 3.1. Official Electoral Results and Ethnic Minorities' Vote for the Labour and Conservative Parties in the United Kingdom, 1974–2010

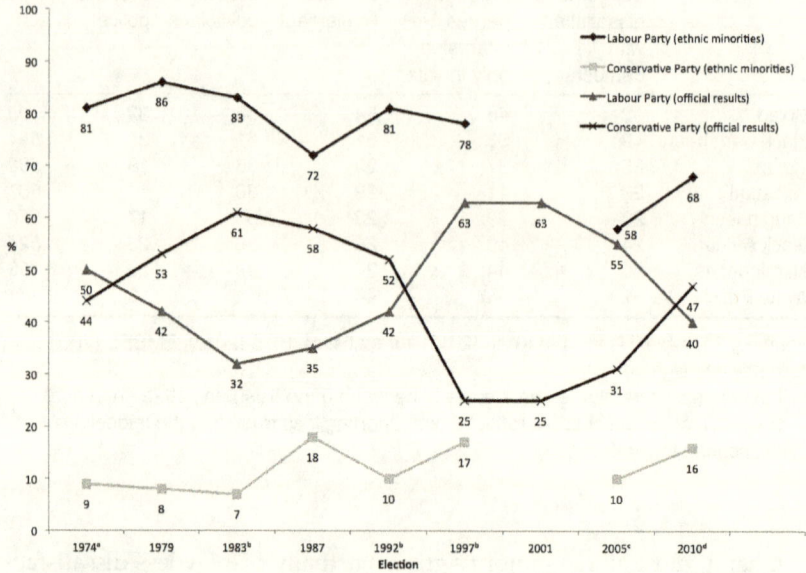

Sources: Adapted from Saggar (2000); UK Electoral Commission (2005); Heath and Khan (2012).
[a]   October 1974 general election.
[b]   Figures represent recalculated average of Asian and black support levels.
[c]   Respective shares of three-party split (Labour, Conservative, Liberal Democrat).

their voting preferences, the former preferring in large proportion the Labour Party. This phenomenon has been referred to – in my own work – as the "iron law" of ethnic-minority voting patterns (see Saggar 2000). As indicated in Figure 3.1 below, in all national parliamentary elections going back to the mid-1970s (the period for which reliable data has been gathered), somewhere around four in five ethnic minorities who registered and turned out to vote supported the Labour Party.

Most recently, a more in-depth data investigation for the 2010 British election presents some evidence consistent with the above claim. Table 3.4 below describes the overall breakdown of the national vote by ethnic-minority group, drawing on the 2010 BES and its over-sample of ethnic minorities. Overall, we can see that the average share of ethnic-minority votes in favour of Labour remained close to 7 in 10, although,

Table 3.4. Reported Vote Shares by Ethnic-Minority Group, 2010 General Election, United Kingdom (%)

	White	All ethnic minorities	Indian	Pakistani	Bangladeshi	Black Caribbean	Black African
Labour	31	68	61	60	72	78	87
Conservative	37	16	24	13	18	9	6
Liberal Democrats	22	14	13	25	9	12	6
Other	11	2	2	3	1	2	1
N (unweighted)	2,805	2,787	587	668	270	597	524
N of voters	2,125	1,768	409	449	185	371	298

Sources: For whites: BES (2010); for ethnic minorities: EMBES (2010).

of course, the variance around this average was considerable: from almost 9 in 10 (black African voters) to just 6 in 10 (Indians and Pakistanis). Nevertheless, the structural hallmarks of the iron law remained recognizable – ethnic-minority voters backed the Labour Party with more than twice the intensity of their white counterparts. In this regard, Labour's bond held, especially given the steep decline in the party's national fortunes in the run-up to the 2010 defeat (down from 55 per cent in 2005 to 40 per cent in 2010 in the national official results).

This was (and remains) undoubtedly an astonishing level of partisanship since it is hard to imagine any other socio-demographic subgroup of the population backing one party to the extent that ethnic minorities have embraced Labour. This bond is further reinforced when account is made for the fact that this lengthy period comprises a number of electoral defeats for Labour as well as a lengthy period (1979–97) of electoral wilderness for the party. Put another way, ethnic-minority voters have remained loyal to Labour in good years and bad, and they have shown a degree of resilience that has been largely unaffected by the changing mood of the electorate as a whole. In short, ethnic minorities have been the most loyal of loyal, thereby ensuring that Labour's electoral failures, however serious, have not become irrecoverable electoral routs. A similar pattern of preferences for large centre-left parties – although generally not at these high levels – is observed in other Western democracies, including the Netherlands (see Chapter 1), Belgium (see Chapter 2), Canada (see Bilodeau and Kanji 2010), and Australia and New Zealand (see White, Bilodeau and Nevitte 2015). This is an important interim finding of comparative research and is worthy of further exploration to analyse the structural underpinning of social and political sentiment among immigrants and ethnic minorities in such democracies.

In light of such strong and long-standing Labour support among ethnic minorities in the United Kingdom, the question is as first articulated by the late Le Lohe (1998): when might the iron law become strained and/or be broken? The most striking response is that long-run backing for Labour is subject to the long-run rise and fall of the electoral fortunes of the major parties. Certainly, the erosion of Labour's large lead would be considerably less likely against the backdrop of the party's significant electoral dominance starting in the mid-1990s and ending towards the late 2000s. Another way of describing the conditions necessary for erosion, therefore, would be to identify a period in which there has been general Conservative electoral revival. Le Lohe (1998) specifically argued that the broad revival of Tory (and Labour's other opponents') fortunes would be the largest influence affecting ethnic minorities' voting preferences. Such a distinctive spell has been pinpointed after the 2005 general election, culminating in the Conservatives' partial national victory and the formation of a coalition administration in spring 2010. And this pattern of Conservative momentum has been significantly extended in 2015. According to this line of argument, then, we would expect some degree of Tory breakthrough to be apparent when examining the voting patterns of ethnic minorities in that particular national election.

Data for the 2010 election, however, contain scarcely any proof of a Tory breakthrough among ethnic minorities, as indicated in Table 3.4 and in Figure 3.1 above. The only exception is in the one-in-four level of support for the Conservative Party among the Indian electorate. Indians are numerically larger than other ethnic minorities (around a quarter of this electorate) and more geographically dispersed, thereby creating a larger impact on Tory revival efforts in 2010 and its further gains in 2015. The anatomy of the Indian electorate's relationship with the Conservatives is the subject of considerable interest and research, some of which has been to estimate how much it reflects general socio-economic class interests (Saggar and Heath 1999). But, by 2010, this partial breakthrough amounted to a quite modest harvest for the Conservatives, who, on and off, have been committed to broadening their support among ethnic minorities for over three decades (*Economist* 2012).

Another question, then – first advanced by Anthony Messina (1998) – interrogates the reasons for this enduring loyalty of ethnic minorities' partisan support for the Labour Party. Different explanations may account for the party's success. A first one posits that the long-standing position of the party is closer than its rivals in temperament and empathy to Britain's ethnic minorities and their concerns. For instance, in addressing racial discrimination, it has been Labour that, in government, has sponsored important extensions of anti-discrimination law from 1965 (the first Race Relations Act) through 1968 (inclusion of the job and housing markets) and 1976 (introducing a ban on indirect discrimination) to 2010 (the Equality Act, which contains further powers to build proactive equality capacity in public bodies). Asian and black voters may have been sensitized to this fact and, as a consequence, been prepared to reward Labour electorally. Otherwise, the party has tended to be seen as more liberal on issues of immigration, even though, of course, it has regularly acted and led in a restrictionist manner (e.g., the 1968 Kenyan Asian crisis, the 2007 introduction of the points-based migration system). The upshot, according to this explanation, is that Labour has been more ethnic minority–friendly.

One strict interpretation of this perspective is that ethnic minorities are therefore driven by a minority political agenda that is distinct and separate from the agendas of others. Another interpretation is that the ethnic-minority experience informs and nourishes a certain prism through which all political issues and concerns are understood (Saggar 2000). Those issues and concerns are typically common across the electorate, but, in the case of ethnic minorities, they add an additional twist that ensures a crucial difference. Bilodeau and Kanji (2010) proposed a similar explanation for the Canadian case, suggesting that, for many years, the Liberal Party of Canada may have "owned" the issue of immigrants and ethnic minorities.

A second explanation has built on this argument but rather characterized Labour's success as a reflection of Conservative failure. In particular, the Tories' own efforts to groom support among ethnic minorities have been undermined by the voices of an unreconciled strand of opinion that have rejected mass immigration and spoken in most ethnic minority–unfriendly terms. In Tory circles, this strand has been periodically large and vocal, often referred to as "sub-Powellite" after Enoch Powell, a notable anti-immigrant champion within the party in the late 1960s. This tenet has been coupled with a strain of English nationalism that has certainly been off-putting to younger, darker, and female voters. In some books, such a strain has been a reflection of outdated values and outlooks that have little credibility in shaping winning electoral strategies in an ethnically plural, cosmopolitan Britain (Ashcroft 2012). Some have pointedly argued that these have been the same elements that resulted in the party being seen as the "nasty party" of British politics. In particular, Labour has prospered as a result of the Conservative Party's periodic obsession with matters of race and with tough grassroots language that openly criticizes efforts to secure a multi-ethnic national identity (*Economist* 2012). The result is that Labour's dividend has been largely unearned, and its long-run sustainability therefore lies not in its own hands. Recent wholesale efforts to modernize the Conservatives and establish greater direction from the party's central leadership are an obvious threat to Labour's enjoyment of this dividend.

A third account has been couched in terms of Labour's historic attachment to issues of disadvantage and to its purpose in tackling social injustice – core Labour values. Ethnic minorities have been drawn to the party that best encapsulates the experiences of those excluded and hampered by discrimination, bias, and hidden unfairness. It is similar to the claims of any progressive-left party to speak for the voiceless. The historic exclusion and bias experienced by women is another basis for the party's special claim to represent the political interests of the disadvantaged. Therefore, Labour's strong electoral lead among ethnic minorities, according to this account, is a reflection of values and purpose. It means that the party may carry on enjoying a bounty so long as the politics of social exclusion and disadvantage remain salient currency in British politics. That said, the bond is not without checks and balances. These may result from Labour's rivals seeking to borrow similar if not identical values and priorities. Equally, Labour's dilution of its traditional class consciousness can also weaken its appeal to disadvantaged groups, such as ethnic minorities.

A final explanation is closely linked to the third, and it centres on the traditional ties between Labour and working-class interests and voters. This is especially relevant in relation to ethnic minorities, who are more likely than their white counterparts to occupy lower or weaker occupational roles and socio-economic positions. Labour's lead would therefore largely reflect this socio-economic context and also its appeal to such interests. In this sense, the iron law would have very little to do with ethnic or racial considerations and would merely be the by-product of social class structures and sensitivities in contemporary Britain. Data presented in Table 3.5 below tend to discard this class explanation, however, indicating quite clearly how ethnic background appears to trump social class background.

Table 3.5. Relationships between Vote and Manual/Non-manual Occupational Class, 2010 General Election, United Kingdom – White and Ethnic-Minority Voters Compared (%)

	White voters		Ethnic-minority voters	
	Non-manual	Manual	Non-manual	Manual
Labour	24	36	68	73
Conservative	44	34	15	13
Liberal Democrats	26	21	15	13
Other	6	9	2	1
N	2,125		1,768	

Sources: For whites: BES (2010); for ethnic minorities: EMBES (2010).

Ethnic Minorities in Westminster

To begin our investigation into ethnic minorities' representation in Westminster, it is helpful to remind ourselves of the current picture at the national parliamentary level and the changes over the past quarter-century. Table 3.6 below presents the descriptive results from a study by Cracknall (2012), presenting the names and party affiliations of the 28 ethnic-minority members of Parliament (MPs) in January 2012, the bulk of whom were returned in the May 2010 general election.

While 17 of the 28 ethnic-minority MPs represent the Labour Party, 11 represent the Conservative Party. In terms of ethnic background, of these 28 representatives serving at Westminster, 18 came from a South Asian background; the remaining 10 were from a black African or Caribbean background.

But the interesting aspect of this group of 28 is that it is composed of several cohorts elected to Parliament in general and by-elections over more than 25 years, thereby gradually expanding the overall levels of ethnic-minority presence in the national legislature. But within this story has been the particular surge in Conservative ethnic-minority MPs (11 of whom were returned in 2010, contrasting with the much earlier foothold and expansion among Labour black and Asian MPs). A further point of significance is that these Conservative MPs have made breakthroughs that broadly align with their party's geographic areas of strength and that, in turn, tend to have very low or modest levels of ethnic-minority residents. Table 3.7 below tells the story: 10 of the 11 Conservative ethnic-minority MPs have been elected in constituencies

Table 3.6. Ethnic Minorities in Parliament, January 2012

Name		Constituency	Party
Abbott	Diane	Hackney North and Stoke Newington	Labour
Afriyie	Adam	Windsor	Conservative
Ali	Rushanara	Bethnal Green and Bow	Labour
Chishti	Rehman	Gillingham and Rainham	Conservative
Grant	Helen	Maidstone	Conservative
Gyimah	Sam	East Surrey	Conservative
Hendrick	Mark	Preston	Labour
Javid	Sajid	Bromsgrove	Conservative
Khan	Sadiq	Tooting	Labour
Kwarteng	Kwasi	Spelthorne	Conservative
Lammy	David	Tottenham	Labour
Mahmood	Khalid	Birmingham Perry Barr	Labour
Mahmood	Shabana	Birmingham Ladywood	Labour
Malhotra	Seema	Feltham and Heston	Labour
Nandy	Lisa	Wigan	Labour
Onwurah	Chi	Newcastle Central	Labour
Patel	Priti	Witham	Conservative
Qureshi	Yasmin	Bolton South East	Labour
Sarwar	Anas	Glasgow Central	Labour
Sharma	Alok	Reading West	Conservative
Sharma	Virenda	Ealing Southall	Labour
Singh	Marsha	Bradford West	Labour
Ummuna	Chuka	Streatham	Labour
Uppal	Paul	Wolverhampton South West	Conservative
Vara	Shailesh	North West Cambridgeshire	Conservative
Vaz	Keith	Leicester East	Labour
Vaz	Valerie	Walsall	Labour
Zahawi	Nadhim	Stratford upon Avon	Conservative

Source: Cracknall (2012).

Table 3.7. Ethnic Diversity of Constituencies Represented by Ethnic-Minority MPs, 2010

Percentage of ethnic-minority residents	Party	0–10%	10–20%	20–40%	Above 40%	Total
	Labour	2	3	4	7	16
	Conservative	10	–	1	–	11

Source: Sobolewska (2013).

Table 3.8. Ethnicity of MPs Elected in General Elections, 1987–2010

Year	Labour	Conservative	Liberal Democrat	Other	Total
White					
1987	255	376	22	23	646
1992	266	335	20	24	645
1997	409	165	46	30	650
2001	400	166	52	29	647
2005	342	196	62	31	631
2010	242	295	57	29	623
Non-white					
1987	4	0	0	0	4
1992	5	1	0	0	6
1997	9	0	0	0	9
2001	12	0	0	0	12
2005	13	2	0	0	15
2010	16	11	0	0	27
Totals					
1987	229	376	22	23	650
1992	271	336	20	24	651
1997	418	165	46	30	659
2001	412	166	52	29	659
2005	355	198	62	31	646
2010	258	306	57	29	650

Source: Cracknall (2012).

made up of between 0 and 10 per cent minorities. By contrast, 7 of the 16 Labour ethnic-minority MPs represent seats that have over 40 per cent levels of minority concentration.

Table 3.8 above, meanwhile, describes the broad trends in ethnic-minority representation at the national parliamentary level from 1987 onwards. The data present a clear increase in the number of ethnic-minority MPs, moving from 4 to 16 for the Labour Party, and from 0 to 11 for the Conservative Party, between 1987 and 2010. While the increase for the Labour Party appears to have been progressive, it appears spectacular for the Conservative Party, jumping from 2 to 11 between the 2005 and 2010 elections. This change in Conservative ethnic-minority MP representation may be the result of the emerging party leadership, internal disciplinary management and the priority attached to widening the social profile of the Tories in Parliament.

Although it is increasing, ethnic-minority representation in the United Kingdom remains disproportionately below that of white citizens. Indeed, while representing about 15 per cent of the national population, in 2010 ethnic-minority MPs still only represented about 4 per cent of all MPs in Westminster. The question is, why are ethnic minorities less likely to run for office and then to be elected? As explained by Bird in Chapter 10, the answer to this question can be divided between what can be called "supply" and "demand" factors – that is, ethnic minorities' willingness to run for office and their acceptance by the parties and the population.

Put together, ethnic minorities have made inroads as elected representatives of major parties in national electoral politics. This can also be assessed from the perspective of their respective parties' strength in the national legislature. For Labour, the current group of 17 MPs amounts to 6.6 per cent of the total – although it should be remembered that the absolute number of Labour MPs is lower than that of the Tories as the party is currently in Opposition. For the Tories, their 11 ethnic-minority MPs make up just 3.6 per cent of the party's parliamentary ranks.

Ethnic-Minority MPs: Supply-Side Considerations

On the supply side, it is not difficult to see that the supply of minorities may be affected by underlying factors. For instance, different ethnic minorities have rather different levels and forms of human capital; these condition their overall chances to access and succeed in employment markets generally and in certain sectors of employment specifically, such as the legal profession or journalism, which are traditionally aligned with political recruitment (Bell and Casebourne 2008; Clark and Drinkwater 2007). Related to this, ethnic minorities can also experience a poor skills mismatch with what is known about successful political candidacy and active career management. An early parliamentary shadowing scheme sponsored by Operation Black Vote and the Electoral Commission found that this difficulty was compounded by poor levels of political knowledge and strategic awareness about the candidate-recruitment patterns and practices of political parties (Saggar 2001). Finally, it has also been suggested that some ethnic-minority family structures and cultural norms add limited value to the pursuit of a political career, but this has yet to be demonstrated.

To these factors can be added day-to-day financial barriers, which can result in would-be candidates being deterred because they cannot meet out-of-pocket costs. In many respects, such circumstantial obstacles mirror those identified by Emily's List, an influential campaign group that routinely awarded small bursary-type awards to female candidates seeking parliamentary nominations during the 1990s and 2000s. The essential point is that a number of practical barriers can act to limit the overall numbers of candidates, although they are often able to sustain several bids to acquire a parliamentary nomination (IfG 2011). In addition, there can be other, less tangible barriers that restrict the support, confidence, backing, and ultimately expectations of "making it" in national political life. A recent study of women in the Conservative Party highlighted the continuing problem of potential candidates seeing themselves in background, supportive roles as opposed to a potential candidate-representative role (Childs and Webb 2011). These softer, indirect conditioners have not been assessed systematically in respect of ethnic-minority potential candidates, but it is prudent to assume that their reach in certain cases may be significant.

Ethnic-Minority MPs: Demand-Side Considerations

Turning to the demand side of the equation, several factors stand out. Chief among these is the role and posture of political parties themselves (Stegmaier, Lewis-Beck, and Smets 2012). More specifically, parties can limit the underlying level of demand for particular kinds of candidates on the basis of existing beliefs and assumptions about the ideal type of political candidate and/or the roles and pathways that suit particular kinds of would-be candidates. In the Conservative Party, these have combined historically to limit the scope for female candidates, and until the selection processes leading to the 2010 general election, these norms remained largely unchallenged by the national party leadership. Jo Silvester's work (2009) has demonstrated the importance of introducing – with national leadership – fresh, objectively defined competency frameworks to even out the effects of pre-existing beliefs and prejudices among party members and managers.

In the Labour Party, ethnic-minority hopefuls who have found their aspirations channelled towards seeking nominations in seats with large ethnic-minority electorates have felt the biggest consequences. The fact that such seats have grown in number as the voting-age ethnic-minority population has swollen – a result of demographic trends – has meant that such candidacies have been relatively attractive within the party. Three additional constituencies were created following the 2011 census, and ethnic-minority populations represented over 40 per cent of the total population (joining an existing list of 23 such constituencies). However, there has been a real risk of effectively ghettoizing such candidacies.

Moreover, where selection has been achieved in the past, it has typically been in constituencies where ethnic-minority candidates have poor or no prospects for actual election, all other things being equal and given their parties' national popularity. This has meant that there is a higher chance of having to serve a longer apprenticeship in a series of such no-hope constituencies, thereby extending the lead time before a safe or winnable nomination is secured. This matters for the obvious reason that such an assault course creates a high degree of attrition as hopefuls fall by the wayside. Some withdraw and/or scale back their efforts, recognizing that as time proceeds, so their absolute chances also recede. Others reduce their pace of industry and attempt to adopt new strategies aimed at realistic nomination contests. But many, inevitably, conclude that their energies are better spent elsewhere, beyond a parliamentary career. This precariousness is capped when the small number who are selected in winnable seats are eventually returned but face the prospect of being unseated by quite small electoral swings. Such political careers are thus often short-lived, fragile while they last, and simply unable to provide enough traction for individuals to build alliances within their parties at Westminster. This general picture is not unique to ethnic-minority politicians, by any means. Indeed, it was first empirically sketched by Rasmussen's (1981) pioneering research on women's political careers in British politics a generation ago.

But even this aspect of candidacy should be viewed in the context of a growing trend towards a younger, more professionalized political class. Successful parliamentary-constituency candidacy strategies have gradually shifted away from hopefuls with a long, established track record of achievement beyond formal politics. This now means that the Westminster pipeline is becoming narrower in its social and economic background, while it is also becoming more diverse in ethnicity and gender. How far ethnic-minority political hopefuls are able to capitalize on this shift remains uncertain. But, at the time of writing, it is worth noting that a further five ethnic-minority candidates have been selected for moderately to highly safe Conservative constituencies against no additional Labour hopefuls in similarly attractive constituencies. Meanwhile, a further 100 minority candidates have been selected to fight in the 2015 general election in marginal seats.

Finally, the fear of voter discrimination is also likely to limit the demand for ethnic-minority candidates in mainstream parties. Party members, managers, and selectors may be caught in a spiral of imputed discrimination. That is to say – and echoing the findings presented by Bird in Chapter 10 – while they will be keen to avoid any sense of overt discrimination against ethnic minorities, they will implicitly worry that voters may continue, at the margin, to be hostile or less welcoming to black and Asian candidates. If parties sense that voters see ethnic minorities as liabilities, it is no huge leap to see why they may remain cautious and sceptical. Forms of soft rejection or rebuff (imputed discrimination may be too strong an interpretation) may be the result of parties internalizing the belief that voters remain sceptical at best. It would be distinctively odd to think that as vote-maximizing agents, party officials could and would remove from their thoughts the worry that some potential voters might punish parties for embracing ethnic-minority candidates.

The general association among major parties between ethnic-minority voters and a distinctly ethnic political constituency can then further compound the problem of perceived voter bias. The tendency to run so-called ethnic campaigns is an obvious manifestation of this association, with attendant detrimental consequences for long-term political integration (see Saggar and Heath 1999).

These are formidable difficulties – on both supply and demand sides – and they invite the question: why do so many ethnic-minority candidates succeed at all? A few decades ago, running such candidates was assumed to guarantee certain defeat. This perception was originally driven, in large part, by several high-profile cases of "failed" Labour candidacies before the mid-1980s. In 1992, the perception was further strengthened as a result of the failure of John Taylor to win Cheltenham following a series of ugly exchanges between parts of the local constituency association and the Conservative Party Central Office. For instance, a prominent figure in the Cheltenham Conservative Association responded to Taylor's selection by calling him a "bloody nigger" (Webster 1990). Taylor later complained – in hindsight – that his party had found it too uncomfortable to confront naked prejudice and bigotry in its ranks. For a decade at least, the Taylor episode haunted the question of ethnicity and political candidacy in Tory ranks, reinforced by the sluggish performance by a small number of high-profile ethnic-minority candidates in Tory-winnable seats in 1997 and 2001.

Much has changed since then, particularly in the Labour Party in the 1990s and in the Conservative Party during the 2000s. Both parties boast a sizeable handful of ethnic-minority MPs, several of whom have served at a high ministerial level or are on track to do so. In the Labour administration that governed between 1997 and 2010, the United Kingdom experienced its first black Cabinet appointee (Paul Boateng, a Treasury minister with full Cabinet rank). Since Labour's defeat in 2010, Sadiq Khan and Chuka Umunna have cemented their position at the most senior level in the Shadow Cabinet (serving as Shadow justice secretary and business secretary, respectively). And, in the Tory-led coalition administration that followed, the Conservative Party's chairwoman, Sayeeda Warsi, held full Cabinet rank between 2010 and 2012. (In the autumn 2012 reshuffle, despite a formal demotion to minister of state level, Lady Warsi retained her right to attend Cabinet before finally resigning in protest from her party's front bench in August 2014, ostensibly over the government's response to that summer's escalation of the Israeli-Palestinian conflict.)

Finally, David Cameron's premiership has also been linked with a rapid rise in ethnic-minority MPs holding second-tier party and government posts, which provide the crucial training ground for Cabinet selection. Helen Grant, a junior minister in the Ministry of Justice (and then in Culture, Media and Sport), Sajid Javid (first a junior Treasury minister and later at Cabinet rank as secretary of state for culture), Rushanara Ali (a junior Shadow minister in International Development until autumn 2014, when she resigned over the renewed use of military action in Iraq) are all examples of this. Labour, noticeably, has been keen to favour ethnic-minority nominees in many of its urban heartlands that now contain substantial numbers of ethnic-minority voters (Martin 2012). Indeed, any sense of voter penalty has mostly given way to neutrality, or even a sense of an "ethnic premium," whereby particular candidates have been able to demonstrate their ability to mobilize dense ethnic networks.

Conclusion

This chapter has probed and discussed the degree to which ethnic minorities have political outlooks that converge with those of the rest of the population by examining whether they vote, for whom they vote, and whether they run for office and are elected.

First, this chapter has provided evidence somewhat contradicting common knowledge. Indeed, we first saw that although voter registration is significantly lower among some ethnic-minority groups – and that is a core concern – once these voters are registered, reported turnout levels approximate those of the rest of the British population. It is interesting to note that this is somewhat at odds with the general beliefs about the negative political consequences of ethnic minorities' greater socio-economic marginalization.

Second, this chapter has provided consistent cross-time evidence in support of what I have called earlier the iron law of ethnic-minority

voting, meaning the long-standing and overwhelming support of ethnic minorities for the Labour Party. As chapters 1 and 2 indicate, and
as research on Canada (Bilodeau and Kanji 2010), Australia, and New
Zealand (White and Bilodeau 2014) supports, this strong preference of
ethnic minorities for large centre-left parties is not unique to the United
Kingdom. However, the specific reasons for such an allegiance remain
to be demonstrated in this country and elsewhere.

Third, the chapter has provided evidence pointing to the increased
representation of ethnic minorities in Westminster over the years, and to
a diversification of the parties represented by ethnic minorities, trends
also observed in the Netherlands and Belgium (see chapters 1 and 2).
The different reasons – supply and demand – for this continuous under-
representation were discussed. Moreover, I would add that beyond the
immediate arena of political representation of ethnic-minority candidates, there are a number of important influences shaping who obtains
elected office and why. Among these has been the professionalization of
the political-recruitment pools that are patronized by national political
parties; and with such professionalization, it can be argued that traditional resource-centred models for candidate selection and career progression count for less than they once did. Or these resources may count
for more, remembering that the resources themselves have altered.
Time, money, and networks continue to be important – but alongside
these, to get ahead in national parliamentary politics (and, by extension,
in executive government), ethnic minorities need to be familiar with,
and gain experience with, an increasingly narrow set of think tank, media, and advisory roles.

British politics no longer favours Labour and Conservative hopefuls
with general profiles in the public or private sector. Instead, it now leans
towards those who enter professional politics early, along highly pro-
scribed routes, and who remain embedded with a comparatively small
peer group. Although these issues have not been the primary focus of
this chapter, it is clearly a high priority to begin to link general studies of
ethnic-minority political representation and integration with the findings of narrower studies of elite political socialization and recruitment.

Finally, the chapter has linked the above observation to a familiar question regarding the role and importance of ethnicity in shaping political
preferences, electoral choice, and political careers. The traditional default
view accepted across the bulk of empirical research has suggested that
ethnicity serves to limit political careers and ghettoize the political interests of ethnic minorities within a limited, constrained set of issues and

places. Indeed, there is reason to think that both careers and substantive representation are hindered as a result. A more nuanced perspective, however, points in a more balanced direction. Certainly the origin of ethnic-minority candidates now counts neutrally or even positively in the bulk of Labour-held, urban seats. And the recent growth of ethnic-minority candidate prospects in Tory ranks appears not to have been met with any significant backlash. In terms of political issues and agendas, the larger question of indirect bias and unfairness in public policy is reasonably well embedded in how parties approach the challenges of equity and efficiency across the board. So, while ethnicity may remain a double-edged sword, it is not quite accurate to say that the political concerns of ethnic minorities are entirely lost in national electoral competition. The distinction that matters far more is the degree to which such interests are seen as distinctive and stand-alone, as opposed to signifying a wider set of interests rooted in equality, sensitivity, and fairness.

All of these questions flow effortlessly into larger considerations and debates regarding the part played by ethnicity and ethnic identity in shaping UK electoral outcomes. At the time of writing (early 2013), an incumbent, unpopular, Conservative-led coalition faces tremendous electoral challenges, leading many to argue that its chances of re-election are perhaps already lost. In this context, the Tories' capacity to attract support from traditionally unlikely quarters becomes pressing. This chapter has highlighted just how uphill a task this will be. Moreover, any assessment of long-term ethnic-minority political integration has also to take into account whether, or how far, the factors that shape partisan choice overall in the United Kingdom are also true among discrete population subgroups. And, more generally, integration assessments will have to be set against the general electoral prospects of the major parties. In short, this chapter has set out to encourage the use of a wider lens in agreeing on and debating the terms of ethnic-minority political integration in the United Kingdom and beyond.

NOTES

1 *New Commonwealth* refers to those countries – principally in South Asia, the Caribbean and sub-Saharan Africa – that became independent of the former British Empire after the Second World War, the vast majority of which subsequently joined (and have remained) members of the Commonwealth.

4 Does Prior Socialization Define Patterns of Integration? Mexican Immigrants and Their Political Participation in the United States

MICHAEL JONES-CORREA

Of the approximately 320 million residents of the United States, 45 million are foreign-born – 14 per cent of the population – with approximately one million new foreign-born residents arriving every year. During the 1990s alone, over 14 million immigrants arrived in the United States (Meissner et al. 2006), with another 13 million arriving between 2000 and 2010.[1] In 1970, soon after the passage of the landmark 1965 immigration act that would trigger dramatic changes in the composition of immigration to the country, a majority of the immigration flow was still from Europe. Forty years later, arrivals from Europe made up only about one in 10 immigrants. Immigrants now arrive largely from Latin America and Asia: 29 per cent arrive from Mexico alone and, together with other Latin American immigrants, make up almost half of all new immigrants to the United States. In the post-1965 period, new immigrants, particularly those from Mexico, come with varying experiences with democratic participation: Mexico itself went through a transition in the 1990s from a single-party system to a contested multi-party democracy.

One question raised by US policymakers as they debate the country's immigration policies is, How will new immigrants, who come with varying experiences of democratic engagement, in turn participate in the United States? Another question that can be posed is, When immigrants arrive in the United States, do they learn new political orientations and behaviours, or does their prior political engagement continue to shape their attitudes and behaviours even in their new setting?

As pointed out by White in Chapter 9, the question of persistence in political learning versus change through adulthood is a continuing debate in the political socialization literature, one that connects closely with the political integration of immigrants (see also Ajinkya and Jones-Correa 2007; Sigel 1989). The issue is the extent to which the political orientations of immigrants either persist or shift in new political environments. The existing literature on immigrant political integration provides mixed evidence on this question. Some researchers see immigration as a break leading to re-socialization into a new political context (Hoskin 1989). Cain, Kiewiet, and Uhlaner (1991) argue that immigrant groups – in their analysis, Asians and Latinos in California – acquire partisanship in the United States over time, with greater partisanship exhibited over generations. This is not the result of the effects of age, they write, but rather of experiential learning though time (ibid., 398–9). Black, Niemi, and Bingham Powell Jr. (1987) make a nearly identical argument for immigrants in Canada – they point to socialization occurring over time, rather than simply as the result of aging, as the explanation for the behavioural differences they find between recent and more established immigrants. A number of studies find that acquisition of English language and US citizenship – both correlated with time in the United States – are associated with greater participation in electoral and non-electoral politics in the receiving country (Junn 1997; Jones-Correa 1998; Cho 1999; Wong 2000; Ramakrishnan 2005), again suggesting a process of adult re-socialization among immigrants.

However, a number of scholars emphasize continuities rather than breaks in socialization (Finifter and Finifter 1989; Black 1987; Bilodeau 2008; Bilodeau, McAllister, and Kanji 2010). Two earlier works – by Wilson (1973) and Gitelman (1982) – examine immigrant political behaviour in Australia and Israel, respectively, noting the prevalent continuities in political orientations among immigrants in both countries. These studies also note differences in integration into their new political context among immigrants of distinct countries of origin. In short, the existing literature finds that immigrants do acclimate themselves to their new political contexts over time but that prior socialization also carries through to immigrants' new political context.

The literature on immigrant political participation pays little attention, however, to individuals' political behaviours before immigration. There are some notable exceptions, though: Wals's recent work (2006, 2008, 2011) on the prior socialization of Mexican immigrants, Ramakrishnan's discussion (2005) on the effects of dual nationality, Lien's research (2001) on transnationalism, Black's study (1987) on the transferability of political skills among immigrants in Canada, and Jones-Correa's work (2001) on contexts and their effects on naturalization and participation.

All touch on aspects of pre-immigration socialization, pointing to the lingering effects of immigrants' prior experiences in their country of origin. Much of the reticence in the literature can largely be explained by the absence of data; existing studies often rely on data collected for other purposes, as explained in the Introduction to this volume. These data have not tracked immigrants' political behaviour before and after migration and, in general surveys including immigrant respondents, have asked very little about immigrants' life before immigration.

This chapter explores two central aspects of the political socialization debate – whether immigrants' experiences with politics in their country of origin leads to persistent political learning that carries over into the new context, despite the changes brought about in the course of immigration, and whether *variation* in immigrants' experiences with democracy has differential effects on civic participation in their host country.

Data and Methodology

To explore the above questions, this chapter focuses on immigrants from a single country: Mexico. The advantage of focusing on Mexican immigrants alone is that it keeps country of origin constant, thus minimizing a wide range of institutional and historical variance deriving from unique country-of-origin characteristics, while at the same time allowing analysis of the substantial variation in political contexts at the state level in Mexico. The analyses rely on the 2006 Latino National Survey (LNS),[2] fielded in the United States.

There are two ways in which prior socialization is indicated by the data. The first is directly, reflecting individuals' own political behaviours in Mexico (their experience with voting and with volunteering in party, labour, and other organizations). The second is indirectly, as a function of the contexts of the Mexican states in which these individuals were born and lived (measured by turnover in governing party control and percentage of seats controlled by any one party in the state legislature).

Beginning in the 1980s, Mexico underwent a transition from a one-party regime to a multi-party democracy with competitive elections. This transition took place in Mexico's 31 states at different times during the period from 1980 to 2000; but it was not uniform, with some states transitioning to competitive elections and shifts in party control earlier than others (see Lackey 2007). Accordingly, there is considerable variation in experience with competitive democracy at the sub-national level (Cleary and Stokes 2006; Beer and Mitchell 2004). Cleary and Stokes

(2006) point out that in some Mexican states, political clientelism still dominates (e.g., Michoacán and Puebla), while in other states, open elections and a high level of electoral participation are common (e.g., Baja California and Chihuahua). The structure of the LNS, because it collects information on Mexican immigrants' state of origin in Mexico, and also uses data on both immigrants' age and year of arrival in the United States, allows us to analyse the effects of state-level democratic transitions in Mexico on immigrants' political experience before immigrating to the United States. Every individual respondent's political experience is situated both in a *place* (the state of birth in Mexico) and a *time* (the political context in the Mexican state at the time of migration), and this dual perspective offers a more precise indication of the effects of contextual variance in Mexican democratic politics on individual attitudes and behaviour.[3]

For this reason, the focus of the analysis here are the foreign-born – specifically, those from Mexico. Two-thirds of the respondents in the LNS are immigrants, and Mexican-origin respondents make up 66.1 per cent of the foreign-born sample. Put another way, of the sub-sample of Mexican-origin respondents, more than two thirds (or 3,879) are born in Mexico and have immigrated to the United States. The analysis is further limited to Mexican-born immigrants who were 19 years of age or older when they arrived in the United States and who immigrated after 1970. We exclude people who were 18 years of age or younger when they entered the country because we are interested in respondents' political participation before their arrival, and Mexican citizens can participate in elections only when they turn 18. Individuals who arrived before 1970 are also excluded from the analysis because contextual data for Mexico is simply non-existent before then. The potential sample – limited to Mexican immigrants arriving at the age of 19 or over after 1970 – consists of 1,867 individuals. After restricting the sample to observations with non-missing values in all relevant variables, the sample for the analysis ultimately consists of 1,547 observations. Sample sizes for the regression models vary somewhat with the dependent variable in the models.

Dependent Variables

Table 4.1 below describes the coding and sample distribution of the four variables used as indicators of participation. The first variable is an attitudinal one, for which respondents answered whether they (strongly) agree or disagree with the statement "People are better off avoiding

Table 4.1 Dependent Variables, Definitions, and Questions

Question	Variable name	Measurement	%
Agree or disagree: People are better off avoiding contact with government	"avoid contact with government"	categorical variable: 1 = disagree strongly 2 = disagree somewhat 3 = agree somewhat 4 = agree strongly	1: 32.5 2: 25.2 3: 22.2 4: 20.0
Have you ever tried to get government officials to pay attention to something that concerned you, either by calling, writing a letter, or going to a meeting?	"get government attention"	1 = yes, has tried 0 = no	19.5
Do you participate in the activities of one social, cultural, civic, or political group; more than one such group; or do you not participate in the activities of any such groups?	"group participation"	1 = yes (participate in one or more) 0 = no	9.3
Are you naturalized American?	"naturalization"	1 = naturalized 0 = not naturalized	20.8

contact with government." This "avoid contact with government" variable is a four-level Likert item. About 45 per cent of Mexican-born immigrants in the sample agree that avoiding contact with government makes them better off. The other three variables measure non-electoral political participation in the United States. "Get government attention" is a dummy variable, indicating whether respondents reported to have ever tried to have government officials in the United States pay attention to something that concerned them; 19.5 per cent of Mexican-born immigrants in the sample reported having tried to contact government officials. "Participation in activities" is also a dichotomous variable, indicating whether respondents reported that they participate in the activities of a voluntary club, association, or community organization in the United States; 9.5 per cent of the Mexican-born immigrants in the sample participate in these types of activities.

The fourth variable, "naturalization," indicates whether respondents are naturalized as American citizens. Conceptually, this variable is somewhat distinct from the others: naturalization is a one-time process rather than a repeated action, leading to the possibility of engagement in other kinds of political behaviours, such as voting. Since naturalization is available only to individuals who entered the country legally, those who reported to be in the United States without legal documents were excluded from the analysis. This model also drops from the sample people who arrived in the country after 2001 who would be ineligible to be naturalized at the time of the interview, even if legal. With these modifications, 20.8 per cent of Mexican-born immigrants in the sample are naturalized Americans. It should be noted that registration and voting – the focus of much of the literature on political participation – were not included here because relatively few Mexican immigrants in the sample had become both citizens and active voters in the United States.

Independent Variables

Table 4.2 below describes the coding and means of the independent variables. Age of respondent captures possible "life cycle" effects with respect to civic engagement. This variable aims to control for the fact that Mexican immigrants might be more likely to engage in political activities at certain times of their lives – when married, for instance, or when their children are grown. Respondents' level of education has been shown to increase the set of skills and information that individuals can apply to political behaviour (Verba, Schlozman, and Brady 1995). Elementary schooling is the reference category in the regression, and "some high school" and "some college" are the included variables. In these regressions, ownership – whether a respondent is a homeowner in the United States and also in Mexico – is both an indicator of rootedness in the community of residence and a proxy for wealth.

Contrary to what Verba, Schlozman, and Brady (1995) hypothesize, Jones-Correa and Leal (2001) provide evidence that the lower levels of participation of Latinos in American politics is not straightforwardly related to Catholic affiliation. However, to control for the possible relationship between religious denomination and civic engagement, this chapter includes a dummy variable coded as 1 when the individual identifies as Catholic. Regular attendance at church services is also included as a proxy for non-political associational membership, which a number of authors have argued is a significant predictor of other forms of participation (Verba, Schlozman, and Brady 1995). The percentage of a respondent's life spent in the United States is a proxy measure of assimilation.[4] The greater relative amount of time that people spend in the receiving country, the more likely it is that they will assimilate and that the strength of ties to sending countries will decrease (Fraga et al. 2012).

Previous research has found that the propensity of immigrants to believe that they will eventually return to stay in their country of origin is a drag on their attachment and integration into the US political system

Table 4.2. Independent Variables, Definitions, and Means

Name	Definition	Mean or %
Individual variables		
Male	1 = male; 0 = female	0.45
Age	number of years	37.79
Elementary	1 = 8th grade or below; 0 = else	0.38
Some HS[a]	1 = at least some high school; 0 = else	0.45
Some college	1 = at least some college	0.18
Property MX	1 = owns land, house, or business in Mexico; 0 = does not own	0.40
House US	1 = owns house in US; 0 = does not own house	0.35
Catholic	1 = Catholic; 0 = else	0.79
Relig. Attend.	1 = attends religious services; 0 = never attends	0.90
% life in US	years in US/age	28.38
No legal docs	1 = without legal documents; 0 = else	0.22
Remain in US	1 = plans to stay all life/until retirement; 0 = less than 5 years or other	0.76
Contextual variables US		
% people w. HS or more	% of population 25 years and over with high school or higher	84.04
% registration	total registered/total population 18 years or over	70.89
% Latino regist.	Latino registered/Latino population 18 years and over	27.28
% turnout	total voters/total population registered	88.08
% Latino turnout	Latino voters/Latino registered	79.54
Vote difference	difference in votes between winning and losing party/total votes	20.56
% union members	workers who are union members/number of employed workers	10.67
NGO density	non-governmental organizations per 1 million inhabitants	4,676
Political participation before migration		
Voted MX	1 = voted in Mexico; 0 = did not vote	0.57
Political activity	1 = joined/participated in political organization; 0 = else	0.15
Contextual variables MX		
% literate	people 15 and over who are literate/total population 15 years and over	85.95
% registered	registered/population 18 and over	93.42
% turnout	voters/registered	57.76
Alternancia[b]	cumulative number of voters switching parties	0.27
% seats majority party MX	number of seats in local Congress held by majority party/total number of seats	64.59
N		1,547

Sources: Current and pre-migration individual data: LNS; US data: US Census Bureau; US Department of Labor; National Center for Charitable Statistics; Mexican data: 1970, 1980, 1990, 2000, 2005 census; local Congress web pages; Banamex-Accival.
[a] High school.
[b] Turnover in party control, with the opposition elected to the state governorship and legislature.

(Jones-Correa 1998). We thus expect to find a positive relationship between the variable "remain in US" and all forms of political participation. Finally, not having legal documents is expected to be negatively associated with political participation.

In addition, we expect that the political attitudes and behaviours of Mexican immigrants will to some extent be shaped by their current environment in the United States. Varying socio-economic, political, and social contexts might make immigrants more (or less) prone to participation. To account for this possibility, a number of US state-level characteristics were merged to the individual-level data in the LNS. These variables, all measured at the state level, include average educational level, registration and turnout for all voters and among Latinos, vote margins by political party, percentage of residents with union membership, and non-governmental organizations per capita.

This chapter's main focus, however, is on the effects of Mexican immigrants' civic and political engagement *before* they arrived in the United States. Building on the findings of the political socialization literature summarized above, which argues for the early establishment of patterns of political engagement, we hypothesize that participation in Mexico will be an important predictor of current political choice. The regressions thus control for respondents' participation in elections as well as in political, labour, student, or paramilitary organizations before immigration.

These behaviours – experience with voting and with volunteering in party, labour, and other organizations – are *direct* measures of immigrants' engagement in their country of origin. We also expect that political engagement will be shaped *indirectly*, reflecting the political contexts of the states in Mexico in which immigrants were born and lived. Among these contextual variables are indicators of Mexico's transition to a competitive democracy. While individual Mexican states transitioned to contested elections in the 1980s, opposition parties began succeeding the previously hegemonic Partido Revolucionario Institucional in controlling state governorships and state legislatures only in 1989; this, among other factors, ultimately paved the way for Vicente Fox's election as president in 2000, running on the ticket of the opposition centre-right Partido Acción Nacional. As a measure of this national democratic transition, we added a dummy variable, indicating whether a respondent immigrated after 1990 (i.e., after the transition to some significant state-level democratic competitiveness was underway).

In addition, contextual, state-level political variables, indicating political conditions in each respondent's state of birth just before migration to the United States, were merged with individual-level data. The Mexican state-level contextual variables include education (measured as a percentage of those literate), the percentage of population registered to vote, electoral turnout in the election before the migrant's departure, *alternancia*, and the percentage of seats occupied by the majority party in the local Congress.[5]

Since all of the dependent variables are dummies, the behaviours are modelled with logistic regressions. An exception is the "avoid contact with government" variable, for which we use an ordered logit model.[6] In addition, because Mexican immigrants residing in the same US state who immigrated in the same year from the same Mexican state are assigned identical values of state-level variables, we report robust standard errors that account for clustering at the US and Mexican state levels.

Results

Table 4.3 below shows the logit coefficients of the variables explaining the civic and political behaviours of Mexican immigrants in the United States. As already noted, the naturalization model excludes those who were not eligible to be naturalized. Consequently, the model does not include the variable specifying whether respondents had documentation allowing them to stay in the United States as legal residents.[7]

According to the results of Table 4.3, the only individual characteristic that is consistently significant in each of the models is the respondents' level of education; all else being equal, being more educated increases immigrants' likelihood of political participation, a finding reflected in much of the literature on political participation (see Verba, Schlozman, and Brady 1995). Some of the variables are not significant in any of the models: gender, property ownership in Mexico, and church attendance.

There are important positive findings, however, with regard to socialization and integration into the American political system. *Ceteris paribus*, both age and the percentage of a respondent's life spent in the United States are positively associated with both the *naturalization* and the *contact* models. People who would like to remain in the country were more likely both to have tried to contact government officials and to have naturalized as US citizens. In contrast, characteristics of current US state of residence do not seem to be significantly correlated to Mexican immigrants' political attitudes and behaviours in the United States.

Given this chapter's focus on immigrant civic and political engagement, the variables indicating the respondents' political activity in Mexico

Table 4.3. Civic and Political Behaviours of Mexican Immigrants in the United States

Dependent variable	Contact		Attention		Participation		Naturalized	
Model fitted	Ordered logit		Logit		Logit		Logit	
Current individual characteristics	B	RSE	B	RSE	B	RSE	B	RSE
Male	−.00	.12	.06	.15	−.24	.20	.12	.17
Age	.02*	.01	.02	.01	.00	.01	.05***	.01
Some high school	−.28*	.12	.34*	.17	.42	.27	.54**	.20
Some college	−.59***	.17	.67***	.20	1.35**	.27	1.23***	.23
Owns property in MX	−.07	.11	.20	.15	−.17	.20	−.28	.19
Owns house US	−.07	.12	.12	.14	.41*	.20	.41*	.18
Catholic	.11	.14	−.16	.19	−.71**	.22	.04	.19
Attend. in place of worship	−.31	.23	−.04	.25	.65	.38	−.08	.31
% life spent in US	.00	.01	.04***	.01	.00	.01	.06***	.01
Do not have legal docs	.09	.13	−.12	.18	.55*	.22		
Wish to remain in US	−.06	.14	.43*	.19	.18	.28	.32	.27
Characteristics of current US state of residence								
% high school educ. or more	−.02	.02	.01	.03	−.02	.04	−.06	.04
% registration	.01	.02	−.00	.03	−.00	.04	.04	.04
% Lat. voter registration	−.00	.01	−.01	.01	−.02*	.01	−.01	.01
% voter turnout in 2004	−.05	.04	−.02	.05	.03	.07	.01	.06
% Lat. voter turnout in 2004	.00	.01	−.01	.02	.00	.02	.01	.02
Vote diff. major parties 2004	−.02*	.01	−.00	.01	.02	.01	−.03	.02
% union membership	.01	.01	.03	.02	.03	.02	−.00	.02
NGO density	.00	.00	.00	.00	−.00	.00	−.00	.00
Individual characteristics before person arrived in US								
Voted in MX	−.25*	.11	.28	.16	.40	.22	−.38*	.18
Political activity	−.09	.15	.12	.18	.25	.25	.60*	.25
Characteristics of the former state of residence in MX								
% literate	−.02*	.01	.01	.01	.00	.01	−.00	.01
% registered	.01	.01	.02	.02	−.00	.01	.00	.01
% turnout	−.01	.00	−.01	.01	.00	.01	.00	.01
Alternancia	.07	.12	.39*	.19	.15	.23	−.80*	.38
% seats largest party	−.01	.01	−.02*	.01	.02	.01	−.01	.01
Year (pre-/post-1990)			−1.20	2.38				
Year × % turnout			.00	.01				
Year × % seats larg. party			.03*	.01				
Year × % registered			−.01	.02				
Cut 1: disagree somewhat	−7.88**	2.78						
Cut 2: agree somewhat	−6.80*	2.78						
Cut 3: agree strongly	−5.70	2.78						
Constant			−2.13	4.15	−5.35	5.31	−4.56	5.56
N	1,416		1,544		1,547		1,150	

* p < .05, **p < .01, ***p < .001

and the political context of their home state are of particular interest. With regard to their political involvement before arriving in the United States, we first observe that those Mexican-born immigrants who were active in political or organizational activity in Mexico are more likely to become naturalized citizens in the United States, but were no different than other Mexican-born immigrants in the other three forms of political engagement. Our predicted probabilities indicate that Mexican-born immigrants who engaged in political or organizational activity in Mexico are 5 percentage points more likely to disagree with the idea that individuals are better off avoiding government.

Second, having voted in Mexico was significant in both the model for "avoiding contact with government" and for naturalization in the United States. It is interesting that while experience with voting in Mexico was correlated with less scepticism about government in the United States, it was negatively correlated with naturalizing there, perhaps suggesting that those with commitments to politics in Mexico may have difficulty transferring those commitments to politics in the United States. This finding has implications for the ongoing debate on the effects of transnational ties on participation in receiving countries.

With regard to the political context in the Mexican home state, the analyses report only some systematic results across the four forms of political activity in the United States. First, the most consistent results concern the non-effect of the proportion of registered voters or the level of turnout in the Mexican home state for any of the four forms of participation in the United States. Whether Mexican immigrants come from a state in Mexico where turnout and voter registration were high or low has no significant impact on their political participation in the United States. Second, whether respondents' home states experienced *alternancia* is significantly and positively correlated with contacting officials as immigrants in the United States, but, as with voting in Mexico, is significantly and negatively correlated with naturalizing as a US citizen. This latter finding suggests that respondents who experienced and participated in democratic practices in Mexico are less likely to engage in a shift of political allegiance to US citizenship and that this shift in allegiance might be more desirable to those who have not experienced democracy than to those who have. Lack of experience with democracy in immigrants' country of origin may translate into a greater willingness to take on a permanent shift in allegiances, perhaps with democratic participation in the United States as part of the attraction.

Third, on the opposite side of the coin, immigrants from states in which a larger percentage of the state legislature is controlled by a single party are less likely to contact government officials once in the United States. Fourth, respondents born in Mexican states with lower levels of literacy are also more likely to report wanting to keep their distance from government in general, but no relation is observed to the other forms of political activities.

Fifth, the move to a contested democracy in Mexico also seems to have no systematic effect on the impact of the pre-migration context on the way Mexican-born immigrants relate to US politics. Only the interaction of the variable for immigrants migrating after 1990 – the year when contested democracy began to take hold in Mexico – with the percentage of seats controlled by a single party in the legislature of their state of birth is significant and *positively* associated with their contact with government once in the United States. The other interaction variables are not significant.

In sum, experience with contested democratic politics in Mexico seems to have a positive effect on Mexican immigrants' initiative to make contact with government once in the United States, but a negative effect on their decision to naturalize: both outcomes provide evidence for the effect of prior political engagement on immigrants' decisions to participate in civic and political life in their new country of residence.

Conclusion

Focusing on Mexican immigrants, this chapter examined the evidence for the effects of immigrants' prior socialization and their political participation in their state of origin in Mexico and how this shapes their decisions to engage in civic and political life in the United States. The evidence from the LNS suggests that Mexican immigrants' experience of politics in Mexico does influence their approach to, and engagement with, American politics. There are two ways in which prior socialization is indicated by the data: directly, reflecting individuals' own political behaviours in Mexico (their experience with voting and with volunteering in party, labour, and other organizations), and indirectly, as a function of the contexts of the states in Mexico in which they were born and lived (measured by turnover in governing party control and percentage of seats controlled by any one party in the state legislature).

Both direct and indirect prior socialization have effects on immigrants' political attitudes and behaviours in the United States. These are seen in three of the four models presented in Table 4.3: gauging avoidance of government as a strategy, asking whether the respondent has tried to contact government officials to address an issue of concern, and asking whether the respondent has naturalized as a US citizen. The results of only one of the models – on voluntary activities in the United States – is unaffected by immigrants' prior political experience. The evidence presented above suggests that for the three models in which some form of prior political experience or socialization is significant, the effect of this prior socialization does not always reinforce participation in the United States. In some cases, rather, experience with contested democracy in Mexico seems to lead to some reticence on the part of immigrants to fully commit to politics in the United States – perhaps because immigrants with a positive experience of Mexican politics are precisely those who see a system in Mexico that holds some promise and to which they can see themselves returning.

These results both elaborate and reinforce the findings in the previous literature. Like other studies, this research finds some evidence for adult re-socialization for some kinds of participation – particularly contacting government officials and naturalizing as a US citizen. In both cases, the chances that an immigrant will engage increase with the proportion of their lives that they spend in the United States and with age, suggesting that immigrants learn new practices over time in their host country.

The central findings of the study, however, support arguments for important continuities in political socialization and engagement, particularly in the areas of trust in government, contact with government officials, and naturalization in the United States. This research corroborates key findings in the field (Wilson 1973; Gitelman 1982; Black 1987; Black, Niemi, and Bingham Powell Jr. 1987; Finifter and Finifter 1989; Yang 1994; White et al. 2008) about the continuities in patterns of political engagement, particularly continuities in the political socialization of Mexican immigrants (Wals 2007, 2008, 2011) but expands this research in important ways, notably by taking advantage of the natural quasi-experiment offered by the course of democratization in Mexico, in which different states became politically competitive at different times.

By noting the political context in their state of origin at the time of Mexican immigrants' migration to the United States, this research is able to note much more precisely the effects of political context on immigrants' subsequent civic and political engagement in their new country of residence. The key finding is that prior experience with democratic practices in Mexico – whether directly, through voting, or indirectly, living through turnover in party government at the state level – is *negatively* correlated with naturalization as a US citizen. Mexican immigrants with the most negative experiences of Mexican politics are the most likely to make a commitment to the United States and naturalize. These conclusions echo some of the findings in the literature – in particular, arguments that immigrants from socialist regimes (Yang 1994) and/or those migrating for political reasons (Portes and Rumbaut 2006) are more likely to naturalize as US citizens. However, the findings in the literature emphasize the difficulty of return as the explanation for why immigrants from non-democratic countries adapt more quickly to civic and political life in the United States. This cannot be the case for the Mexican migrants we examine here. Rather, the explanation hinges on disenchantment with the political system in the sending country.

The approach taken in the research presented here differs from the earlier literature on immigrant engagement and prior socialization in emphasizing the experiences, and the contexts of those experiences, of individuals rather than their skills and social capital (although these surely matter). The emphasis here is on the role of institutional contexts, and experiences with these contexts, in shaping individual political attitudes and behaviours. This shift in emphasis, from the individual to the contexts in which individuals operate, and from the psychological to the institutional, is present in some of the more recent literature on socialization, but is not usually made explicit. This chapter suggests that more attention to the contexts, institutional and otherwise, that individuals find themselves in, and the ways in which these shape their political actions and attitudes, merit further investigation.

NOTES

1 See US Census Bureau, "Community Population Survey – March 20 Detailed Tables," 2010, Table 2.1 "Foreign-Born Population by Sex, Age, and Year of Entry: 2010," http://www.census.gov/population/foreign/data/cps2010.html.

2 The LNS is a state-stratified random sample of 8,634 Latino residents in 15 states as well as metropolitan Washington, DC, representing 90 per cent of Latinos in the United States. The national margin of error for the sample is approximately ±1.05 per cent. The data, along with a description of the survey and its methodology, are publicly available at http://www.icpsr.umich.edu/icpsrweb/DSDR/studies/20862.

3 The analysis here examines outcomes for migrants from all 31 states.
4 Other researchers use "years in the US" to capture similar effects; however, the measure for "years" does not account for the difference between an individual arriving in the United States at age 10, who spends the next 20 years in the country, and an individual who arrives at age 40, who, similarly, lives in the United States for the next 20 years. While both have spent the same amount of time in their new country of residence, at the end of 20 years, the younger individual will have spent half of his or her life there, while the older individual will have spent only a third of his or her life there. The argument here is that proportion of time spent in the United States matters.
5 We also included a variable measuring the percentage of violations of human rights at a state level. Data to construct this variable is available starting in 2000. The substantive results presented in this chapter did not change when this variable was included in regressions similar to the ones presented here using a sub-sample of individuals who arrived in the United States after 2000. Results are available on request.
6 Note that we did not present multilevel hierarchical linear modelling (HLM) here because we do not expect the cases to cluster within states either in Mexico or in the United States. HLM modelling does not significantly change the results.
7 Since the estimated parameters of binary (or categorical) outcomes do not provide directly useful information for understanding the relationship between the independent variables and the outcomes, I calculated the predicted probabilities for the statistically significant variables. Because binary outcomes are non-linear, changes in predicted probabilities depend not only on the value of the independent variable of interest but also on the values of all predictors of the model (Long 1997). For this reason, changes in predicted probabilities are computed with a reference point: an individual representing the plurality of the sample for the following characteristics: elementary schooling or less, Catholic, usually attending church, having no property in Mexico or the United States, voting in Mexico before coming to the United States, and planning to remain in the United States if possible. (These are dummies for which calculating a mean is not possible.) The rest of the variables were evaluated at their sample means (see Table 4.2).

5 How Strong Is the Bond?
First- and Second-Generation Immigrants and Confidence in Australian Political Institutions

JULIET PIETSCH AND IAN MCALLISTER

Beyond participating in political affairs, immigrants will develop in the process of integration a set of orientations towards the political system of their host country. One such orientation will be the amount of confidence that they express for the various political institutions – or the perception of fairness with which individuals expect to be treated by institutions (Listhaug and Wiberg 1995, 299). Confidence in political institutions is central to maintaining the stability of political regimes. It provides authorities with greater capacity to meet commitments and make important decisions (Gamson 1968, 42), and, in difficult times, confidence helps preserve a minimum level of support necessary for the functioning of the political apparatus (Easton 1975). But if confidence cannot be too low, neither can it be too high. A certain level of public scepticism is essential to keep public officials responsive to the people and keep the public vigilant (Almond and Verba 1963; Gamson 1968, 46–8). Thus, unconditional trust in government and political institutions is not necessarily better than the absence of trust. In this chapter, therefore, we explore how much confidence immigrants exhibit for the political institutions of their host country.

As presented in the Introduction to this volume, not many studies have examined the issue of political support among immigrants, and even fewer have addressed the specific issue of confidence in political institutions. This chapter examines levels of confidence in political institutions among immigrants in the Australian context. Between 2001 and 2011, the percentage of first-generation immigrants in Australia as a proportion of the overall population increased from 31 per cent to 35 per cent. In addition, about 20 per cent of the population was born in Australia of a mother and/or father born overseas – what we often refer to as second-generation immigrants. In total, therefore, around 55 per cent of the population was either born overseas or had one or two parents who were born overseas.[1] Australia is thus a particularly important case study for examining the amount of confidence that immigrants develop for the political institutions of their host country.

Two questions are asked. First, do first- and second-generation immigrants exhibit similar levels of confidence in the political institutions of their host country? While considerable research has been conducted on the political integration of first-generation immigrants, less attention has been paid to second-generation immigrants (see Ramakrishnan and Espenshade 2001). Because they are born in the host country, members of this increasingly large group are often considered to have fully adapted to the local political dynamics, yet they are often caught between the values of their immigrant parents and those of the broader society. This chapter builds on previous debates on immigration and political integration, which focus primarily on the experience of first-generation immigrants. Observing the second generation as distinct from the first generation offers some important insights into immigrant integration and overall confidence in democratic institutions.

The second question is, Do some groups of immigrants develop more easily than others confidence in the political institutions of their host country? More specifically, we compare the situation of immigrants from authoritarian and democratic countries. Two main considerations justify such a comparison. In recent decades, an important proportion of immigrants who have settled in Australia – and in many other liberal democracies – have come from political regimes that are partly democratic or not democratic at all. Bilodeau, McAllister, and Kanji (2010) estimate this proportion to be higher than 50 per cent in Australia. This raises many questions for host governments as to the ease with which these newcomers make their transition to democracy, and, accordingly, governments place an increasing emphasis on the need for immigrants to express an allegiance to a shared political culture that promotes democratic norms and practices (Ichilov 1990).

Moreover – and closely related to the first consideration – several studies have demonstrated that citizen values and behaviours are profoundly influenced by the authoritarian attitudes of the society in which they received their formative years of socialization (Linz and Stepan 1996; Jacobs and Shapiro 2000; Linz 2000; Stevens, Bishin, and Barr 2006). For example, studies in Australia and Canada indicate that the more severe the experience of authoritarianism is, the more likely it is that immigrants will exhibit a dual loyalty: both to democracy and to non-democratic forms of governments (Bilodeau, McAllister, and Kanji 2010; Bilodeau 2014). The preceding chapter on Mexican immigrants provides evidence, as do the other studies cited above, with regard to the lasting impact of pre-migration political orientations. It is not clear, however, whether such orientations marked by authoritarianism and other pre-migration influences are transferred to the second-generation immigrants born in the host country. If certain segments of immigrants from authoritarian backgrounds experience difficulty in adapting to the norms, attitudes, and expectations of liberal democracy, it is possible that some of these difficulties may be transferred to their children.

The chapter also examines the role of the performance of political institutions in structuring immigrants' level of confidence. While the perspective presented above highlights the importance of political background and the carry-over of attitudes from one political setting to another, performance theories place greater emphasis on contemporary adult experience and perceptions of government performance. This viewpoint is largely influenced by the psychological tradition that shows that "humans have the capacity to change across the entire life span" (Brim and Kagan 1980, 76). This means that successful political integration is not a one-way process. For example, studies have shown that several contextual factors may be critical for a successful integration – such as socio-economic background, labour market access, and feelings of alienation from the political process – particularly among the unemployed (see McAllister and Makkai 1992). In addition, successful immigrant integration is often dependent on immigration programs and citizenship regimes (Freeman 2004). The role of policies is probably best demonstrated by Bloemraad in her study of naturalization rates in Canada and the United States (2006). The question is thus worth asking, What is the role of institutional performance and immigrants' expectations in structuring their confidence in political institutions?

We investigate the above three questions using the Australian Election Study (AES) for 2001 and 2010. Given the large immigrant population in Australia, these two random studies of the Australian population contain sizeable samples of first- and second-generation immigrants. It is important to note that because the samples for these two studies were drawn from the electoral roll, all immigrant respondents in our study hold Australian citizenship. Accordingly, it does not represent all immigrants in Australia, but rather those who have acquired citizenship.[2]

Methodology

To investigate these questions, the first task is to determine whether AES respondents are first- or second-generation immigrants to Australia. To do so, we rely on questions asking respondents in which country they were born and in which country their mother and father were born. The second task requires determining whether respondents have democratic or authoritarian political origins. Such a task is, in principle, straightforward given the range of measures available for categorizing countries according to the degree of freedom in their political institutions. However, the analysis is complicated by the fact that we do not know when respondents or their parents migrated to Australia. For example, how should we classify an immigrant from a country such as Hungary if we do not know when he or she migrated to Australia? A person who migrated from Hungary to Australia in 1960 at the age of 18 would have spent their formative political years in an authoritarian state, while the same person migrating in 2000 would have spent their formative years in a democratic country. The data do not permit us to make this distinction. To partly address this limitation, we categorize countries according to whether they have been continuously democratic since 1950 or whether they have been continuously authoritarian over the same period. Countries that have moved between democracy and authoritarianism represent a third category.[3]

Determining the political origins of second-generation immigrants presents another set of challenges as the mother's and father's origin may be different. However, the challenge is somewhat alleviated by the fact that we know where each parent was born and that, in practice, both parents were often born in the same country. The correlation between the birthplace of fathers and mothers for the second generation is .70. Given the limited sample size available for our analyses, we do not seek to differentiate the political effects of fathers and mothers. When parents were born in countries of different political contexts, they are classified as being of "mixed" political origins.

Classifying birthplace by democratic, mixed, and authoritarian country, then disaggregating the results by generational status, results in the distribution shown in Table 5.1 below. Among the first generation, who constitute about a quarter of the Australian electorate in our sample, about 54 per cent came from a continuously democratic country, and just 9 per cent came from an authoritarian country; the remaining 37 per cent

Table 5.1. Political Origins by Generation (%)

	Democratic	Mixed	Authoritarian	N	Column
First-generation immigrants	54	37	9	993	25
Second-generation immigrants	82	15	3	654	18
Local population	100	0	0	2,322	57

Sources: AES (2001, 2010).

came from countries that have moved between democracy and authoritarianism. The second generation, those who were born in Australia from two parents born overseas, constitutes 18 per cent of the sample of respondents. The majority of the parents from this group, 82 per cent, come from continuously democratic countries, and just 3 per cent come from authoritarian countries. Such a figure is not too surprising given that groups of immigrants from authoritarian countries have arrived in Australia more recently than other groups. Accordingly, many of their children may not yet have reached adulthood, or they may have just reached it. This would explain why their representation in the AES is marginal. Finally, about 57 per cent of respondents were born in Australia of two parents born in Australia; for the sake of simplicity, we refer to this last group as the "local population."

The 2001 and 2010 AES include a battery of items designed to measure confidence in major public institutions, from Parliament and political parties to the armed forces and the police. Table 5.2 below shows the results of a factor analysis, which indicate that, across the electorate, the 10 items form two distinct dimensions.[4] First, we observe a dimension of confidence in political institutions, including Parliament, the federal government in Canberra, political parties, the political system as a whole, the public service, and the legal system. Second, we also observe a dimension of confidence in security institutions, including confidence in the armed forces and the police.

Even though there is some commonality in the confidence that respondents express for each type of institution within each dimension, absolute levels of confidence vary significantly across institutions. Thus, among political institutions, while confidence is highest for the Australian political system as a whole (54 per cent of Australians report having a great deal or quite a lot of confidence), confidence is lowest for political parties (32 per cent). Similarly, for security institutions – as observed in a different context (see Newton 2007) – confidence is significantly higher for the armed forces (88 per cent) than for the police (74 per cent).

Table 5.2. Confidence in Public Institutions among All Australians

	Percentage saying "a great deal" or "quite a lot" of confidence	Factor loadings 1	Factor loadings 2
Political system			
Federal Parliament	47	.88	.11
Federal government in Canberra	47	.84	.15
Australian political parties	32	.82	.13
Australian political system	54	.77	.10
Public service		.63	.14
Legal system	38	.53	.32
Security			
Armed forces	88	.05	.84
Police	74	.23	.74
Eigenvalues		3.85	1.13
Percentage variance explained		43	18

Sources: AES (2001, 2010).
Notes:
The question was, "How much confidence do you have in the following organizations?" Figures are factor loadings from a varimax rotated factor analysis, with unities in the main diagonal.

The different confidence items for each of the two factors were combined into a single scale and re-scored from a low of zero to a high of 10. The mean values for each of the scales are shown in Table 5.3 below, disaggregated for the three groups identified earlier (first generation, second generation, and local population). Both first- and second-generation immigrants exhibit variations based on the democratic/authoritarian experiences of the respondents. Among first-generation immigrants, confidence in political institutions seems to decrease with the democratic experience. Although the differences are marginal, confidence is highest among first-generation immigrants from authoritarian countries (5.29), followed by immigrants from countries with mixed democratic experiences (5.11), and lowest among immigrants from democratic countries (5.01).

McAllister and Makkai (1992) observed a similar pattern in Australia with immigrants from authoritarian countries: they exhibited higher levels of trust in government than immigrants from non-authoritarian countries; this finding was also corroborated by Maxwell (2010a) among immigrants in Europe. It is interesting that the opposite is observed for confidence in security institutions, and the differences among our

Table 5.3. Confidence in Public Institutions by Generation

	Political institutions	Security	N
First generation			
Democratic	5.01	6.84	525
Mixed	5.11	6.35	337
Authoritarian	5.29	5.91	87
Second generation			
Democratic	4.96	6.86	515
Mixed	4.55	6.01	94
Authoritarian	4.54	6.04	16
Local population	4.98	6.88	2,199

Sources: AES (2001, 2010).
Note: Figures are mean scores from zero to 10 based on the factors in Table 5.2.

three groups are larger. Confidence in the police and armed forces is highest among first-generation immigrants from democratic countries (6.84), followed by immigrants from countries with mixed democratic experiences (6.35), and lowest among immigrants from authoritarian countries (5.91). Immigrants from authoritarian regimes are possibly more hesitant to trust what they might consider the repressive instruments of the state.

By contrast, for second-generation immigrants, confidence in both political and security institutions seems to be highest among those born of parents from democratic countries. While the mean score is 4.96 among second-generation immigrants from democratic countries, it is 4.55 among those from mixed political systems. The difference is even larger for security institutions, with mean scores of 6.86 and 6.01, respectively, for our two groups. Levels of confidence are also quite low among second-generation immigrants from authoritarian countries, although the sample is very small for this group of respondents ($N = 16$). Finally, it is important to note that levels of confidence for both political and security institutions among first- and second-generation immigrants from democratic countries approximate quite closely those of the local population.

The differences reported above suggest that the political origins of immigrants – even second-generation immigrants – seem to exert a certain influence on their levels of confidence in political and security institutions. Other considerations, however, can potentially account for the differences across groups. As explained earlier, the evaluation of institutional performance is thought to exert a significant influence on one's

Table 5.4. Evaluation of Institutional Performance and Socio-demographic Profile

		First generation			Second generation			Local population
		Democratic	Mixed	Authoritarian	Democratic	Mixed	Authoritarian	
Country's prospective economic situation	5 = a lot better 4 = a little better 3 = same 2 = a little worse 1 = a lot worse	3.13	3.10	3.09	3.26	3.14	3.18	3.17
Effect of government policies	3 = good effect 2 = no difference 1 = bad effect	1.97	1.96	2.00	2.03	2.08	2.25	2.00
Left-right position	0 (left) to 10 (right)	5.23	5.41	5.19	5.27	4.99	5.36	5.21
Interest in politics	4 = a good deal 3 = some 2 = not much 1 = none	3.32	3.15	2.96	3.20	3.13	2.71	3.19
Age	In years	56.37	54.63	55.89	54.40	53.15	53.00	54.56
Gender	1 = male 0 = female	.51	.49	.46	.45	.54	.47	.46
University education	1 = yes 0 = no	.19	.22	.37	.21	.30	.35	.21
Family income	Quintiles	2.78	2.67	2.74	2.96	3.35	3.17	2.92

level of confidence. Moreover, the respondents' levels of confidence could also be associated with their specific socio-economic situation.

First, could the observed group differences be attributed to different evaluations of institutional performance? Descriptive data presented in Table 5.4 above suggest that it is unlikely the case. Our data indicate that mean scores on evaluations of institutional performance among those with different political origins are fairly similar. All groups hold broadly similar evaluations of Australia's economic future, and all groups broadly agree on the limited impact of government policies on the economy.

Second, could the observed group differences be attributed to distinct socio-economic profiles? The data in Table 5.4 indicate no significant difference in terms of age or income level. The data do indicate, however, that immigrants from authoritarian regimes – both first and second generations – exhibit higher levels of university education. Moreover, interest in politics is slightly lower among first- and second-generation immigrants from an authoritarian background compared to immigrants from a democratic background. This is an interesting paradox: first- and second-generation immigrants from authoritarian countries exhibit higher levels of education but lower levels of interest in politics.

To sort out which of these considerations has the greatest effect on group differences in levels of confidence, multivariate analyses are conducted. The analyses rely on ordinary least-squares regression methods. We proceed with two regression analyses. The first one compares first-generation immigrants to the local population, while the second one compares second-generation immigrants to the local population. For each one, we proceed in two steps. In Model 1, we include only variables indicating whether the respondents (for first-generation immigrants) or the parents' respondents (for second-generation immigrants) were born in democratic, mixed, or authoritarian political systems. In Model 2, we include our control variables – evaluation of institutional performance and socio-demographic profile – and examine whether these can account for group differences. Our hypotheses predict that for the first generation, a person's country of birth – democratic or authoritarian – will influence his or her confidence in public institutions. For the second generation, we predict that the same effect will occur through the parents' country of birth.

Results

The results of the analyses are shown in Table 5.5 below. For the first generation, they suggest that the type of country that respondents or

Table 5.5. Confidence in Political Institutions and Regime Type

	First generation		Second generation	
	Model 1	Model 2	Model 1	Model 2
Respondent was born in[a]				
Democratic	.01	−.01	n/a	n/a
Mixed	.02	−.01	n/a	n/a
Authoritarian	.03*	.02	n/a	n/a
Parents were born in[b]				
Democratic	n/a	n/a	−.00	.00
Mixed	n/a	n/a	−.05**	−.04**
Country's economic situation		−.16***		−.19***
Government effect on economy		−.17***		−.15***
Left-right position		.07***		.04*
Interest in politics		.15***		.16***
Age		.00		.02
Gender		−.09***		−.07**
University education		.08***		.09***
Family income		.07***		.06**
Adjusted R-square	.00	.14	.00	.15
N	3,145	2,349	2,819	2,087

Sources: AES (2001, 2010).
Note: Ordinary least-squares regression analysis showing standardized (beta) coefficients predicting confidence in institutions. See text for details of variables and scoring.
[a] The reference category is the local population.
[b] The reference category is the local population; there is no category for "authoritarian" because the sample size is too small.
* $p < .10$, **$p < .05$, ***$p < .01$

their parents were born in does seem to have a small but significant effect on their confidence in Australian political institutions. As suggested in Table 5.3, first-generation immigrants from authoritarian countries appear somewhat more confident than other immigrants and the local population. Once controlling for the socio-economic situation as well as their evaluation of institutional performance, however, the difference does not remain statistically significant. What seems to matter most for first-generation immigrants is good governance. The results show that those who believe that the economy is performing well and that the government has had a positive effect on the economy tend to have more confidence in political institutions compared to those who believe that the government has performed badly. Social background also matters. Women and those with a higher education and income are more likely to value political institutions positively. Political interest is also important for levels of confidence. Those who show an active interest in politics are also more likely to view political institutions positively compared to those who show little interest in politics.

The situation is different for second-generation immigrants. As suggested in Table 5.3, those of mixed political origins seem to be less confident than other second-generation immigrants and the local population. Here, however, the lower confidence of second-generation immigrants from mixed background remains significant once the control variables are included in the model. Thus, even though evaluations of the economy and other socio-economic variables, such as education and interest in politics, relate to confidence in Australian political institutions, they fail to account for the lower confidence in political institutions among second-generation immigrants of mixed political origins.

We also examined the relative importance of political origins, institutional performance, economic evaluations, and social background on confidence in security institutions. The results for Model 1 in Table 5.6 below, for both first- and second-generation immigrants, are consistent with those observed in Table 5.3. Those immigrants of mixed or authoritarian political origins exhibit lower levels of confidence in security institutions than other immigrants and the local population. Moreover, in contrast to our analyses for political institutions, including the control variables in Model 2 for security institutions, this does not explain the lower levels of confidence observed for first- and second-generation immigrants from authoritarian and mixed political origins. Once again, even though evaluations of the economy, interest in politics, and education – to name a few – significantly relate to confidence in the police and the armed forces, first- and second-generation immigrants from authoritarian and mixed political origins appear less confident in security institutions than other immigrants and the local population.

Conclusion

Many of the chapters presented in this volume have focused on immigrant political participation – a reflection of the dominant trend in the field, as highlighted in the Introduction. In the present chapter, we decided to explore another dimension of immigrant political integration – namely, confidence in the political institutions of the host country. Such confidence is essential for the smooth functioning of a democracy. The chapter also looked at confidence in what we called security institutions – more specifically, the police and Australian armed forces. Two questions were investigated.

Table 5.6. Confidence in Security Institutions and Regime Type

	First generation		Second generation	
	Model 1	Model 2	Model 1	Model 2
Respondent was born in[a]				
Democratic	−.01	−.03	n/a	n/a
Mixed	−.09***	−.11***	n/a	n/a
Authoritarian	−.09***	−.09***	n/a	n/a
Parents were born in[b]				
Democratic	n/a	n/a	−.01	−.01
Mixed	n/a	n/a	−.08***	−.06***
Country's economic situation		−.07**		−.05*
Government effect on economy		−.05*		−.04*
Left-right position		.12***		.10***
Interest in politics		.04*		.07***
Age		.03		.02
Gender		−.02		−.02
University education		−.04*		−.03*
Family income		.01		.03*
Adjusted R-square	.01	.04	.01	.02
N	3,220	2,381	2,884	2,121

Sources: AES (2001, 2010).
Note: Ordinary least-squares regression analysis showing standardized (beta) coefficients predicting confidence in institutions. See text for details of variables and scoring.
[a] The reference category is the local population.
[b] The reference category is the local population; there is no category for "authoritarian" because the sample size is too small.
* $p < .10$, **$p < .05$, ***$p < .01$

The first question was, Do immigrants of first and second generations exhibit similar levels of confidence as the local population in Australian political and security institutions? It seems, however, that the answer to this first question cannot be provided without simultaneously answering our second question, Do some groups of immigrants develop confidence in Australian institutions more easily than others? The answer seems to be that some groups of immigrants – such as those from democratic political systems – exhibit levels of confidence in Australian institutions similar to those of the local population and that this holds for both first- and second-generation immigrants. In contrast, however, other groups of immigrants are distinct from the local population – more specifically, those from authoritarian or mixed political origins. Do these latter groups exhibit more or less confidence in Australian political and security institutions than the local population? Once again, the answer is conditioned upon two considerations: which institutions – political or security – and which generation of immigrant – first or second – are we talking about?

For political institutions, once the model controlled for differences in socio-economic status or for different evaluations of institutional performance, second-generation immigrants from authoritarian and mixed political origins also appeared to have less confidence than the local population, but not first-generation immigrants of these origins. The question is, then, When looking at confidence in political institutions, why are immigrants' political origins seemingly determinant for second-generation but not for first-generation immigrants? These findings present quite a paradox and challenge the causal mechanism at play here. Can we talk about the influence of immigrants' political origins – or pre-migration influences – when looking at second-generation immigrants born and raised in Australia, especially when no such effect is observed among first-generation immigrants? Something other than pre-migration influence is arguably the key to explaining these findings.

For security institutions, the pattern is straightforward. Both first- and second-generation immigrants from authoritarian and mixed political origins exhibit less confidence in security institutions than the local population and other immigrants. Moreover, these differences do not appear to be attributable to socio-economic status or to evaluations of institutional performance. So what explains the lower levels of confidence in security institutions among first- and second-generation immigrants from authoritarian and mixed political origins? Here the pre-migration influence appears more plausible. One common key characteristic of authoritarian countries and those with a mixed political history is the role that repressive instruments of the state, such as the police and the army, have played in threatening, silencing, or physically oppressing populations. To a varying extent, it is exactly what many immigrants from authoritarian and mixed political origins experienced before coming to Australia.

It is, then, not too surprising to observe lower levels of confidence in these institutions among these immigrants, even when living in Australia. Immigrants from these countries might be carrying with them a deeply entrenched fear of those repressive instruments of the state. As for the second-generation immigrants, born and raised in Australia and thus never having a first-hand experience with these repressive forces in their parents' country of origin, how can we explain their lower levels of confidence? It seems not too extravagant to speculate that such fear of political repression can be easily transmitted from parents to their children through the process of socialization. Hence, although they did not themselves experience the repressing power of these institutions, second-generation immigrants could have inherited from their parents the fear of those institutions, in any country.

Our pre-migration explanation, however, is based on quite a distant inference – namely, national political origins. Accordingly, we do not highlight the precise causal mechanism at play here. And not everything points to this pre-migration explanation. For instance, as mentioned above, why are we not observing a similar pattern for both first and second generations when it comes to confidence in political institutions? It seems that we could have expected the same pattern as that observed for security institutions. Accordingly, it appears appropriate to propose at least one other possible explanation to make sense of the lower levels of confidence in security institutions among first- and second-generation immigrants from authoritarian and mixed political origins.

In Chapter 8, Gidengil and Roy examine the racial divide in immigrant political integration in Canada between those of visible minority background and other immigrants; perhaps one such possibility would be worth exploring to make sense of the findings presented in our chapter. We know that the relationship between the police and some immigrants and ethnic minorities is not always easy, with the police sometimes being accused of practising what has been called "racial profiling," and a substantial proportion of immigrants from authoritarian and mixed political origins are of an ethnic-minority background that would fall under the "visible minority" category in the Canadian context. It seems that such an explanation might also have some credence here, although, if it is supported, we would expect the effect to be stronger for confidence in the police than for confidence in the armed forces.

All in all, our chapter, like the preceding one examining Mexican immigrants in the United States, offers some support for what seems to be the transfer of political values with migration, especially when the country of origin was authoritarian and repressive (Bilodeau 2008; Bilodeau, McAllister, and Kanji 2010; Bilodeau 2014). Furthermore, although it does not provide a definitive answer to the question, it helps to understand the constraining influence of authoritarianism on political attitudes – even across generations born and raised in the host country.

NOTES

1 See ABS, "Reflecting a Nation: Stories from the 2011 Census, 2012–2013," Cat. no. 2071.0 (Canberra: ABS, 2012).

2 The AES is a national, post-election, mail-out/mail-back, self-completion
   survey of voters. While two AES surveys were conducted between 2001
   and 2010, they did not include questions on confidence in political institutions. For full details of the survey methodology for the 2001 and 2010
   AES surveys, see McAllister and Pietsch (2011, App. B). The AES has been
   conducted for each general election since 1987. The data are available from
   http://assda.anu.edu.au.

3 In categorizing country of origin, we distinguish between countries that
   have been continuously democratic since 1950, using the criteria developed by Lijphart (1999), and countries that have been continuously authoritarian for the same period. Countries in the former category are
   Australia, Austria, Belgium, Canada, Denmark, Finland, France, Iceland,
   Ireland, Italy, Japan, the Netherlands, New Zealand, Norway, Sweden,
   Switzerland, the United Kingdom, and the United States. Identifying
   countries that are in the latter category is more difficult. For this purpose,
   we use the Freedom House ranking and classify any country that has a
   score of 3 as continuously authoritarian. The countries in this category are
   Brunei, Burma, Cambodia, China, Egypt, Gaza and the West Bank, Hong
   Kong, Iran, Iraq, Russia, Sri Lanka, Syria, Vietnam, and Zimbabwe. All
   other countries are coded as mixed.

4 Four further items in the battery – the legal system, trade unions, the public service, and universities – either added little explanatory power to the
   scales or cross-loaded and were therefore excluded.

6 How Much Do They Help?
Ethnic Media and Political Knowledge in the United States

CHRIS HAYNES AND S. KARTHICK RAMAKRISHNAN

Political scientists have long recognized the important role that knowledge of politics plays in enabling citizens to make decisions that are in line with their interests. Although we have a relatively good understanding of the content, determinants, and consequences of political knowledge among the general population (Delli Carpini and Keeter 1997; Bartels 1996; Bennett 1995; see Galston 2001 for a review), we know little about the role and consequences of political knowledge in the American context for fast-growing minority groups such as Asians, Latinos, and African Americans (Pantoja and Segura 2003; Nicholson, Pantoja, and Segura 2006). What we do know, however, is that a sizeable knowledge gap exists among Latinos, African Americans, and the rest of the population, even after controlling for other factors, further compounding other ethnic inequalities based on class and racial discrimination (Delli Carpini and Keeter 1997; Nicholson, Pantoja, and Segura 2006; de la Garza et al. 1992; DeSipio 1996).

Moreover, we know from various studies of political news consumption in these communities that ethnic media play an important part in the lives of many individuals in these subgroups. This was perhaps most dramatically evident during the massive pro-immigration marches of 2006, as millions of Latinos participated in peaceful street demonstrations, with political messages and strategies that were coordinated by Spanish-language radio personalities and widely reported by television news anchors (Voss and Bloemraad 2010). This is also evident in presidential campaigns as candidates attend primary debates sponsored by Spanish-language news organizations and nominees attend national gatherings of ethnic-minority groups that are heavily covered by ethnic news media.

While some have explored the role of ethnic-media consumption on political behaviour (Abrajano 2010; Panagopoulos and Green 2011), surprisingly little research has been done on the consequences of ethnic-media consumption on political knowledge. Here we bring these two concerns together to examine whether, and how, the consumption of ethnic news media relates to political knowledge among Latinos, Asian Americans, and African Americans. We seek to answer three fundamental questions. First, is the consumption of ethnic media related in any significant way to knowledge of American politics? Second, which ethnic media (television, newspaper, radio, or the internet) has the greatest relationship to knowledge of American politics among ethnic-minority groups? And third, do these associations vary across groups? Thus, like the previous chapter on confidence in political institutions in Australia, we shift the focus away from immigrant political participation.

While our chapter analyses these relationships among African Americans as well as Latinos and Asian Americans, it is important to point out that African Americans are different than the other groups primarily because of their unique process of socialization, including slavery and a longer history of living in the United States. This history shows how black media have served as a crucial link between African Americans and their leaders (Dawson 1994). This linkage may indeed motivate African Americans to obtain and retain their political information from ethnic-media sources. And while some might cite this as a reason for not analysing African Americans alongside Latinos and Asian Americans, we disagree. We point out that many of the experiences and factors that forged this linkage for African Americans and black media are there for Latinos and Asian Americans as well. In fact, the proliferation and success of Latino and Asian news sources bolsters this claim.

The Role of Ethnic Media

News media that cater to ethnic minorities in the United States is not new. The first African American newspaper, *Freedom's Journal*, was founded in New York in 1827, after the abolition of slavery in the state. While much of its editorial focus advocated for the political rights of free blacks in the North and countered the pro-slavery messages of other newspapers in New York, *Freedom's Journal* also provided freed blacks in the North with features that were typical of other newspapers (local, national, and international news; classifieds; birth and death announcements), but often customized to this audience (Bacon 2007).

African American newspapers proliferated in the 19th century with the growth of African American communities in the North before the Civil War and even after the implementation of segregation following the end of Reconstruction. And they continued to grow in the 20th century with the Harlem Renaissance and various movements for political empowerment throughout the civil rights era of the 1960s. Since the 1970s, many African American newspapers have gone out of business, but other types of media have grown in size and stature, including African American radio and cable television and African American–oriented websites (Barlow 1999; Jones 1990; Harris-Perry 2004).

Perhaps an even greater transformation of the news media landscape in the past few decades has been the rise of ethnic media catering to Latinos and Asian Americans. For both groups, the growth of newspapers, radio, and television has all been driven by the growth of immigrant communities – first in gateway states and cities in the two decades following the liberalization of immigration policy in 1965 and, subsequently, after the settlement of immigrants in new destination regions in the Midwest and the South. As with African American newspapers from the 19th century, these ethnic-media outlets serve a range of purposes, from providing entertainment and community-specific business information, coverage of local events, and coverage of homeland politics and US foreign policy that do not typically appear in mainstream media (Zhou and Cai 2002). While the earlier formations of ethnic media were focused primarily on helping immigrants maintain a sense of connection to their homelands, more recently these newspapers, radio shows, and television programs have increasingly paid attention to domestic politics, in line with a greater bi-national orientation among immigrant-serving organizations (Levitt and Schiller 2004; Ramakrishnan and Viramontes 2010).

This greater focus on US politics was perhaps most dramatically evident in the widespread pro-immigration marches of spring 2006. In December 2005, the US House of Representatives passed H.R. 4437, a measure that classified undocumented immigrants, and anyone who assisted them, as felons. In response, immigrant activists and allied organizations such as the Catholic Church and service unions led a series of marches and demonstrations, starting in February 2006. The demonstrations were larger than many had expected, from 10,000 in Philadelphia on 14 February to 100,000 in Chicago on 10 March, followed by a protest of 750,000 in Los Angeles on 25 March and over a million demonstrators across the country on 10 April and 1 May. The magnitude of the marches, especially the early demonstrations in Chicago and Los Angeles, caught many in the mainstream media by surprise. By contrast, many ethnic-media outlets knew about these demonstrations well before they occurred. Indeed, Spanish radio and newspapers in Chicago and Los Angeles played a key role in mobilizing Latinos to participate, even shaping the kinds of messages displayed and sent by the demonstrations – with advice on wearing white T-shirts, marching with family members, and waving American flags alongside Mexican ones (Ramírez 2011).

While scholarship on immigrant politics in the United States is starting to pay more attention to the role of ethnic news media in shaping protest activity and less contentious processes of political representation, we know virtually nothing about whether consumption of ethnic media has any bearing on political knowledge. Since Delli Carpini and Keeter published their seminal work on the state of American political knowledge in 1996, the ethnic-media landscape has changed dramatically. Not only is this evident in the growth of large national television networks such as Univision and Telemundo, which air programs that sometimes rank in the top 10 of television viewership, there are now over 3,000 ethnic news-media outlets in the United States, with an estimated 57 million Americans consuming such content (Roberts 2011).

If previous theory and research is correct – that Americans obtain much of their political information from news media (Chaffee and Frank 1996) – the rise in ethnic-media consumption could provide some insight as to why we observe such a sizeable political knowledge gap between whites and non-whites in the United States (Delli Carpini and Keeter 1997; de la Garza et al. 1992). While previous research offers some insight, no study to date has explained how ethnic-news consumption relates to political knowledge among these emerging subgroups of Americans.[1]

Data and Methods

We analyse data from the Collaborative Multi-racial Post-election Survey (CMPS) to examine levels of knowledge of American politics in the context of the 2008 general election. This telephone survey – conducted between 9 November 2008 and 5 January 2009 – was the first multiracial and multilingual survey of registered voters across multiple states and regions in a presidential election. The CMPS was available in six languages and contained robust samples of the four largest ethnic groups, with a total of 4,563 registered voters who self-identified as Asian Americans, African Americans, Latinos, and whites. The sample was drawn from 18 states, including the top states with significant Asian American, African American, and Latino populations plus five battleground states containing at least one minority group with 10 per cent or greater of the registered voter population.[2] Interviews were conducted in English, Spanish, Mandarin, Cantonese, Korean, and Vietnamese; 36 per cent of the Asian interviews and 44 per cent of the Latino interviews were carried out in a non-English language.

Given the comparative sizes of the four group samples and the extent of language support for Asian and Latino populations, the CMPS is an ideal data set for our comparative analysis across racial and ethnic groups. In order to explore the robustness of our findings, we also analyse data from the 2008 American National Election Study (ANES), which posed a question about ethnic-media consumption to Latino respondents in the survey. We provide details about the survey questions that are relevant to this chapter in Appendix B.[3]

Our key outcome of interest is political knowledge. Both surveys included factual questions about which political office was then held by John Roberts. The CMPS had one additional question on political knowledge: about which party (Democrat or Republican) held more seats in the US Congress. The 2008 ANES did not have the same question, but it included questions about the offices held by Nancy Pelosi and Dick Cheney.[4]

Our explanatory variable of interest is whether respondents receive their news about politics primarily from ethnic-media sources or mainstream media sources. The CMPS has the richest data in this regard, asking questions about whether respondents obtain their information about politics from particular sources (television, radio, newspapers, or the internet) and whether each of those sources is predominantly in Spanish (for Latinos), is an Asian-language or Asian-oriented source (for Asian Americans), or is black-oriented (for African Americans). The ANES has a composite version of this question, asking Latino respondents whether they obtain most of their information about politics from "Spanish-language television, radio, and newspapers, or from English-language television, radio, and newspapers." (See Appendix D.)

Levels of Knowledge of American Politics

To begin, we look for gaps in knowledge of American politics between the ethnic-minority groups and the white population. Table 6.1 below reports the levels of political knowledge for each ethnic group in both

Table 6.1. Political Knowledge (Proportion Correctly Identifying) (%)

	Latino	Asian	Black	White
Collaborative Multi-racial Post-election Study (2008)				
Majority party in US House	63	68	64	79
Office of John Roberts[a]	10	21	19	29
N	1,576	918	944	1,121
American National Election Study, Post-election (2008)				
Office of Nancy Pelosi[b]	25	–	28	55
Office of Dick Cheney	45	–	51	73
Office of John Roberts[a]	5	–	6	17
N	504	–	568	1,156

[a] Respondent coded as correctly identifying Roberts as a judge, justice, or Supreme Court Chief Justice.
[b] Respondent coded as correctly identifying Pelosi as a member of Congress, democratic leader, or Speaker of the House of Representatives.

the 2008 CMPS and the 2008 ANES post-election surveys. Consistent with previous findings in the literature, we find significant gaps in political knowledge between whites and all other ethnic-minority groups. According to the CMPS, while 79 per cent of whites knew which party held the majority in the US House, this was true of only 63 per cent of Latinos, 68 per cent of Asian Americans, and 64 per cent of African Americans. On the question of what office John Roberts held in 2008, 29 per cent of whites responded with the correct answer; this was true of only 10 per cent, 21 per cent, and 19 per cent of Latinos, Asian Americans, and African Americans, respectively.

Similarly, data from the 2008 ANES show that whites appear to be most politically knowledgeable, followed by African Americans and Latinos.[5] On the question of which office Nancy Pelosi held at the time, only 25 per cent of Latinos and 28 per cent of African Americans were able to respond with a correct answer. In comparison, 55 per cent of whites answered this question correctly, a response that equates to a 30-percentage-point gap with Latinos and a 27-point gap with African Americans. We find similar patterns for the questions asking for the office of Dick Cheney and the office of John Roberts. Thus, Table 6.1 shows that like previous studies on political knowledge, whites appear to be most knowledgeable, followed by Asian Americans, African Americans, and Latinos.

Ethnic-Media Consumption

What about consumption of ethnic media among African Americans, Asian Americans, and Latinos? In Table 6.2 below, we report media usage of ethnic and mainstream sources of news from both the 2008 CMPS and the 2008 ANES post-election surveys. First, we observe that only a minority of Latinos, Asian Americans, and African Americans consume ethnic media exclusively. Second, we find that exclusive use of ethnic media is highest among Asian Americans, followed by Latinos and then African Americans. According to the CMPS, 12 per cent of Latinos, 16 per cent of Asian Americans, and 2 per cent of African Americans report watching only ethnic television stations to obtain their political information. For ethnic consumption of newspapers, we find similarly that 18 per cent of Asian Americans, 4 per cent of Latinos, and 3 per cent of African Americans report receiving most of their political information solely from ethnic news sources. Finally, analysing the ANES data, we find that 13 per cent of Latinos consume most of their political information from Spanish-language news sources, a finding that is almost identical to that revealed by the CMPS (12 per cent).

These patterns – showing that exclusive ethnic-media use is highest among Asian Americans – are consistent with expectations based on patterns of nativity as the proportion of first-generation immigrants is much higher among Asian Americans than among Latinos. These demographic realities are reflected in our data set, in which 71 per cent of Asian American respondents were foreign-born, while only 44 per cent of Latinos were born outside the United States.[6] Furthermore, there is a significant correlation between nativity and ethnic-media use for Latinos (ranging from $r = 0.31$ to 0.49, depending on the source) and Asian Americans ($r = 0.24$ to 0.36, depending on the source).

It is interesting to note that while Asian Americans are the most likely to consume only ethnic media, they are also those most likely to consume only mainstream media, and this holds for all four types of media (television, newspaper, radio, and the internet), although the differences between them and Latinos and African Americans are not always large. Asian Americans thus present the most "forked" pattern of media consumption of all ethnic-minority groups examined.

Accordingly, when we look beyond exclusive use of ethnic media to those who obtain political information from a mix of ethnic and mainstream sources (see Table 6.2), we find that Latinos and African

Table 6.2. Ethnic News Media Usage by Data Set and Racial/Ethnic Group (%)

	Ethnic only	Ethnic and mainstream	Mainstream only	Any ethnic source	No news consumption
Collaborative Multi-racial Post-election Study (2008)					
Latinos					
Television	12	36	41	48	11
Newspaper	4	15	31	19	51
Radio	10	15	23	25	52
Internet	2	9	35	11	54
Asian Americans					
Television	16	16	55	32	13
Newspaper	18	11	34	29	37
Radio	12	7	27	19	54
Internet	8	13	37	21	42
African Americans					
Television	2	44	46	46	8
Newspaper	3	25	29	28	43
Radio	7	28	19	35	47
Internet	2	17	25	19	56

	English	Spanish	Both
American National Election Study, Post-election (2008)			
Latinos			
All types of media	78	13	8

Americans score much higher than Asian Americans. Thus, for example, 36 per cent of Latinos and 44 per cent of African Americans receive their news from a mix of mainstream and ethnic television, while the same is true for only 16 per cent of Asian Americans. Similarly, while 15 per cent of Latinos and 28 per cent of African Americans obtain their news from a mix of ethnic and mainstream radio outlets, only 7 per cent of Asian Americans do so. The group differences on our other two measures (newspapers and internet sources) are not as stark, but even there, African Americans have significantly higher levels of mixed news consumption than Asian Americans.

We also find interesting differences by ethnic group in the type of media source that people favour for their political news. The most preferred source of political-news consumption among those who only pay attention to ethnic media is television for Latinos, newspapers for Asian Americans, and radio for African Americans. Unsurprisingly, when we fold in those who receive their political information from both ethnic and mainstream sources, television news is the most popular media source. However, it is interesting to point out that the second most preferred news source is not consistent across all three racial groups; here we find that while the second most preferred news source for Latinos and African Americans appears to be the radio, Asian Americans instead prefer the newspaper.

Thus, results indicate that while Asian Americans are the most active consumers of ethnic media across all four forms when measured *exclusively*, African Americans tend to be the highest consumers when we include those who consume both mainstream and ethnic media. Most important, however, a significant proportion of each ethnic group obtains at least some of its political information from ethnic-media sources.

Ethnic-Media Consumption and Knowledge of American Politics

How does ethnic-media consumption relate to political knowledge? To arrive at a systematic answer to this question, we conduct ordinary least squares (OLS) regressions since our outcomes are index measures of political knowledge. Separate analyses are conducted for Latinos, Asian Americans, and African Americans (see Table 6.3 below). Given the relatively small sample sizes of Latino and African American respondents who consumed ethnic media exclusively, we operationalize the ethnic-media consumption variable as *any* ethnic-news consumption compared to mainstream-news consumption and no news consumption (no ethnic, no mainstream). In the discussion of the results, we will note any areas where our findings for "exclusive ethnic-media use" vary from the "any ethnic-media use" measure.

In addition to ethnic-news consumption, we consider the potential effect of several other factors on political knowledge among ethnic-minority groups in the American electorate. First, we consider nativity. Scholars observe that those who are born outside the United States have lower levels of political knowledge because of their lower levels of interest in politics and their lack of exposure and familiarity with American political culture (DeSipio 1996; Wong 2000; Ramakrishnan 2005). Second, we consider socio-economic factors such as age, gender, and educational attainment. Most scholars agree that level of education is one of the most important factors in determining a person's level of political knowledge (Bennett 1994); age also matters for political knowledge as repeated exposure to the American political system is hypothesized to increase a person's chances of learning important facts

Table 6.3. Predictors of Formal Political Knowledge

	Latinos				Asian Americans				African Americans			
	Model 1		Model 2		Model 1		Model 2		Model 1		Model 2	
	B	SE	β	SE	β	SE	B	SE	β	SE	B	SE
Newspaper												
None	−.04	.06	.01	.06	−.07	.10	−.07	.12	**−.08***	.09	−.04	.09
Mainstream[a]	**.07***	.07	**.06***	.07	.02	.11	−.01	.13	.01	.1	.03	.1
Radio												
None	−.03	.06	−.03	.06	−.02	.11	−.04	.12	.02	.08	.01	.08
Mainstream	**.09***	.07	**.07****	.07	.01	.13	−.01	.14	.04	.11	.02	.11
Television												
None	0	.08	−.01	.09	.05	.13	.06	.14	**.09***	.13	**.09****	.13
Mainstream	**.11***	.06	.04	.06	.02	.1	.02	.12	**.14****	.08	**.12***	.08
Internet												
None	**−.23***	.08	**−.18***	.08	**−.18***	.09	**−.16***	.11	**−.13***	.09	**−.10****	.1
Mainstream	**−.10****	.08	**−.10****	.09	.05	.11	.06	.12	.03	.11	.03	.11
Foreign-born			**.05***	.05			−.02	.08			**.08****	.13
English interv.			**.07****	.06			**−.08***	.1			−.01	.7
Age			**.11***	.00			**.07***	.00			**.08****	.00
Educ.			**.23***	.00			**.13***	.01			**.13***	.01
Political contact			.03	.05			−.02	.08			**.07****	.07
Strength party ID			.04	.02			**.08****	.04			.03	.04
R-squared	.09		.14		.06		.08		.06		.09	
N	1,564		1,476		897		749		920		874	

Source: CMPS (2008).
Note: Significant coefficients are in bold.
[a] Mainstream: Mainstream only.
* $p < .1$, ** $p < .05$, *** $p < .01$

about that political system and the actors involved in it (Delli Carpini and Keeter 1997). Scholars have noted a significant gender gap in political knowledge, which reinforces the disadvantages that women face in politics in relation to men (Delli Carpini and Keeter 1997; Bennett 1994).

Third, we consider motivational factors. One of the strongest predictors in this category is a person's level of political interest (Bennett 1994). Another variable related positively to political knowledge is internal political efficacy or the belief that one can understand politics well enough to participate effectively in the process of democratic representation (Delli Carpini and Keeter 1997). Finally, scholars have found that partisan strength is strongly related to political knowledge:

the stronger a person's attachment to a political party (e.g., Republican, Democrat), the higher a person's level of political knowledge (Delli Carpini and Keeter 1997; Bennett 1994).

In Model 1, we report the results of the analyses when only the media variables are included – with any ethnic-news consumption as the omitted variable. In Model 2, we report the results of analyses that control for the variables listed above.

Latinos

For Latinos, we find that consumers of ethnic media – whether it be newspapers, television news, or radio news – have the same levels of political knowledge as those who consume no news at all. This means that those who consume Spanish newspapers, television, or radio have no knowledge advantage in comparison to those who do not consume any news media. For these three media types, those who are exclusive consumers of mainstream news have the highest levels of political knowledge. The consumption of Spanish-language news on the internet, however, has a different effect. Here such ethnic-media consumption has a significant and positive relationship with knowledge of politics: those who know the most are those who consume some ethnic media on the internet, suggesting a different selection mechanism into internet news sources. Of course, other factors such as nativity, education, and English proficiency may also account for variation in political knowledge among Latinos, and it is important to see whether these ethnic-media effects persist after controlling for these other factors.

As we can see from our multivariate analysis in Model 2, age, education, and English proficiency are indeed significant and positive correlates of political knowledge among Latinos. Nativity is also significant, but, contrary to expectations, foreign-born Latinos have a higher level of political knowledge when compared to native-born Latinos. However, it is important to note that this relationship appears only after controlling for education and language of interview, factors that are strongly tied to nativity among Latinos. Absent these controls, foreign-born Latinos have lower levels of political knowledge than native-born Latinos, as expected.

More important, even when we control for these factors, in addition to political contact and party identification, we still find that Latinos who consume ethnic newspapers and ethnic radio have a significantly lower level of political knowledge than those who consume mainstream news sources. Only in the case of television news do we find that the information deficit from ethnic-media consumption no longer holds.

Finally, it is important to note that when we disaggregate those who consume ethnic news *exclusively* from those who consume ethnic news in combination with mainstream news, we find that deficits in political knowledge are greatest for those who consume a mix of both sources (results not presented). The relationship is also negative for those who consume ethnic news exclusively when compared to those who consume only mainstream news. However, this difference is statistically significant (at p < .10 or less) only for ethnic radio. Likely, the relatively small proportions of Latinos who consume Spanish-language newspapers only – or the internet – explain why this difference fails to reach statistical significance (see Table 6.2). Thus, overall, Latinos appear to know most when they consume mainstream media exclusively than when they consume only ethnic media; and, finally, they appear to know least when they consume both ethnic and mainstream media. As we indicate below, however, we find a more linear relationship using the ANES data; this suggests that further surveys with information on political knowledge and detailed ethnic-media use will help resolve the question of whether those who consume a mix of ethnic and mainstream news sources are in an intermediate stage with respect to political knowledge or in a separate stage altogether.

Asian Americans

Interestingly, for Asian Americans – the largest immigrant group in this study – ethnic-media consumption does not generally have a significant bearing on their knowledge of American politics. Indeed, even mainstream news consumption is not significantly related to political knowledge among Asian Americans, with the notable exception of internet news consumption; those who consume mainstream and ethnic internet news are likely to have the same level of political knowledge, and have more political knowledge, than those who consume no internet-based news. Thus, for Asian Americans overall, there is little evidence of a relationship between media consumption (ethnic or mainstream) and knowledge of American politics. While we do not observe any media effect for Asian Americans, we nevertheless observe that English proficiency, age, education, and party identification play important roles. It is intriguing that those who responded to the questionnaire in English express lower levels of knowledge. Otherwise, as expected, age and education correlate positively with knowledge of politics. Finally, after controlling for these other factors, nativity does not have any bearing on levels of political knowledge among Asian Americans.

African Americans

Turning finally to the analyses for African Americans, we observe in Model 1 that consumers of ethnic newspapers and ethnic internet news have significantly greater levels of political knowledge when compared to those who consume no news at all ($\beta = .08$ and $\beta = .13$, respectively). On the other hand, those who consume black television news display lower levels of political knowledge than those who consume main-stream television news as well as those who consume no television news at all. This negative relationship between ethnic television-news consumption and political knowledge remains significant even after we introduce our various controls, and it remains true not only when we compare consumers of ethnic-television news to those consuming main-stream news ($\beta = -.09$) but also to those who consume no television news at all ($\beta = .12$). This suggests that there is something about the content of black-television news, or the selectivity of such viewers beyond their age and education, that accounts for lower political knowledge among African Americans. As observed for Latinos and Asian Americans, African Americans who are older and more educated tend to know more about American politics than younger and less-educated African Americans. It is interesting to note that African Americans born abroad seem to know more than those born in the United States.

Replication from Other Studies

The ANES is one of the few other surveys containing information on ethnic media use and political knowledge, and it does so only for Latino respondents. In Table 6.4 below, we report our multivariate find-ings after regressing an index of political knowledge on ethnic-media consumption and a host of available controls.[7] Although the ANES is limited in its coverage of Asian Americans and lacks questions on ethnic-media use among African Americans, it contains a fuller range of variables, including internal efficacy and interest in politics. As with the CMPS, we find that ethnic-media consumption has a negative relation-ship to Latinos' level of political knowledge, even after all of the control variables are included in the model.[8] Substantively, those using both

Table 6.4. Predictors of Formal Political Knowledge among Latinos

	Model 1		Model 2	
	B	SE	B	SE
Mainstream and ethnic	−.09**	.12	−.10**	.12
Ethnic only	−.26***	.11	−.27***	.13
News from newspapers	.05	.02	−.03	.02
News from TV	.08*	.02	.05	.02
News from radio	.12***	.02	.06	.02
News from the internet	.18***	.02	.07	.02
Foreign-born			.09*	.11
English interview			−.06	.14
Age			.18***	.00
Education			.33***	.01
Political interest			−.16***	.03
Internal efficacy			−.08*	.03
Strength of party ID			−.02	.04
Contacted/mobilized			.05	.08
R-squared	.16		.31	
N	441		410	

Source: ANES (2008).
Note: Significant coefficients are in bold.
* p < .1, **p < .05, ***p < .01

ethnic and mainstream media are about 18 per cent less knowledge-able than those who rely only on mainstream media, and those who use Spanish-language media exclusively are 50 per cent less knowledge-able. Including the control variables in Model 2 does not change these findings. Once again, age, education, and interest in politics appear to be significant predictors of Latinos' knowledge of American politics. And, once again, Latinos born abroad appear more knowledgeable than those born in the United States, but those who are appear to know less about politics.

Overall, our regression results from both surveys tend to support our expectations that consumption of ethnic media has a negative relation-ship to political knowledge. Or, to be more specific, those who consume ethnic media often do not know more than those who consume no news media at all. Not surprisingly, then, consumption of ethnic media seems to bring no benefits in knowledge of American politics. There is one no-table exception that merits further exploration: Latinos who obtain their political information from Spanish-language websites are more knowl-edgeable than those who do not consume internet-based news at all.

Conclusion

Prior studies have recognized that there are significant gaps in political knowledge between whites and non-whites. However, short of speculating about the origins of these gaps, few studies have provided a comprehensive account of why these gaps occur. Moreover, no study has yet explored the role that ethnic news-media consumption might have on the political-knowledge levels of individuals in these ethnic-minority groups (i.e., Latinos, Asians), who have been the source of most of the recent population growth in America. The question asked in this chapter was, Do ethnic media help consumers learn about politics in the United States? Here we argue that because of the increase in access to and consumption of ethnic news media, and because of the qualitative differences in programming, informational content, and nature of the coverage of ethnic news media vis-à-vis more mainstream media, ethnic-media consumption might not provide the same knowledge benefits as those associated with mainstream media and, hence, might partly account for the knowledge deficit among Latinos, Asian Americans, and African Americans. Specifically, we expect that because of the tendency for ethnic news to provide less frequent and narrower coverage of American political events, policies, and processes, such consumption does not help consumers among any of these ethnic-minority groups learn more about American politics.

Our findings tend to support our expectations. For Latinos in the ANES and for both Latinos and African Americans in the CMPS, we find that consumers of ethnic media often do not know more than those who do not consume any news media at all. Asian Americans are the only group for whom such a relationship does not appear. Our findings compel us to better understand why ethnic-media outlets tend not to increase political knowledge among their consumers. What is it about the coverage, the people who consume it, or both that result in such findings? If it is the quality of coverage, what does that mean? In other words, what are the selection and/or causal mechanisms that produce these relationships? A related question is, If previous research is correct that lower levels of political knowledge can lead a person to form incorrect preferences, make incorrect political decisions, or otherwise inadequately participate in the democratic political process, is it incumbent upon elites at more ethnic-media outlets to integrate more domestic political information into their broadcasts?

Perhaps ethnic media could be an instrument to integrate new American immigrants into the political system in the same way that

racial coalitions and party machines of the past did for previous waves
of immigrants. To better understand this potential, it is important that
future surveys of ethnic-minority populations include detailed information on ethnic and mainstream news consumption. Measures of political knowledge at the local and international levels, in addition to the
national level, would also help paint a more comprehensive picture of
how ethnic-media consumption relates to the political integration of
immigrants and ethnic minorities.

NOTES

1 Relevant research on Latinos has found generally low levels of political
   knowledge among Latinos (de la Garza et al. 1992; DeSipio 1996; Neuman
   1986; Nicholson, Pantoja, and Segura 2006). Most scholars attribute this
   gap to factors already included in previous models of political knowledge,
   including income, education, and political interest, and new factors, such
   as nativity and political context (Pantoja and Segura 2003).
2 The 18 states were Arizona, California, Colorado, Florida, Georgia,
   Hawaii, Illinois, Michigan, Nevada, New Jersey, New Mexico, New York,
   North Carolina, Ohio, Pennsylvania, Texas, Virginia, and Washington.
3 More details on the CMPS methods can be found at the study's web site at
   http://www.cmpstudy.com.
4 In both surveys, the set of knowledge questions were loaded onto one underlying factor, which we term "formal political knowledge" (from a
   principal-component factor analysis retaining factors with eigenvalues
   greater than 1.0).
5 The 2008 ANES post-election survey does not report Asian as a racial category because of the low incidence of Asian Americans in the data set.
6 We include those born in Puerto Rico as being "born outside the US" because the territory has no representation in the United States and political
   communication is conducted primarily in Spanish. The Puerto Rican–born
   population represents 5 per cent of our Latino sample, and our findings on
   Latinos and ethnic-media use are unaffected by whether we use "United
   States" or "US and Puerto Rico" as constituting the native-born.
7 The full model we use to analyse data from the 2008 ANES includes the
   following independent variables: foreign-born, English interview, age,
   education, internal political efficacy, partisan strength, contacted by campaign, news from newspapers, news from TV, news from radio, news from
   internet, and use of ethnic media.

8 The ANES partial model consists of the five media (mainstream and ethnic) independent variables: news from newspapers, news from TV, news
   from radio, news from the internet, and use of ethnic media. Unlike the
   CMPS, the ANES does not ask detailed questions on ethnic-news consumption for any medium.

7 Enabling Immigrant Participation: Do Integration Regimes Make a Difference?

MARC HELBLING, TIM REESKENS, CAMERON STARK,
DIETLIND STOLLE, AND MATTHEW WRIGHT

What kinds of factors condition the political participation of immigrants? The other chapters in this volume have answered this question by looking at the situation of immigrants in individual countries (Canada, the United States, Australia, the United Kingdom, the Netherlands, and Belgium). In this chapter, we employ a comparative strategy. Such a strategy allows us to explore the role of different sets of considerations influencing immigrants' political integration. More specifically, we ask whether integration policies help to erase the participation gap that other chapters have revealed between immigrants and the native-born. Such policies work to transfer resources to new immigrants as well as providing pathways to politics and civil society. They might entail removing barriers to immigrant participation (e.g., opening voting rights before naturalization at the local level, as seen in Chapter 1 for the Netherlands and in Chapter 2 for Belgium), creating attachment to the host nation state, enabling and supporting employment opportunities for immigrants, and many others. Symbolically, then, these policies are an open hand rather than a closed fist – at least in theory. In practice, we know relatively little about whether such policies actually *work* in systematic ways: above all, do they help to close the distance between immigrants and the native-born and thereby foster a more harmonious and equitable society?

In this chapter, we examine a large cross-national sample of Western democracies to answer this question in a way that one-country studies or small-n comparisons cannot. Our ingredients are the European Social Survey (ESS) (four waves from 2002 to 2008), combined with statistical measures of integration regimes from the 2007 classification of the Migrant Integration Policy Index (MIPEX).

Explaining Immigrant-versus-Native-Born Gaps

There is broad agreement that substantial gaps exist between natives and immigrants in levels of political activity and other aspects of social capital.[1] But these gaps tend to vary over place and time, as demonstrated in many of the chapters in this volume, thus begging the question of the conditions under which immigrants are best able to participate in their host country's political process and civil society. While research to date has focused mainly on immigrant characteristics, aspects of the origin country, and characteristics of the destination or host country to explain participatory disparities between immigrants and the native-born, relatively little attention has been focused on the nature of integration regimes.

Some scholars point to the importance of the welfare-state regime in a given country, whereas others emphasize immigration-policy regimes (mainly how they affect the acquisition of citizenship), and still others examine the impact of multiculturalism versus assimilationism (Sainsbury 2006; Entzinger and Biezeveld 2003; Wright and Bloemraad 2012). A classic focus is on the significance of citizenship regimes in defining immigrants' rights and limitations within a state, claiming that countries with civic-based rather than ethnic-based citizenship are better able to accept immigrants into their society (Kymlicka 1995; Bloemraad 2000).

The story emerging from this literature is mixed – at least in terms of policy effects. On the one hand, a series of studies has argued on behalf of assimilationism versus multiculturalism in closing the immigrant-versus-native-born gap. Koopmans, for example, claims that states with more assimilationist policies or those with less generous welfare states (and particularly a combination of the two) are more successful in integrating immigrants (Koopmans 2010; see also Joppke 2007; de Wit and Koopmans 2005). The idea here is that the lack of a social safety net forces immigrants to leave ethnic enclaves and "acquire the linguistic and cultural skills that are necessary to earn a living" (Koopmans 2010, 21).

Most studies, however, find that such policies do not have much effect (van Tubergen, Mass, and Flap 2004; Fleischmann and Dronkers 2010; Dinesen and Hooghe 2010). This debate notwithstanding, the same issues tend to occur time and time again: these studies focus on socio-economic integration at the expense of the "softer" indicators of social and political community (van Tubergen, Mass, and Flap 2004; Fleischmann and Dronkers 2010), use rather crude indicators (van Tubergen, Mass, and Flap 2004), or are based on few cases (Koopmans 2010; Ersanilli and Koopmans

2010). For example, van Tubergen, Mass, and Flap (2004, 711) simply differentiate among destination countries based on whether they use a point system for allocating visas, and Koopman's conclusions are based on studies that include only three to eight countries.

The main argument in this chapter is that turning the focus to attitudes towards and behaviour within the political community allows us to better understand the role of integration policy in closing the gaps between natives and immigrants. The assumption is that a variety of integration policies might help to reduce engagement gaps. For example, labour-market-integration policies provide immigrants with the socioeconomic resources essential to participation (Verba, Schlozman, and Brady 1995). Others, such as removing legal barriers to participation, seem to be straightforward enough to encourage participation by simply allowing it: voting rights for immigrants or the inclusion of immigrant consultation bodies at all levels of political decision-making should help equalize political opportunities for immigrants.

The role of integration policy is not simply to transfer resources or break down legal barriers. These obviously matter, but it is also true that strong integration efforts might foster attachment to state institutions and the nation state and thus reduce the participation gap. The relationship between national attachment and political and civic engagement has been demonstrated (Huddy and Khatib 2007; Schatz, Staub, and Lavine 1999). Furthermore, one of the foundational expositions of this perspective, T.H. Marshall's *Citizenship and Social Class* (1950), suggests that a vital means of bringing about social solidarity is providing civil rights, which lead to political and ultimately social rights. From this perspective, the failure to accord equal citizenship to immigrants should impinge on their sense of identification with the adoptive nation and, in turn, on their active engagement in its affairs (see also Crepaz 2008, 171). For example, policies targeted at reducing the time and effort necessary for permanent residence as well as nationality should link immigrants early on to the political opportunities and culture in their host country. Even early voting rights and consultative policies should be able to draw immigrants into political issues and institutions in the host country. While we cannot test these causal mechanisms directly, this chapter can help establish a relationship between integration policy and native-immigrant differences in political engagement.

Of course, integration regimes might have little or no effect, even when the focus is on the broad conception of integration favoured here. In this view, macro-level policy regimes might be too abstract to influence immigrants in countries where xenophobia runs rampant and participation depends more on individual resources than fuzzy-sounding tropes about social harmony. Further, if the "assimilationists" are right, it could be that certain types of integration policies enable immigrants to retain elements of their own culture and language at the expense of broader integration (see Koopmans 2010). For example, integration policies that foster family reunification and thus the creation of family networks of immigrants might help build strong immigrant communities, but they might also shelter them from interactions and contact with mainstream society. Given this line of thinking, liberal family-reunification policies might even prevent immigrants from participating in broader societal and political issues. At the same time, even expressly political forms of integration – which seem innocuous enough in their attempt to involve immigrants in politics – might backfire if they lead to political conflict with natives over resources; in such cases, these policies could (somewhat ironically) fail through their very success (Paskeviciute and Anderson 2007). It might, however, also be that these policies create resources that consist in access to existing networks and social ties, thereby easing integration efforts (Portes and Sensenbrenner 1993) and making it easier for immigrants to participate in the political process.

This chapter addresses some of the discussed weaknesses in the literature in that it focuses systematically on general political attitudes and behaviours of immigrants, in comparison to the native-born, as a measure of political integration. These measures include political attitudes such as political interest, political efficacy, and political trust as well as behavioural measures that tap into electoral and non-electoral modes of political participation. Second, we use a large cross-national sample of Western democracies and thereby go beyond other studies, which are based on a small sample of countries. Finally, we will employ a comprehensive policy index measuring several dimensions of integration regimes.

Data, Measures, and Methodology

Data

We bring several sources of data to bear on the questions raised above. First of all, for individual-level information, we measure not just attitudinal "outcomes" but also behavioural ones by measuring actual participation in a variety of political acts. To do this, we rely on the four waves of the European Social Survey (ESS), with emphasis on indicators that have recurred over time. These data enable a uniform and detailed measure of immigrant status as the survey is collected among immigrants and natives, thus allowing us to make comparisons between these two groups. Contrary to other surveys, the ESS also provides detailed information not only on the countries of origin of the respondents, but also on whether their parents have immigrated. We classified respondents as immigrants of the first generation if they were not born in the country of destination; respondents were classified as belonging to the second generation if they were born in the country, but at least one of their parents was not.

Besides its high quality and within-country representativeness, the ESS is the only data set that allows us to compare a large number of countries and thus transcend the one-country, or small-n, comparisons that dominate extant literature. Eighteen Western European countries were included to reduce a variety of dissimilarities (see Table 7.1 below). These 18 countries can be much more easily categorized as "advanced, immigrant-receiving democracies," where most immigrants arrived in the second half of the 20th century or at the beginning of the 21st century. Countries in Eastern Europe have not been traditional receivers of immigrants and have just recently started to be so. Although our estimation strategy is mindful of the longitudinal structure of the data set, in this chapter we are not interested in time effects; having four waves available to us simply allows us to capture a sufficiently large immigrant sample for rigorous analysis.

Table 7.1 presents general information about the countries under study, including the waves in which they participated, the total number of respondents surveyed, and the number of those respondents who are first- or second-generation immigrants. For reference, we include the proportion of foreign-born inhabitants in each country in 2005, as recorded in the United Nations Human Development Report. The foreign-born proportion of the survey sample and the actual population often diverge, but, in most cases, the number of first-generation immigrants surveyed provides a sufficient sample on which to base our analyses. Sample-size problems become more apparent when moving to the second generation, where, in countries like Italy and Finland, strikingly low numbers were surveyed. All of this stems from some combination of a given country participating in fewer ESS rounds, historically limited immigration histories, and immigrants being underrepresented in ESS sampling frames and response rates. These are not

Table 7.1. Country Characteristics

Country	ESS round(s)				Total	Foreign-born population			Second generation	
					Survey	Actual[a]	Survey	Survey	Survey	Survey
					N	(%)	(%)	N	(%)	N
Austria (AT)	1	2	3		6,905	14.0	7.8	542	2.0	136
Belgium (BE)	1	2	3	4	7,233	8.5	8.9	644	3.7	271
Switzerland (CH)	1	2	3	4	7,804	22.3	19.3	1,504	3.9	307
Cyprus (CY)				4	1,215	13.9	7.9	96	0.6	7
Germany (DE)	1	2	3	4	11,452	12.9	8.0	921	2.0	226
Denmark (DK)	1	2	3	4	6,091	7.8	5.6	341	0.8	48
Spain (ES)	1	2	3	4	7,842	10.7	7.4	578	0.3	22
Finland (FI)	1	2	3	4	8,113	3.3	2.7	216	0.1	11
France (FR)	1	2	3	4	7,368	10.6	8.7	643	3.9	289
Great Britain (GB)	1	2	3	4	8,691	9.7	9.7	843	2.5	216
Greece (GR)	1	2		4	7,024	8.8	8.7	608	4.2	293
Ireland (IE)	1	2	3		6,119	14.8	8.7	530	0.2	13
Italy (IT)	1	2			2,736	5.2	2.2	61	0.1	2
Luxembourg (LU)	1	2			3,185	33.7	30.4	969	7.3	232
Netherlands (NL)	1	2	3	4	7,911	10.6	8.4	666	1.6	127
Norway (NO)	1	2	3	4	7,093	8.0	7.3	515	0.4	27
Portugal (PT)	1	2	3	4	8,136	7.2	5.9	476	0.7	56
Sweden (SE)	1	2	3	4	7,701	12.3	10.8	828	2.0	156

Source: Survey data pooled ESS (2002–08).
[a] 2005 values, UNDP (2008).

issues that can be definitively "solved," and as a result, we must proceed with the utmost caution when interpreting specific results in these cases. In our analyses below, we highlight cases that include fewer than 20 immigrants in the entire sample (per wave) and eliminate them from analyses of the role of immigration regimes.

Measures

INDEPENDENT VARIABLES

Any attempt to gauge the putative effect of integration policy will not go far without a suitable measure of it. By far the most comprehensive cross-national indicators are the MIPEX scores, produced under the auspices of the European Union (Niessen, Huddleston, and Citron 2007). MIPEX was designed to measure "policies that promote integration in European societies" (ibid., 4), implying that the policies it quantifies ought to close gaps between natives and immigrants. These data catalogue a huge array of policies pertaining to immigrant integration against a standard of "best practice" drawn from Council of Europe conventions and European Community directives.[2] When national policies meet these best practices, countries receive the maximum score of 3; when they are halfway there, they receive a score of 2; and when they do not meet these best practices, they receive the least favourable score of 1.

Despite its aim to benchmark against what MIPEX refers to as the "highest European or international standards aimed at achieving equal rights, responsibilities and opportunities for all its residents" (Huddleston et al. 2011, 7), this "best practice scoring" is sometimes criticized for being overly normative and not based on clear criteria. It is often unclear, for example, why selected policies receive higher scores than others (Howard 2009, 34–5). To give but one example of the arbitrary nature of the coding, we can point to how MIPEX quantifies language requirements to acquire naturalization. Whereas the European "best practice" is an absence of language requirements or only an A1 level (the beginner level), and thus receives the maximum MIPEX score of 3, it can be argued that a language requirement should be seen as being supportive of integration, thus receiving a higher score. Nonetheless, various tests have shown that the MIPEX data are highly reliable as they correlate strongly with alternative indicators that are based on concrete criteria but available only for a restricted number of countries (Koopmans 2012; Koopmans, Michalowski, and Waibel 2012; Howard 2009, 33–5). To an increasing extent, cross-national studies addressing immigrants' integration success rely on the MIPEX composite index or its sub-dimensions (Dinesen and Hooghe 2010; Fossati 2011; Dronkers and Vink 2012).

MIPEX canvasses integration policy with respect to the following domains: labour market access (such as job eligibility for immigrants and their rights as workers), family reunification (broadly concerning the rights of immigrants to sponsor family members for immigration and eventual citizenship), long-term residence (the rights associated with attaining and retaining the status of a "long-term resident" over that of a "temporary alien"), political participation (broadly speaking, the freedom of immigrants to participate in national politics through voting or party membership), access to nationality (pertaining to the ease with which immigrants can acquire and maintain citizenship), and anti-discrimination (the existence of policies designed to reduce ethnic, linguistic, or religious discrimination in the country). All of these have been collapsed into one overall index, largely because they tend to be sufficiently intercorrelated that we lack the analytical leverage necessary to pry them apart through statistical analysis. Our analyses have shown that they form a reliable scale (Cronbach's alpha: 0.83).

DEPENDENT VARIABLES

We examine a diverse set of outcomes, all tapping into some aspect of political engagement. These include both electoral and non-electoral political participation, political trust, political interest, as well as perceived political efficacy. The measure of political trust comprises seven individual questions, asking whether a respondent trusts politicians, parties, the national parliament, the legal system, police, the United Nations (UN) and the European Parliament.[3] Political interest is a single indicator, while political efficacy is made up of two questions assessing the difficulty a respondent has making political decisions and how complicated the respondent thinks politics is. The separation of electoral and non-electoral participation is based on theoretical differentiation (Verba, Schlozman, and Brady 1995), confirmed here through factor analysis of the eight participatory acts included in the ESS battery. The scale of electoral participation includes party membership, working for a party, contacting politicians, and working in an organization. Non-electoral participation includes wearing a political badge or sticker, signing a petition, publicly demonstrating, and boycotting a product for ethical or political reasons.

All dependent variables are standardized from 0 to 1 to allow for comparisons across the various predictors, and they are shown in Table 7.2 below, along with the Cronbach's alpha for the scale (if applicable). Also included are the means, standard deviations, and sample sizes for the three groups of interest: native-born, second-generation immigrants, and first-generation immigrants. Even at this level, differences quickly emerge among these groups, although coarse descriptions obviously do not account for country-specific levels or individual-level factors. For example, the second generation may be younger, on average, and immigrants from high-participating countries may drive their average up, while native-born respondents from low-participating countries may drive their average down. However, second-generation immigrants score, on average, higher on non-electoral participation, first-generation immigrants have higher average levels of political trust,

Table 7.2. Descriptive Statistics of the Dependent Variables

Dependent variable	α[a]	Native-born			First generation			Second generation		
		Mean	SD	N	Mean	SD	N	Mean	SD	N
Political trust	.88	.50	.18	108,957	.53	.19	10,904	.50	.19	2,432
Political interest	–	.48	.30	109,070	.46	.32	10,943	.46	.31	2,431
Political efficacy	.61	.48	.23	108,776	.46	.24	10,845	.46	.24	2,424
Electoral participation	.56	.11	.20	109,243	.08	.17	10,977	.09	.18	2,438
Non-electoral participation	.54	.16	.23	109,060	.14	.23	10,956	.18	.24	2,435

Source: Survey data pooled ESS (2002–08).
[a] Cronbach's alpha.

and non-immigrants score higher on the remaining measures. Since the above-described country-specific effects should, indeed, mute the differentiation among immigrant types in Table 7.2, we must conduct multivariate analyses to capture the differences we are interested in: immigrant-native gaps.

Methods

ESTIMATING THE GAPS
The first task is to estimate the gaps between immigrants and their native-born counterparts on a country-by-country basis. In all multivariate models, individual-level factors known to have an impact on political variables are controlled. These include the respondent's gender, education, age, employment status, and income. Employment status includes a dummy variable, indicating whether the respondent has ever been unemployed. Subjective income is measured, rather than actual reported income, because equivalent income scales have been available only since wave 4, and the objective income measure yielded a high level of item–non-response.[4] Dummy variables for the different ESS rounds are also included to control for changes in the dependent variables over time.

ESTIMATING THE POLICY EFFECTS
To gauge the effect of the policy measures on immigrant–native-born gaps, a random-intercepts multi-level model on the pooled ESS sample of 18 countries is estimated. The aim is to determine immigrant-mainstream gaps and assess how the size of these gaps varies according to contextual-level policy measures (all else being equal). In this analysis, the focus is on first-generation immigrants, for both practical and

conceptual reasons: the former provide the most reliable sample of immigrants in the data set; as to the latter, it makes sense to assume that integration policies should be most relevant for first-generation immigrants.

These models include the individual-level predictors of political engagement as well as aggregate-level controls for the proportion of immigrants living in each country and its overall level of economic prosperity (estimated here, as elsewhere, using a measure of gross domestic product per capita).[5] To control for temporal effects, the ESS wave corresponding to each respondent is included. In addition, a contextual-level variable captures the average level of the dependent variable among natives in a given country. By creating an interaction between this and the first-generation immigrant indicator, we allow for the possibility – noted in the literature reviewed – that the immigrant-native gap is conditioned by the overall level of the dependent variable among natives in a country (Aleksynska 2008; see also Dinesen and Hooghe 2010, who use a similar model for social trust). The parameter of interest is a cross-level interaction between the MIPEX score and the first-generation immigrant indicator variable. By creating this interaction, it is possible to estimate the size of the immigrant-native gap on the outcome measures as a function of policy regimes.[6]

Results

Multivariate Gaps

The results of the estimation of country-specific immigrant-native gaps are presented in Table 7.3 below. For lack of space, we do not present the full results of all of the regression models here,[7] but rather the linear combination of coefficients comprising the immigrant–native-born gaps for each country and immigrant type. In the interest of clarity, Table 7.3 includes only those (negative) coefficients considered significant at the 95 per cent confidence level. Positive and statistically significant gaps are denoted with a + sign. The table is sorted first by average-gap magnitude and then by the number of significant negative gaps. Total gaps for each dependent variable and immigrant type are presented at the bottom.

As was apparent in Table 7.2, Table 7.3 shows a number of statistically significant *positive* gaps in political trust between first-generation immigrant and native-born respondents. Indeed, 12 of 18 countries exhibit this pattern (see also Maxwell 2013), with only Denmark demonstrating a negative gap (which is, in turn, the smallest of all gaps in

Table 7.3. Multivariate-Gap Coefficients

Country	Number of gaps	Average gap	Political trust		Political interest		Political efficacy		Electoral participation		Non-electoral participation	
			1st	2nd	1st	2nd	1st	2nd	1st	2nd	1st	2nd
LU	7	−.09	+	+	−.11	−.10	−.08	−.10	−.11	−.07	−.06	
CY	5	−.09			−.09		−.13		−.08	−.11	−.06	
IT	2	−.09								−.09ᵃ		−.08a
NO	2	−.07	+	−.10					−.03			
DE	4	−.06	+		−.06		−.06		−.05		−.08	
GR	4	−.06	+	+	−.06	+	−.08		−.04		−.04	+
ES	3	−.06	+		+				−.04	−.04	−.09	
AT	3	−.06			−.06				−.09		−.03	
GB	1	−.06	+			+					−.06	
FI	1	−.06	+						−.06			
CH	6	−.05	+	+	−.04	−.03	−.03		−.07	−.04	−.06	
DK	5	−.04	−.02				−.06	−.07	−.03		−.04	
SE	3	−.03					−.02		−.03		−.03	
BE	2	−.03	+		+				−.03	−.03		
NL	2	−.03	+				−.02		−.03			
FR	1	−.03	+								−.03	
IE	0	−										
PT	0	−	+		+							
Total number of negative gaps			1	1	6	2	8	2	13	6	11	1

Source: Survey data pooled ESS (2002–08).
ᵃ Gap does not include a sufficient number of respondents (< 20).

Denmark). This could be a result of immigrants migrating from "oppressive" regimes and thus finding their host countries' political actors and institutions comparably trustworthy (Bilodeau and Nevitte 2003).

Turning to the second generation, systematic gaps occur only in electoral participation, although they are not nearly as marked as they are with regard to first-generation immigrants. The overall absence of significant gaps between second-generation immigrants and the native-born confirms what Dinesen and Hooghe (2010) have already found with regard to trust – namely, that second-generation immigrants tend to adapt better to the level of engagement of natives in the destination country than do first-generation immigrants. With current discussions about the difficulty of incorporating second-generation immigrants into European society, this result is quite surprising. However, because of low sample sizes for this group, we cannot dwell on this finding much longer.

For first-generation immigrants, negative gaps are present in a number of countries when it comes to political interest (6), political efficacy (8), and both electoral (13) and non-electoral (11) participation. With some exceptions, the negative gaps are fairly small, ranging from 2 to 13 per cent. Still, they are systematically negative across four of our five measures, despite the fact that some countries have conductive integration policies in place.

At first sight, it is difficult to see any pattern in which the gaps could be explained by country-specific characteristics or policies. Among the countries with the largest number of gaps, Luxemburg (7) and Switzerland (6) also have the highest ratios of immigration. While some analyses have indeed revealed a positive correlation between the number of integration gaps and immigration rates, this result is exclusive to the two outliers of Luxembourg and Switzerland. If we exclude these two cases, the correlation disappears as if there were no relationship between immigration rates and the average integration gaps. However, the two countries that do not reveal any gaps, Ireland and Portugal, do have an average proportion of immigrants, thereby not confirming this hypothesis.

If we compare the average gaps with the overall MIPEX scores of the individual countries, we recognize a pattern that seems to confirm our main argument: Cyprus, which shows the highest average gap, ranks second last on the overall MIPEX scale. On the other hand, Portugal, the Netherlands, Belgium, and Sweden, cases with no or very small integration gaps, belong to the group of countries with the most highly developed integration policies and thus very high MIPEX scores.[8] Looking at the overall figures, therefore, it appears that integration policies have an impact and close the gaps between immigrants and natives of the destination countries.

Policy Effects

In what follows, we test whether the observations we made in Table 7.3 hold up in a multivariate analysis. Table 7.4 below, then, presents the condensed results from five models for the overall MIPEX index on all five political outcome variables. Each column represents one of our political outcomes, and the MIPEX index is added to the baseline model. For presentation purposes, displayed in the table for each model is the estimate of the first-generation immigrant dummy interacted with MIPEX, which models the difference in the immigrant-native gap between lowest MIPEX (0) and highest MIPEX (1) countries, all else being

Table 7.4. Policy Slopes for Composite Index of MIPEX

	(1) Political trust		(2) Political interest		(3) Political efficacy		(4) Electoral participation		(5) Non-electoral participation	
	B	SE	B	SE	B	SE	B	SE	B	SE
Native levels of DV	.23***	.01	.18***	.02	.11***	.03	.12***	.02	.19***	.01
Natives × immigrants	−.06***	.01	−.05***	.01	−.05***	.01	−.07***	.01	−.04***	.01
Being an immigrant	.10***	.01	−.10***	.02	−.05**	.02	−.05***	.01	−.06***	.01
MIPEX index	−.00	.00	.00	.00	−.01	.01	−.00	.00	.00*	.00
Immigrant × MIPEX	−.00***	.00	.02***	.00	.01***	.00	.01***	.00	.01***	.00
Covariates	Yes		Yes		Yes		Yes		Yes	
Constant	.52***	.01	.15***	.03	.40***	.04	−.06**	.02	−.03*	.02
N	111,957		112,071		111,735		112,249		112,084	
G	18		18		18		18		18	

Note: Cell entries are the estimated coefficients from five separate random-intercept multilevel models, including contextual- and individual-level controls.
* p < .05, **p < .01, ***p < .001

equal. The information provided in Table 7.4 does not allow one to assess whether a gap is eliminated by a specific policy or whether the effect of native levels counteracts or reinforces the effect of policy, but it provides a summary indication of whether policy matters in reducing the gaps. A positive and significant immigrant × MIPEX interaction term indicates that more inclusive integration policies close the gap between immigrants and the native-born, whereas a negative and significant interaction term implies that more inclusive policies widen the native-immigrant gap.

For the political indicators included in this study, the short answer is that policy *does* matter.[9] The MIPEX policy measures appear to reduce many immigrant-native gaps in political engagement; that is, they are positive and different from zero. But we must be mindful that this effect is associated with the difference between the absolute lowest-policy country and the highest. The only exception of all political engagement indicators appears, again, to be the political trust index, which seems to show that the effect of policy is negative. The positive average coefficient for the immigrant dummy indicates that policy serves to reduce the gap, but in a direction opposite to that of most other political variables. In this sense, integration policy seems to be related in all cases to the reduction of the immigrant–native-born gaps, whether they are

Figure 7.1. Selected Relationships between Immigrant-Native Gaps
and MIPEX Scores

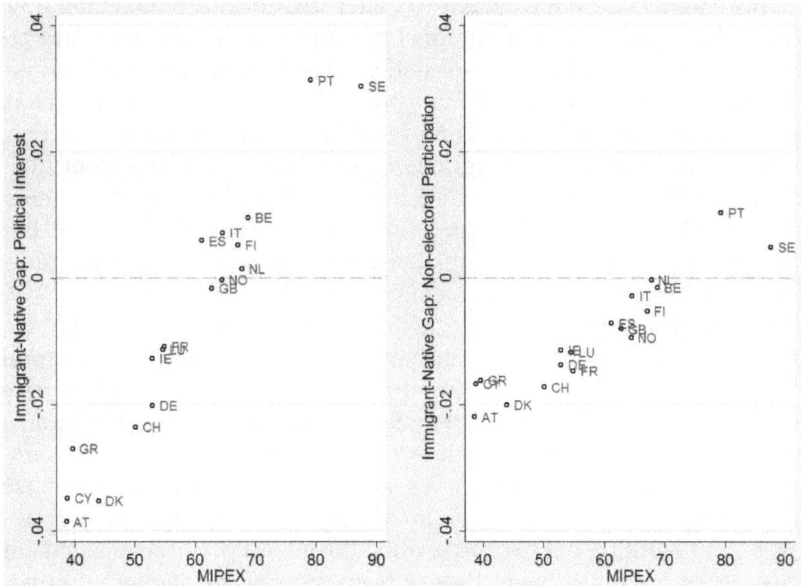

positive (in case of political trust) or negative (in the case of the other
outcome variables).

In Figure 7.1 above, we examine the relationship between our estimated gaps and the countries' MIPEX scores, while simultaneously
controlling for native level and other variables, included in the analysis
in Table 7.4, for a visual test of policy effects. We present the results
for the relationship between MIPEX and the two indicators political
interest and non-electoral political participation (the graphs look similar for the remaining three indicators). In the graph on the left, we see
the strong positive relationship between a country's MIPEX score and
the estimated gap in political interest between immigrants and natives.
Indeed, in those countries with the highest policy scores, immigrants'
and natives' estimated averages of political interest are virtually indistinguishable, while immigrant averages in many lower-scoring countries are significantly below native averages. In the graph on the right,
we observe a very similar pattern. However, the relationship between
integration policies and non-electoral participation is smaller.

Conclusion

In this chapter, we have sought to better understand the comparative political integration of immigrants by examining the character and institutional sources of immigrant-native gaps. It is perhaps not too surprising to discover that immigrants participate least in societies that are, overall, least engaged. What is more interesting, from our perspective, is the question of why immigrants in some contexts differ from their native counterparts on these civic measures than immigrants in other contexts. Overall, controlling for a variety of factors, we found small but fairly consistently negative gaps between first-generation immigrants and natives on many political engagement indicators.

More to the point, we asked whether integration policy played a role in lowering immigrant-native disparities in political engagement (presumably because they remove important legal and institutional barriers to immigrant engagement or transfer useful resources to immigrants and strengthen their attachment to the nation state of their host country). Our answer at this point is yes, at least in a correlational sense: we showed that countries with the most comprehensive and immigrant-friendly integration policies also exhibit the lowest political engagement gaps. From the policy view, then, integration policies seem to do their share of better pulling immigrants into the polity. However, different causal mechanisms must be at work in the case of political trust, where immigrants score significantly higher than the native-born, yet in countries with immigrant-friendly integration policies, the gap between immigrants and the native-born is lower.

While we have gained several new insights in this analysis, much is left to be done to strengthen these results. Policy effects could be further ascertained by looking at policy change over time. The longitudinal nature of the ESS and MIPEX data (even though for only a short period) lends itself to this next analytical step. Furthermore, policy effects should be strongest for those who have experienced the policies captured by the MIPEX data. The variable that measures when immigrants arrived in their host country could be used in such an analysis. Third, policy effects might differ across various ethnic groups and might not apply equally to everyone. Characteristics of the country of origin, home experiences, and group conditions might all affect native-immigrant gaps, and these factors should be included in future analyses. Fourth, integration policies might go beyond those measured by MIPEX, and they might include social policy regimes that treat immigrants in different ways and that directly transfer socio-economic resources to them. Integrating their effects on native-immigrant gaps might be an essential expansion of the project. Fifth, the political gaps that we have identified in this article are only part of an entire array of measures that tap political integration. Certainly, political value differences, particularly when it comes to support for human rights and the basic principles of democracy, would be other potential indicators for which we might desire low immigrant-native gaps. Finally, little is known at this point about whether a politically engaged immigrant population is actually helpful or harmful to social harmony more generally; while it is easy to support political action in an abstract sense, it may also give rise to additional divisions over which political battles are fought. Such future extensions of this analysis would make its insights even more valuable and robust.

NOTES

1 See, for example, Aleksynska 2008; André, Dronkers, and Need 2009; DeSipio 2011; Drobnič 2006; Maxwell 2010a; Paskeviciute and Anderson 2007; Phalet and Swyngedouw 2003; Rath 1983; Togeby 2004.

2 The 2007 wave used in this chapter includes 28 countries – the EU-25 as well as Canada, Norway, and Switzerland.

3 A principal-component analysis identified one latent factor accounting for 61 per cent of the variance and a number of smaller factors with eigenvalues below 1.

4 In the literature, objective and subjective income assessments are used as proxies for the concept of "economic vulnerability" (Whelan and Maître 2005). While the objective and subjective measures are distinct concepts, they are theoretically intertwined.

5 The source of these economic and demographic estimates is the UNDP's Human Development Report (2008) (http://hdr.undp.org/en) and the UN's International Migrant Stock Database (http://esa.un.org/migration/), respectively. Because the ESS sample was fielded between 2002 and 2008, these are 2005 estimates for each indicator.

6 Here we use the same logic as in the individual-level model: the gap between immigrants and natives in a given context is the sum of the two groups' unshared effects. Two individuals in the same country – differentiated only by their immigrant status – share all other individual-level effects, the main impact of average native levels of the dependent variable,

and the main effect of the MIPEX policy. What differentiates an immigrant, then, are the effects of the immigrant indicator variable, the interaction with average native levels, and the interaction with MIPEX policy. Since mean native levels and MIPEX scores are available for each country, we are able to estimate country-specific gaps between immigrants and natives, as conditioned by these contextual-level factors.

7 Results are available from the authors on request.

8 See MIPEX scores per country at http://www.mipex.eu.

9 We also estimated random-slope models. This leads to the same overall pattern; the interaction effects are, however, smaller: for political trust, the effect is no longer significant, and for non-electoral participation, it is significant only at the 0.1 level.

PART TWO

Immigrant Political Integration in Canada

8 Is There a Racial Divide? Immigrants of Visible Minority Background in Canada

ELISABETH GIDENGIL AND JASON ROY

Along with augmenting over the past few decades – as shown in the Introduction to this volume – immigration flows have become increasingly diverse over the past 50 years. According to the 2006 census, fully three-quarters of immigrants who had arrived in Canada since 2001 were visible minorities.[1] This reflects a dramatic shift in the main sources of immigration. Before 1961, the overwhelming majority of newcomers (90.5 per cent) were born in Europe. By 2006, this proportion had dropped to 16.1 per cent. Asia has become the main source region, accounting for fully 58.3 per cent of immigrants who arrived between 2001 and 2006, up from 12.1 per cent in the late 1960s (Chui, Tran, and Maheux 2007).

Despite this massive influx of visible minority immigrants, we know very little about their political integration. Studies suggest that they may face greater challenges in regard to political representation (Bird, Saalfeld, and Wüst 2011; Black 2011), adapting to institutional and societal norms and to the new political system (Bilodeau 2008; Black 1982, 1987; Black, Niemi, and Bingham Powell Jr. 1987; Reitz et al. 2009; White et al. 2008) as well as participating more generally in the host country's political organizations (Berger, Galonska, and Koopmans 2004; Bevelander and Pendakur 2009; O'Neill, Gidengil, and Young 2012; van Londen, Phalet, and Hagendoorn 2007; Tillie 2004). These challenges may be amplified depending on the country of origin or the ethno-racial group.

Intuitively, the more difficult political integration of visible minority immigrants could be related to a generally negative racialized experience in the host country. There is abundant evidence that immigrants from visible minority backgrounds suffer from discrimination and greater social and economic marginalization (Plante 2010; Skuterud

2010, 878). It is therefore possible that the lower levels of political activity on the part of visible minority immigrants reflect the racial biases that still permeate Canadian society. In the American context, Michelson (2003) has observed that the trust relationship with public authorities worsens when immigrants become aware of discriminatory experiences. In this chapter, we investigate whether visible minority immigrants in general suffer from a more difficult political integration on a wide range of dimensions, and we examine a number of possible reasons why they are not as politically involved as other immigrants.

Visible Minority Immigrants: Is the Political Divide Really about Race?

While the generally negative racialized experience of visible-minority-background immigrants could explain their more difficult political integration, other considerations should also be taken into account.

Younger Immigrants Learning the Political Ropes?

A first possibility is that visible minority immigrants are less active politically simply because they tend to be younger. There is a wealth of evidence that young Canadians are less likely to vote or to belong to a political party (Gidengil et al. 2004). If the age profile of visible minority immigrants were the explanation, any participation deficit would simply be part of the larger problem of youth disengagement from electoral politics. However, this explanation offers little leverage here as the proportion of newcomers in the 15-to-24 age group is very similar to the proportion of Canadian-born youth in the same age bracket. It is actually the 25-to-54 age bracket that is over-represented among recent arrivals (Chui, Tran, and Maheux 2007).

Learning about an Unfamiliar Political Environment?

Another possible explanation is that visible minority immigrants are more likely to be recent arrivals. The initial years of settlement are going to be the most challenging for newcomers. Finding a job, adapting to new cultural norms, and putting down roots in the community are likely to take precedence over learning how to navigate an unfamiliar political system. Moreover, learning the political ropes takes time. Immigrant turnout has proved to be very much a function of accumulated experience with the host country's political system (White et al. 2008). Whether this is equally true of other forms of political involvement remains an open question. If their length of time in Canada were to explain why visible minority immigrants participated at lower levels than other Canadians, there would be little cause for any special concern. Like those who arrived before them from the traditional European source countries, they would become more involved as their exposure to Canadian politics increased.

The lack of familiarity with the Canadian political environment could have deeper roots, though. Prior experience with politics can be an important factor in immigrants' political integration. For example, newcomers to Toronto in the early 1980s who were already interested in politics and had participated in politics in their country of origin were able to draw on their prior political experience in adapting to their new political setting (Black 1982, 1987; Black, Niemi, and Bingham Powell Jr. 1987). This *transferability* was not contingent on the nature of the political system in the immigrant's country of origin. Note, however, that the only visible minority immigrants in the sample originated from the British West Indies. Many visible minority immigrants today are likely to have had very different experiences of politics in their country of origin than their counterparts from the traditional source countries, and the experience of repression could explain their greater difficulty in participating actively in the new political environment. There is evidence from the United States, for example, that being from a repressive regime somewhat reduces voter turnout on the part of foreign-born citizens (Ramakrishnan and Espenshade 2001). The dampening effect may be much more evident in the case of protest activities, whether out of fear of speaking out or because the habit has not been formed (Bilodeau 2008).

The Reflection of a Geographical Reality?

Another explanation relates to where visible minority immigrants settle. In 2006, 96 per cent of the visible minority population was concentrated in Canada's major metropolitan areas (Statistics Canada 2008a). Settlement patterns are reflected even more sharply in the composition of federal ridings. According to the 2006 census (Statistics Canada 2008b), visible minorities accounted for 50 per cent or more of the population in 24 ridings (out of a total of 308). In four ridings, visible minorities made up fully 75 per cent of the population, a figure that rose to 90 per cent in Scarborough–Rouge River.[2]

Research on the impact of settlement patterns on immigrant integration suggests that settling in areas with high concentrations of immigrants helps newcomers to find employment and shelter when they first arrive (Forsander 2004; Greenwell, Valdez, and Da Vanzo 1997). The influence of settlement patterns on immigrants' political integration has received much less attention. We cannot necessarily assume that the effects will be similarly beneficial: living in proximity to other immigrants may ease the short-term social and economic costs of resettlement, but it could conceivably make it more difficult to meet the long-term costs of political integration. If living in an immigrant enclave limits contacts with the host country, immigrants may have fewer opportunities to learn about the country's political life or be mobilized to become politically active. Indeed, a study of Asian immigrants in the United States found that co-ethnic concentrations typically diminished the turnout of registered voters (Cho, Gimpel, and Dyck 2006). Similarly, immigrant concentrations appear to depress the turnout of immigrant groups in Swedish local elections (Togeby 1999).

Note, however, that a study of immigrant women living in Canada's two largest cities found very little support for the hypothesis that extensive ties within the ethnic community impeded their long-term political integration (Gidengil and Stolle 2009). Indeed, there is evidence that immigrant enclaves may actually facilitate immigrants' political integration in the United States (see Leighley 2001; Ramakrishnan 2005) and in Australia (Bilodeau 2009).

The Reflection of a Social Integration Reality?

Living in an ethnic enclave could impede visible minority immigrants' political integration if it limits their opportunities for associational involvement beyond their own ethnic group. Participation in voluntary associations is assumed to foster democratic learning and to mobilize citizens to participate in politics (Teorell 2003; Putnam 2000). A number of studies have found that involvement in host country organizations increases the political involvement of visible minority immigrants in Germany (Berger, Galonska, and Koopmans 2004) and in the Netherlands (van Londen, Phalet, and Hagendoorn 2007; Tillie 2004). These findings raise the possibility that visible minority immigrants may be less politically active than other immigrants because they are less likely to belong to host country organizations.

It is not clear, however, that involvement in cross-ethnic associations is necessarily more conducive to immigrants' political integration than involvement in co-ethnic associations. Studies of turnout in local elections among immigrants in the Netherlands found positive relationships with membership in and density of ethnic associations (van Heelsum 2005; Tillie 2004; Fennema and Tillie 1999). Meanwhile, in the Canadian context, belonging to an ethnic or immigrant association made no difference to whether immigrant women in Canada's two largest cities vote or not (Gidengil and Stolle 2009). The same was true of immigrants' probability of voting in Swedish local elections (Strömblad and Adman 2009).

A Resource Deficit?

Political involvement requires both cognitive skills and material resources. Proficiency in the language of the host country is clearly a critical resource for immigrants (Cho 1999; Lien 2004; Ramakrishnan 2005; Uhlaner, Cain, and Kiewiet 1989; White et al. 2006). As immigrant flows have become more diverse, the proportion of foreign-born citizens who grew up speaking neither French nor English has increased. According to the 2006 census, 70.2 per cent of the foreign-born population reported a mother tongue other than French or English (Chui, Tran, and Maheux 2007). Resource models of political participation also emphasize the role of education and income (Verba, Schlozman, and Brady 1995). Education helps to instil norms of civic duty and political engagement, and it fosters the cognitive and information-processing skills that are required to deal with the complexities of politics. Following politics and being politically active also require money and time. The sheer effort of getting by may leave people on low incomes with little time or energy for politics. These considerations raise the possibility that difficulties in visible minorities' political integration are linked to problems with their socio-economic integration.

This explanation may not offer much leverage here, however. First, in terms of language proficiency, the vast majority (88.5 per cent) of those who grew up speaking neither of Canada's official languages reported that they could carry on a conversation in English and/or French (Chui, Tran, and Maheux 2007). Second, in contrast to earlier waves of immigrants, those who have arrived since Canada opened the door to non-traditional source countries typically have a relatively high level of education. Therefore, even if many of them struggle to find employment related to their field of study (Plante 2010), they could nevertheless possess the cognitive resources to be politically engaged.

Data and Measures

To investigate why visible minority immigrants have more difficulty learning the political ropes and practising democratic citizenship in Canada, we compare four groups: immigrants who belong to a visible minority and those who do not, and Canadian-born citizens who belong to a visible minority and those who do not. This strategy enables us to assess whether differences between visible minority immigrants and other immigrants reflect differences in the nature of the immigrant experience or a more generally racialized experience that is shared with their Canadian-born counterparts.

The data are taken from the Canadian Election Study (CES). Respondents are classified as belonging to a visible minority based on their responses to the question, "To what ethnic or cultural group do you belong?" Those who responded "Canadian" were asked, "In addition to being Canadian, to what ethnic or cultural group did you or your ancestors belong on first coming to this continent?" The classification in both cases is based on the first group mentioned. To identify visible minorities, we follow Statistics Canada and use the Employment Equity Act definition: "persons, other than aboriginal peoples, who are non-Caucasian in race or non-white in colour" (Statistics Canada 2008c).[3] Groups classified as visible minorities include Chinese, South Asian, black, Filipino, Latin American, Southeast Asian, Arab, West Asian, Korean, and Japanese. To have sufficient cases, we have pooled data from the 2000, 2004, 2006, and 2008 CES. The pooled data set includes 795 visible minority immigrants, 1,680 non-visible minority immigrants, and 223 Canadian-born visible minority respondents. Note that only Canadian citizens 18 years and older are eligible to take part in the CES.

Our first indicator of political involvement is interest in politics as people are unlikely to invest much time and energy in keeping up with Canadian politics, still less in taking an active part in the country's democratic life, unless they are at least somewhat interested in the country's politics. We look at interest in both the federal election campaigns and politics in general, both measured on a zero-to-10 scale. We also look at how much attention people paid to news about the federal elections. Respondents were asked to rate their attention to news on television, in the newspaper, and on the radio using a zero-to-10 scale.

Any form of political activity also presupposes political information (Delli Carpini and Keeter 1996). Respondents in all four election studies were asked to name the leaders of the federal political parties as well as their provincial premier and to answer three other general political-knowledge questions.[4] The political-knowledge measure is a simple count of the number of correct responses. Even if people do not pay much attention to the news, casual conversations with family, friends, neighbours, and colleagues at work can all elicit political information. Political discussion is measured on a three-point scale.

Of course, the bottom-line question is whether people actually participate in politics. The first two measures are voting in the federal election[5] and whether one has ever belonged to a political party. We also have indicators of participation outside of traditional arenas of government – namely, participation in protest activities. We have combined signing a petition, attending a lawful demonstration, and taking part in a product boycott into a simple additive scale.[6]

Findings

There are strikingly different patterns when we compare subjective political engagement and political activity across our four groups (see Table 8.1 below). Immigrants match or exceed the average for Canadian-born citizens on every indicator of political interest and attention to news about an election. This pattern holds for visible minority and other immigrants alike. It is Canadian-born visible minority respondents who score lowest on these measures. However, in the case of visible minority immigrants, higher levels of interest and attention do not necessarily make for higher levels of political knowledge. Visible minority immigrants score lower on this objective measure of political awareness than their levels of interest and attention would predict. Other immigrants, by contrast, are at least as, if not more, knowledgeable about politics than their Canadian-born counterparts.

This contrast between visible minority and other immigrants is heightened when we turn to actual political behaviour. Visible minority immigrants are much less likely to have had several discussions about an election with other people, and they are under-represented in every form of political activity, from belonging to a political party to taking part in a demonstration. Non-visible minority immigrants, by contrast, have clearly attained levels of *participatory* or *substantive citizenship* (Bloemraad 2006, 6) that match or closely approximate those of their native-born counterparts. The former just as clearly have not, despite

Table 8.1. Immigrants' Political Involvement

Type of involvement	Canadian-born		Foreign-born		
	Non-VM[a]	VM	Non-VM	VM	N
Interest					
Political interest (mean, 0–10 scale)	5.5	5.3	6.0	5.6	14,711
Campaign interest (mean, 0–10 scale)	6.1	5.8	6.8	6.2	15,960
News attention					
TV news attention (mean, 0–10 scale)	4.8	4.5	5.2	5.1	15,251
Radio news attention (mean, 0–10 scale)	3.1	2.9	3.6	3.4	15,226
Newspaper attention (mean, 0–10 scale)	3.7	3.8	4.2	4.2	15,233
Knowledge					
Political knowledge (mean, 0–7 scale)	4.2	4.0	4.4	3.9	12,409
Participation					
Discussed election several times (%)	55	47	58	44	12,662
Voted in federal election (%)	87	82	89	80	12,685
Belonged to a political party (%)	18	9	17	10	12,650
Signed a petition (%)	83	72	78	52	5,012
Took part in a boycott (%)	27	20	23	11	4,909
Took part in a demonstration (%)	22	23	26	17	4,927

[a]   VM: Visible minority.

their expressed interest in politics. The question is, what explains this more difficult political integration? To explore why visible minority immigrants participate at lower levels than other immigrants, we have estimated baseline models that compare visible minority immigrants, other immigrants, and Canadian-born visible minority respondents with other Canadian-born citizens (see Table 8.2 below).[7] These models confirm that the differences observed in Table 8.1 with respect to political knowledge, political discussion, and political activity are statistically significant and hold regardless of the particular election study. Visible minority immigrants know less about politics, and, like their Canadian-born counterparts, they are less likely to have engaged in frequent discussions about an election than non-visible minority Canadian-born respondents (the reference group). They are also less likely to have engaged in all of the listed forms of political activity. The pattern is similar for Canadian-born visible minority respondents, but only the turnout gap achieves conventional levels of statistical significance. In contrast to visible minority immigrants, other immigrants are statistically indistinguishable from the reference group when it comes to the probability

Table 8.2. Immigrants' Political Involvement

Type of involvement	Canadian-born VM[a]		Non-VM immigrant		VM immigrant		
	B	RSE	B	RSE	B	RSE	N
Political knowledge (0–7 scale)	.10	.28	.18	.09**	−.35	.14**	10,550
Political discussion (0–2 scale)	−.35	.19*	.17	.08**	−.56	.13***	10,919
Voting in federal election	−.54	.30*	.18	.13	−.54	.18***	10,933
Party membership	−.62	.41	−.01	.11	−.72	.21***	10,909
Protest activities	−.68	.42	−.04	.12	−1.34	.27***	4,399

Note: Estimation was by ordered logistic regression for political discussion and by ordinary least-squares regression for political knowledge. All other models were estimated using binary logistic regression. Controls are included for election year, and cases are clustered by constituency and by type of respondent.
a VM: Visible minority.
* p < .10, **p < .05, ***p < .01

of voting, belonging to a political party, or engaging in protest activities like signing petitions, boycotting, and demonstrating. And they are actually more likely to have engaged in discussions about an election and to be politically informed, although the differences are modest.

These baseline models provide a yardstick by which to judge whether differences in resources and other social background characteristics can help to explain why visible minority immigrants have been less successful in surmounting the challenges of political integration. If these factors are the key, the corresponding coefficients will shrink when these characteristics are added to the baseline models. This is quite obviously the case for voting for both Canadian-born and foreign-born visible minority respondents (see Table 8.3 below) (cf. Tossutti 2007). The coefficient for visible minority immigrants is halved and ceases to be statistically significant. More detailed analysis reveals that this is entirely due to the fact that these immigrants are more likely to have arrived within the previous 10 years. Even controlling for a variety of social background characteristics, the probability of voting is 8 points lower for recent immigrants. Note that first language makes no difference whatsoever to the probability of voting. Growing up speaking neither of Canada's official languages is clearly not an impediment when it comes to voting.

This is not the case for protest activities. People who grew up speaking a language other than English or French are significantly less likely to have engaged in any form of political protest. Being a relative

Table 8.3. Social Background Characteristics and Political Involvement

	Political knowledge		Political discussion		Voting		Party membership		Protest activities	
	B	RSE	B	RSE	B	RSE	B	RSE	B	RSE
Canadian-born VM[a]	.18	.26	−.50	.19**	−.34	.30	−.31	.41	−.54	.45
Non-VM immigrant	−.09	.08	.12	.09	−.10	.15	−.23	.13*	.19	.13
VM immigrant	−.29	.12**	−.54	.14***	−.24	.22	−.65	.27**	−.66	.36*
Recent immigrant	−.60	.18***	−.29	.20	−.76	.25***	−.41	.44	−1.49	.38***
Non-official language	−.20	.09**	−.19	.09**	−.01	.14	−.20	.14	−.52	.14***
Under 35 years of age	−.71	.06***	−.15	.06**	−.84	.08***	−.91	.11***	−.54	.09***
Over 54 years of age	.87	.05***	.22	.06***	1.03	.10***	.83	.07***	−.32	.07***
Did not complete high school	−.87	.07***	−.69	.07***	−.49	.10***	−.36	.10***	−.57	.10***
University graduate	1.03	.05***	.57	.06***	.63	.09***	.47	.08***	.65	.07***
Lowest household income quartile	−.66	.06***	−.35	.06***	−.47	.09***	−.15	.08*	−.24	.08***
Highest household income quartile	.24	.06***	.28	.06***	.26	.10***	.20	.08***	−.03	.08
Female	−.70	.05***	−.21	.04***	.09	.08	−.25	.07***	.19	.07***
Constant	5.44	.06***			1.70	.10***	−1.40	.09***		
R square/ pseudo–R square	.28		.18		.14		.10		0.10	
N	10,550		10,919		10,933		10,909		4,399	

Note: Estimation was by ordered logistic regression for protest activities and political discussion and by ordinary least-squares regression for political knowledge. The remaining models were estimated using binary logistic regression. Controls are included for election year, and cases are clustered by constituency and type of respondent.
a VM: Visible minority.
* $p < .10$, **$p < .05$, ***$p < .01$

newcomer is even more of an impediment; indeed, the probability of having taken part in none of these activities is fully 20 points higher for recent immigrants. Both language and length of time in Canada are clearly important factors in explaining why visible minority immigrants are less likely to have engaged in protest activities. The probability that a visible minority immigrant has not taken part in any of these activities drops from 19 points to 9 points once these two factors are taken into account. However, even allowing for the fact that visible minority immigrants are much more likely to have grown up speaking neither official language (72 per cent, compared with 54 per cent of other immigrants) and to have arrived within the previous decade (28 per cent, compared with 8 per cent of other immigrants),[8] they are still significantly less likely to have signed a petition, taken part in a boycott, or participated in a demonstration than members of the Canadian-born majority.

Neither factor, by contrast, is of any help in explaining why these immigrants are less likely to have belonged to a political party. Introducing these and other social background characteristics into the model has a negligible effect on the coefficient for visible minority immigrants. The CES asked whether respondents had *ever* belonged to a political party. This wording raises the possibility that levels of party membership are lower because these immigrants are more likely to be recent arrivals. However, even controlling for this (and other social background characteristics), the probability of belonging to a political party is an estimated 9 points lower for these immigrants. Income and education certainly affect party membership, but they do not explain why visible minority immigrants are less likely to have belonged to a political party. The same is true of first language, which is unrelated to party membership. Clearly, the low levels of party membership on the part of visible minority immigrants cannot be explained by any lack of resources. Note that other immigrants are also significantly less likely to have belonged to a political party once other social background characteristics are taken into account. This suggests that their probability of belonging to a political party is lower than we would expect given their average age, education, and income. The effect, however, is quite modest (3 points).

Finally, these factors are of little or no help in explaining why visible minority immigrants tend to know less about Canadian politics and are less likely to talk about an election with other people. In both cases, the coefficient for visible minority immigrants is barely affected when controls are introduced for socio-demographic resource and length of time in Canada. It is interesting to note that in the case of political discussion, the negative coefficient for Canadian-born visible minority respondents actually *increases* when factors like age, income, and education are taken into account. This suggests that there is something about belonging to a visible minority per se that may be discouraging political discussion, regardless of whether a member of a visible minority is Canadian-born or came to Canada as an immigrant.

Clearly, then, to explain why visible minority immigrants experience these participation deficits, we need to look beyond their length of time in Canada and their first language. As discussed earlier, one possibility is that visible minority immigrants are less integrated into the country's associational life. To examine the impact of membership in ethnic and cross-ethnic associations, we have created two variables. The first is a dichotomous variable coded 1 if the respondent had been active in an ethnic association during the previous five years. The second counts the number of other associations in which the respondent had been active in the previous five years.[9]

We do not present the full analysis because of space limitations. These analyses indicate, however, that visible minority immigrants are almost as active in voluntary associations as other immigrants: on average, visible minority immigrants had been active in 1.64 associations in the previous five years, compared with 1.73 for other foreign-born citizens. Moreover, levels of associational involvement for both groups are statistically indistinguishable from their Canadian-born, non-visible minority counterparts. It is Canadian-born members of visible minority background who stand out for their low level of associational activity: on average, they had been active in only 1.12 associations in the previous five years. Accordingly, we can rule out the possibility that differences in levels of associational involvement explain the participation deficits on the part of visible minority immigrants. This is not to say that political participation is unrelated to associational involvement. On the contrary, the greater number of associations in which people have been active, the more often they discuss elections with other people, the more they tend to know about politics, and the more likely they are to have belonged to a political party, signed a petition, boycotted a product, or taken part in a demonstration. The point is that differences in levels of associational involvement do not explain why visible minority immigrants lag behind on these measures.[10]

The same is true of being active in ethnic associations. Fully a quarter of visible minority immigrants (26 per cent) and a fifth of their Canadian-born counterparts (20 per cent) have been actively involved in an ethnic association. The comparable figures for non-visible minorities are only 12 per cent for the foreign-born and 3 per cent for the Canadian-born. However, there is no evidence to suggest that involvement in ethnic associations impedes the political integration of visible minority immigrants. It does not affect their frequency of political discussion, and those who have been involved in an ethnic association in the previous five years are actually more likely to have engaged in political protest activities or to have belonged to a political party.[11] Visible minority immigrants who have belonged to this type of association are almost twice as likely (29 per cent) as non-members (15 per cent) to have engaged in at least two protest activities, and party membership increases from a mere 2 per cent to 16 per cent. In the case of political knowledge, visible minority immigrants who belong to an ethnic association score fully one point higher on political knowledge.

Residential concentration, on the other hand, appears to be of some help in explaining why visible minority immigrants are less politically active. Visible minority immigrants are three times as likely (33 per cent) as other immigrants (12 per cent) to live in constituencies where half or more of the population belongs to a visible minority.[12] People who live in constituencies where visible minorities are in the majority are less likely to have belonged to a political party. This pattern holds for the Canadian- and foreign-born alike, whether or not they belong to a visible minority. However, many more visible minority immigrants and their Canadian-born counterparts live in these constituencies, a fact that may help to explain why they are less likely to have been party members. Immigrants who live in these constituencies also talked about an election less often and typically scored half a point lower on the political-knowledge scale. This is the case whether or not they belong to a visible minority. There is no difference in political-knowledge scores for the Canadian-born, and the pattern is actually reversed for political discussion. Finally, fully half of visible minority immigrants living in constituencies with 25 per cent or more visible minorities have not participated in any protest activities, compared with less than a third of those living in constituencies where visible minorities are very much in the minority. The ethno-racial composition of their constituency makes little or no difference to other immigrants' propensity to engage in such activities.

To explore the impact of coming from a repressive regime, we have used the "Freedom in the World" country ratings[13] to classify immigrants' country of origin as democratic (2.00 to 4.99), partly democratic (5.00 to 10.99), or non-democratic (11.00 to 14.00). The classification is based on the average rating for the country of origin for the 15-year period before the year of arrival in Canada. The ratings are available only since 1973, and this necessarily results in a smaller sample because it excludes immigrants who settled earlier. Visible minority immigrants are significantly less likely (14 per cent) than non-visible minority immigrants (47 per cent) to have emigrated from a fully democratic country and significantly more likely (58 per cent) to have left a country that was only partly democratic (compared with 26 per cent of non-visible minority immigrants), although they are no more likely to have originated from a non-democratic country.

Coming from a non-democratic country, however, has much more of an impact on visible minority immigrants. Fully half of visible minority immigrants from non-democratic countries have not participated in any protest activities, such as signing a petition, boycotting a product, or participating in a protest, compared with only a quarter of their non-visible minority counterparts. Similarly, visible minority immigrants from these countries were more than twice as likely (29 per cent) as other immigrants (12 per cent) to report that they had never discussed an election with other people. Tellingly, these differences are confined to activities that involve expressing opinions: there was no significant difference in party membership among immigrants from non-democratic countries, and the knowledge gap was no larger than the gap observed among immigrants from fully democratic countries.[14]

Conclusion

As others have observed before (O'Neill, Gidengil, and Young 2012), the political integration of visible minority immigrants clearly remains incomplete. Other immigrants, meanwhile, are as active – or not – as their Canadian-born counterparts.

Lower turnout on the part of visible minority immigrants can be explained by the fact that they are more likely to be recent immigrants and thus to have less exposure to Canadian politics (White et al. 2008). Being a relative newcomer is also part of the reason that visible minority immigrants tend to know less about politics and are less likely to participate in protest activities, and so is growing up speaking neither of Canada's official languages. However, lack of exposure to Canadian politics and language barriers are by no means the whole story. And these factors are no help in explaining why visible minority immigrants are less likely to have belonged to a political party and are less prone to talk about elections with other people.

Prior experience with a repressive political regime may provide another piece of the puzzle, at least when it comes to activities that involve voicing political opinions. This was especially evident for participation in protest activities. It may also explain why speaking neither official language appears to depress involvement in activities like signing petitions and taking part in demonstrations, given that 83 per cent of visible minority immigrants from non-democratic regimes speak neither English nor French as their first language.

There has been a good deal of debate about the impact of association-al involvement on immigrants' political integration. However, visible minority immigrants are as active in voluntary associations as other immigrants, so we cannot explain the political participation deficits as a lack of integration into Canada's associational life. And we did not un-cover any evidence that being active in an ethnic association depresses involvement in the host country's politics. On the contrary, some of the gaps might be wider were it not for the fact that visible minority immi-grants tend to be more active in ethnic associations. On the other hand, settlement patterns do appear to be part of the reason why visible mi-nority immigrants are not as politically engaged as other immigrants.

Evidence for a racialized-experience explanation, which would be reflected in similarly low levels of political participation on the part of both visible minority immigrants and visible minority Canadian-born, is weak. The one exception is political discussion: both Canadian-born and newcomers of visible minority background are significantly less likely to engage in frequent discussions about elections. Of course, these findings do not rule out the critical role that racial discrimination and marginalization may play in structuring visible minority Canadians' experience with politics. We are not able, however, to directly inves-tigate the impact of personal experience of discrimination and other negative experiences, which may well differ from one visible minority group to another.

We also need to be mindful of the other limitations of the data. Even pooled, the CES data do not provide sufficient cases to undertake more detailed analyses of the impact of factors like involvement in voluntary associations and prior experiences of repression. There are simply too few cases to be able to institute the necessary controls. Similarly, the CES data are limited when it comes to exploring differences *among* vis-ible minority immigrants (see Jedwab 2006).

Overall turnout rates are similar for Canadian-born and foreign-born citizens, but as we have seen, aggregated figures risk obscuring significant differences within the immigrant population. It would be unfortunate if those figures led to a sense of complacency about im-migrant political integration. Just why visible minority immigrants are less politically active than other immigrants has only been partly ex-plained by the factors examined here, and many aspects of their politi-cal integration remain to be explored. As the proportion of immigrants coming from non-traditional source countries continues to increase, the question of what facilitates their integration into an unfamiliar political system will grow in importance as well.

NOTES

1 *Visible minority* is the Canadian term for racialized minority and refers to people who are non-white and/or non-Caucasian. Aboriginal peoples are not visible minorities.

2 Note that these population distributions include all visible minorities residing in the federal riding, not a single visible minority group. There is only one riding – Richmond in British Columbia – where a single visible minority group constitutes more than 50 per cent of the population (based on the 2006 census, 2003 FED profile).

3 Note that the CES question differs from the Employment Equity Act definition because it asks respondents to self-identify the *ethnic or cultural group* to which they belong. While we acknowledge this difference, we believe that self-identified membership in an ethnic or cultural group serves as a reasonable approximation, given that no direct measure of visible minority status is otherwise available from the CES.

4 The political parties were the Liberals, Conservatives, and New Democratic Party (NDP). In Quebec, the Bloc Québécois was substituted for the NDP since the latter held only one seat in the province during the entire period. In 2000, respondents were asked to name Canada's finance minister, the prime minister at the time of the Canada-United States Free Trade Agreement, and the capital of the United States. The 2004 questions asked for the names of Canada's finance minister, the British prime minister, and the female cabinet minister who had run for the leadership of the federal Liberal party. In 2006, respondents were asked to name the British prime minister, a female cabinet minister, and the judge who was heading a commission of inquiry into a political scandal that had featured prominently in the news. In 2008, respondents were asked the names of Canada's governor general, the Republican presidential candidate, and a federal cabinet minister. The scale consisted of a simple count of the number of correct responses. Coefficient alpha ranged from .81 to .83 outside Quebec and from .77 to .80 in Quebec.

5 Note that the CES overestimates voter turnout. This reflects a combination of panel conditioning, social desirability, and the fact that people who are not interested enough to vote are not interested enough to complete the surveys.

6 Note that questions about protest activities were posed only in the self-administered mail-back questionnaire, which reduces the number of cases

available for analysis. No mail-back survey was administered in 2006. Coefficient alpha = .56.

7 Note that panel respondents may appear up to three times in the pooled data set. Accordingly, the cases have been clustered by type of respondent as well as by constituency to take account of the violation of the assumption of independence.

8 The comparable figures for other immigrants are 54 per cent and 8 per cent, respectively.

9 The respondents were asked about 11 types of association: a community service group, business association, professional association, environmental group, women's group, labour union, sports association, religious organization, parents' group, farmers' association, and other association. Note that the questions about associational involvement were asked only in the self-administered mail-back survey; this reduces the sample.

10 This conclusion is confirmed when the number of associations (up to four) in which respondents had been active in the previous five years is added to the models estimated in Table 8.3.

11 Results are available from the authors on request.

12 It is not possible to group constituencies based on the proportion of visible minority immigrants. However, census data are available on the percentage of the population in each constituency that belongs to a visible minority. To the extent that newcomers settle in areas with an established community of co-ethnics, this is likely to be highly correlated with the proportion of visible minority immigrants. Constituencies are grouped into three categories based on whether visible minorities account for a small (less than 25 per cent), sizeable (25 per cent to 49 per cent), or substantial (50 per cent or more) portion of the population. These are similar to the cut-offs used by Bilodeau (2009) in classifying constituencies based on the percentage of immigrants from non-English-speaking countries. Detailed results from the analysis of the impact of residential concentration are available from the authors.

13 "2015 Freedom in the World," Freedom House, www.freedomhouse.org/report-types/freedom-world, accessed 15 August 2012.

14 It is interesting that the differences between visible minority and other immigrants either disappear for immigrants coming from partly democratic countries or are reversed (in the case of party membership and political knowledge). Coming from one of these countries has a particularly negative effect on the propensity of non-visible minority immigrants to engage in protest activities: fully 59 per cent had engaged in none of these activities compared with only 12 per cent of their counterparts from fully democratic countries.

9 Do Younger and Older Immigrants Adapt Differently to Canadian Politics?

STEPHEN E. WHITE

Electoral engagement is an important facet of immigrant integration. Along with obtaining citizenship, the power to recognize and pursue one's political interests through one of the most common forms of political participation is a crucial step towards achieving full political integration. Three aspects of citizen behaviour – electoral participation, attentiveness, and information acquisition – deserve close attention because they are essential requirements for democratic citizenship. As Nie, Junn, and Stehlik-Barry (1996, 15) explain,

> In order for democracy to function, individual citizens must first be able to identify and understand their preferences and political interests. Engagement in politics entails surveillance of the current political landscape and requires attentiveness to and knowledge of politics. Citizens must then also be capable of pursuing and protecting their interests by electing and petitioning representatives in democracy.

These dimensions of "citizen competence" (Kuklinski and Quirk 2001) are at the heart of healthy democratic politics. Electoral participation is a cornerstone of democratic citizenship, not only because it is one of the most common forms of political action but also because it levels the political playing field. Significant disparities among citizens when it comes to many other forms of political participation, and inequalities that emerge because some citizens have more resources at their disposal or are more motivated to act than others, are muted in elections because each citizen is limited to one vote. Elections thus present immigrant citizens with the same opportunities that all other Canadians have to convey support for the political system and the political community and to express their political preferences.

The empirical record is clear: immigrant citizens in Canada and elsewhere take advantage of these opportunities. Election survey data from the 1990s and early 2000s indicate that immigrants in Canada, Australia, and New Zealand exhibit levels of interest in politics, attention to election campaign news, and political knowledge equal to or slightly higher than those of their domestic-born counterparts (Bilodeau and Kanji 2006). In Canada, there are no discernible differences in overall voter turnout between immigrants and those born in Canada (White et al. 2006), although we can observe differences across some groups of immigrant (see Chapter 8). The empirical record in the United States, another traditional immigrant-receiving country, also suggests that immigrants are just as active when it comes to elections as the domestic-born population. Lien (1997), for instance, finds no differences in participation between foreign-born and domestic-born residents in the United States, and Barreto and Muñoz (2003) do not uncover any differences in political activity between foreign-born and domestically born Mexican Americans. Ramakrishnan and Espenshade's research (2001) shows that voter turnout is slightly lower among immigrants in the United States, but increases the longer they reside in the country (see also Ramakrishnan 2005). In Europe, we seem to observe more significant group differences (see chapters 1 and 2).

The above evidence, along with the review of the field of studies on immigrants' political integration, highlight the amount of attention that has been devoted to understanding the level of electoral engagement of newcomers. We know considerably less, however, about the process by which immigrants adjust to electoral politics in their host country. Do they make a smooth transition from one political setting to another? Certainly, the political attitudes and behaviours of immigrants appear to be determined in part by conditions in the countries from which they come (Bilodeau 2008; McAllister and Makkai 1992; Bilodeau, McAllister, and Kanji 2010; Bueker 2005). But immigrants not only arrive from a diverse set of social, economic, and political contexts; they also arrive at different stages in life. For example, although nearly one quarter (24 per cent) of immigrants to Canada between 2001 and 2006 were children under 15 years of age, more than half of newcomers in that period (61 per cent) were 25 years of age or older (Statistics Canada 2007).[1] This variation in age may well have important implications for how they adjust to political life in their host country. This possibility is the focus of this chapter.

Classical theories of political socialization suggest that political predispositions – the political beliefs, norms, and values regulating how people react to novel political stimuli – are acquired relatively early in life and that they are deeply held and fairly resistant to change. These traits have considerable effects on political participation (Blais 2000; Wattenberg 2008; Rosenstone and Hansen 1993; Blais et al. 2002; Almond and Verba 1963; Norris 2002). And yet, for the large numbers of foreign-born Canadians who arrive as adults, these traits were initially shaped in political environments quite different from Canada's. Accordingly, the political predispositions of immigrants who arrive in Canada later in life might be less relevant in the Canadian context than in the political environments in which those outlooks were formed.

Do immigrants who arrive in their host country relatively late in life adapt to their host political system in the same way as immigrants who arrive before adulthood? Do broad political beliefs, norms, values, and affective attachments influence responses to elections in much the same way for domestic-born Canadians and foreign-born citizens who arrive at different stages in life? This chapter uses pooled data from the 2004, 2006, and 2008 Canadian Election Study (CES) (Blais et al. 2007; Gidengil et al. 2009) to examine whether the link between immigrants' political predispositions and their responses to national election campaigns is conditioned by age at the time of migration.

The Role of Predispositions: Empirical Expectations

The focus of this investigation is not on differences in *levels* of electoral engagement, as it is in many of the chapters in this volume, but rather a particular set of *determinants* of engagement: political predispositions. We know that the ways in which individuals react to many kinds of short-term political stimuli, including elections, are heavily influenced by these predispositions, which include dominant political values, norms, and beliefs that individuals acquire through socialization (Eckstein 1988; Sears and Levy 2003). These outlooks shape the extent to which they participate in politics (Almond and Verba 1963; Putnam 2000; Norris 2002), how much they learn about politics (Delli Carpini and Keeter 1997), how they interpret political messages (Zaller 1992), and which types of parties and candidates they support (Campbell et al. 1960). When it comes to foreign-born citizens, however, the impact of predispositions may well be more complex. Adult migrants may, in fact, be different from both domestic-born Canadians and immigrants who arrive in their youth. Moreover, the impact of predispositions might also be moderated by the type of country from which immigrants arrive.

Immigrants Who Arrive as Adults: The Persistence of Early Learning

There are reasons to suppose that political predispositions have a relatively weak impact on how immigrants who arrive in Canada as adults respond to election campaigns. The central idea behind classical theories of political socialization is that people develop inclinations towards certain political beliefs and actions, in the so-called impressionable years between childhood and early adulthood, from sources including schools, the media, family, and peers (Hyman 1959; Searing, Wright, and Rabinowitz 1976; Easton, Dennis, and Easton 1969; Merelman 1980; Sears and Levy 2003). These predispositions are thought to be relatively stable throughout the life course because they structure the ways in which people interpret and react to subsequent political events (Searing, Schwartz, and Lind 1973; Jennings 1987; Niemi and Jennings 1991; Beck and Jennings 1991; Sears and Valentino 1997; Valentino and Sears 1998; Sears and Funk 1999; Jennings 2002). Many immigrants whose "formative years" were spent in a different political environment might retain many features of the core political norms, values, and beliefs they developed before migration. However, it is not clear that political predispositions acquired in their country of origin shape how immigrants react to politics in their host country.

If their perceptions of the Canadian political environment differ dramatically from their perceptions of the politics in their country of origin, then immigrants' political predispositions might not affect how they respond to political stimuli in Canada. For example, because of exposure to political scandals, corruption, or acrimonious political discourse in their country of origin, some immigrants might hold deeply negative views about political leaders and the political process as a whole. Whereas we might typically expect people who are deeply cynical about politics to express relatively little interest in elections and to abstain from voting, that might not be the case for immigrants in Canada whose political cynicism is largely informed by their experiences elsewhere. Instead, they may well sense that their generally negative outlook on politics is misplaced when it comes to Canadian politics in particular. By the same token, some immigrants may arrive in Canada with generally optimistic orientations towards politics, but come to see Canadian politics in an entirely negative light.

One possibility, then, is that the political predispositions of adult immigrants persist after they arrive in their host country (Finifter and

Finifter 1989; Black, Niemi, and Bingham Powell Jr. 1987; White et al. 2008). If the persistence of predispositions is a feature of immigrant adaptation, then the expectation is that the link between electoral engagement and political predispositions is weaker among immigrants who arrive in Canada as adults than it is among other Canadians.

Immigrants Who Arrive before Adulthood:
Adaptation to a Different Political Setting

Unlike their counterparts who migrate to Canada as adults with typically well-developed sets of political predispositions, immigrants who arrive before adulthood are far more likely to be influenced by the Canadian political environment. The transition from old to new political context should be far easier for young immigrants than it is for those who migrate later in life.

The idea that many immigrants make relatively smooth transitions from one political environment to another has some empirical support. This possibility has been referred to as "translation" (Finifter and Finifter 1989) or "transferability" (Black 1987). Immigrants, the argument goes, arrive with predispositions learned in their country of origin, but are able to apply these to new political situations in their host country. This is perhaps because many immigrants are able to transport particularly important generalized skills such as interest in politics from one political environment to another (Black 1987; Black, Niemi, and Bingham Powell Jr. 1987) or because the political-attitude objects they encounter in their host country (parties or leaders, for example) are comparable to those experienced in their country of origin (Finifter and Finifter 1989). At any rate, there is certainly evidence to suggest that immigrants adapt their political outlooks and behaviours fairly quickly as they spend more time in the host country (Black 1982; Arvizu and Garcia 1996; Ramakrishnan and Espenshade 2001; Cain, Kiewiet, and Uhlaner 1991; Wong 2000; White et al. 2008).

The shift from one political context to another, however, should be less unsettling for migrants who arrive in the host country *before* their core political predispositions have deepened and solidified than for those who arrive *after*. The adaptation hypothesis, therefore, should apply only to those who migrate in their youth. The political predispositions of those who make the transition from one setting to another before adulthood ought to be largely shaped by their experiences in the host country. The second expectation, then, is that political predispositions affect the reactions to electoral stimuli of this group of immigrants in much the same way as they do those of domestic-born Canadians.

The Moderating Effects of Country of Origin

A more nuanced approach to the question of whether age at arrival affects how immigrants adjust to electoral politics in the host country is to take into account the kinds of social and political environments in which Canadian immigrants' political norms, values, and beliefs were initially shaped.

Most previous research on immigrant integration that distinguishes among different kinds of immigrants emphasizes differences in ethnicity or country of origin. There is some evidence that the political outlooks of immigrants in Canada, Australia, and the United States are conditioned by where they come from. Bilodeau (2008), for example, finds that immigrants in Canada and Australia who come from repressive political regimes are less likely to engage in political protest. McAllister and Makkai (1992) demonstrate that immigrants in Australia who come from other established democracies express greater trust in political authorities in their host country but also more authoritarian values, and Bilodeau, McAllister, and Kanji (2010) find that Australian immigrants from authoritarian regimes express greater support for non-democratic principles. Bueker's research (2005) indicates that immigrants to the United States who originate from countries lacking a democratic tradition are less likely than others to vote.

The implication is that the age at which immigrants arrive ought to be significant, but only once their origins are also taken into account. Those who arrive during adulthood from countries with social and political systems that are quite distinct from Canada's should be less likely than others to adapt; those from regions with relatively long histories of democratic government, on the other hand, should behave much like their domestic-born counterparts. With these three empirical expectations in mind, we turn to the data.

Data

The relationship between political predispositions and electoral engagement is explored using pooled data from the 2004, 2006, and 2008 CES (Blais et al. 2007; Gidengil et al. 2009). Each of these surveys of Canadian citizens contains a number of common items related to

Table 9.1. Electoral Engagement by Place of Birth, 2004–08 Averages

Electoral Engagement	Domestic-born	Foreign-born: arrived as youth	Foreign-born: arrived as adult
Interest in elections (mean score, 0–1 scale)	0.59	0.66	0.68
Turnout (% voting)	88	89	88
Leader knowledge (% know three or more leaders)	53	54	53

Source: CES (2004–08).

electoral engagement. The item wording and coding for each of the items is reported in Appendix C, and they also ask respondents where they were born. Separately, the surveys contain too few foreign-born respondents to produce reliable estimates of group differences in relationship between political predispositions and electoral engagement, but pooling them generates a sufficient number of foreign-born cases for analysis: in total, the three studies have 9,639 respondents, including 829 foreign-born citizens who arrived in Canada after age 18 and 530 foreign-born citizens who arrived before turning 18.

The dependent variables in these analyses are three dimensions of electoral engagement: election interest, election knowledge (measured by respondents' ability to recall the names of party leaders), and voting. The most recent data available from the CES echo the findings of Bilodeau and Kanji (2006) and White et al. (2006): when it comes to electoral engagement, the differences between immigrant Canadians and their domestic-born counterparts are quite small. More significant is that the differences between immigrant groups – those who arrived before adulthood and those who arrived after – are negligible. Table 9.1 above shows immigrant and domestic-born Canadians' average reported levels of election interest, voter turnout, and knowledge of party leaders across the 2004, 2006, and 2008 general elections. Both groups of immigrants are virtually indistinguishable from domestic-born citizens when it comes to voter turnout and levels of political knowledge. Both groups of immigrant Canadians express slightly more interest in politics than do citizens born in the country. Precisely why this is the case is unclear, but the differences among the groups, at any rate, are rather small.[2]

Much the same pattern emerges with respect to the set of independent variables in this analysis. It is composed of four political predispositions for which there are consistent measures across all three election

Table 9.2. Predispositions by Place of Birth, 2004–08 Averages

Predisposition	Domestic-born	Foreign-born: arrived as youth	Foreign-born: arrived as adult
General interest in politics (mean score, 0–1 scale)	0.56	0.61	0.64
Sense of civic duty to vote (% strongly agree)	80	80	84
Cynicism (mean score, 0–1 scale)	0.58	0.57	0.58
Partisan strength (% fairly strong/very strong)	57	57	61

Source: CES (2004–08).

surveys: general political interest, sense of civic duty, political cynicism, and strength of partisanship. As the data in Table 9.2 above show, the differences among domestic-born Canadians and immigrants who arrived before and during adulthood are trivial. With respect to sense of civic duty, political cynicism, and strength of partisanship, all three groups of citizens are quite similar. Both groups of immigrants express slightly higher levels of general political interest relative to domestic-born Canadians, but the difference is fairly modest.

To reiterate: these results with respect to basic levels of electoral engagement and core predispositions are perhaps not surprising; in fact, they are quite consistent with previous findings. The primary concern of this chapter, however, is how they relate to one another. Generally speaking, a stronger sense of civic duty (Blais 2000; Wattenberg 2008), higher levels of general interest in politics, stronger psychological ties to a political party (Rosenstone and Hansen 1993; Blais et al. 2002), and lower levels of cynicism (Almond and Verba 1963; Norris 2002) ought to be associated with higher levels of interest in an election, more knowledge about the central political figures in the campaign, and a greater likelihood of turning out to vote. The question is whether these relationships are as powerful among all types of immigrants as they are among domestic-born Canadians.

Analysis

To assess whether and how age at arrival matters, the relationship between each predisposition and each dimension of electoral engagement is compared across three groups: immigrants who arrived as adults, immigrants who arrived before adulthood, and domestic-born Canadians. Changes in electoral engagement and predispositions across the three elections are controlled. The estimation method varies, depending on the dependent variable: ordinary least squares (OLS) regression is used to obtain estimates of differences in election interest, while ordered logit is employed for estimates of leader knowledge and binary logit for turnout. In each estimate, the key pieces of evidence are the coefficients for predispositions ("cynicism," for example) and then those for the interactions ("cynicism x adult," for example): the former represent the effects of predispositions on each dimension of electoral engagement among citizens born in Canada, while the latter are estimates of how these effects differ among immigrant citizens. (Those who arrived in Canada before age 18 are labelled "youth," and those who arrived after age 18 are categorized as "adult.")

The findings presented in Table 9.3 below lend considerable support to the first empirical expectation about the persistence of early learning among immigrants who arrived as adults. The results show that the relationships among political predispositions and the three dimensions of electoral engagement are generally weaker among immigrants who arrived in Canada as adults than among their domestic-born counterparts. The results from each of the 12 separate estimations reported in Table 9.3 confirm that among domestic-born Canadians, the impact of predispositions on electoral engagement is in the expected direction and is statistically significant: general interest in politics, sense of civic duty, and strength of party identification are positively associated with all three forms of engagement; political cynicism is negatively associated with all three forms of engagement. More important, however, is that in 10 of those 12 sets of estimates, the effects of predispositions on electoral engagement are smaller among immigrants who arrived as adults, and these differences in effects are statistically significant (at $p = .05$ or lower).

Perhaps the easiest way to see the general pattern that emerges is to compare the direction of the relationship for each predisposition to the direction of the corresponding interaction term for immigrants who arrived as adults. In each and every case, it takes the opposite sign, indicating that whenever a predisposition has a positive (or negative) effect on electoral engagement, the effect is less positive (or negative) among immigrants who arrived as adults.

The logit results presented in Table 9.3 can also be converted to predicted probabilities, which are somewhat easier to interpret than regression coefficients. These probabilities show just how striking the

Table 9.3. Electoral Engagement by Predisposition and Age at Immigration, 2004–08 (Pooled Data)

Predisposition	Election interest[a] B	RSE	Leader knowledge[b] B	RSE	Turnout[c] B	RSE
General interest	.80***	.01	2.50***	.08	3.12***	.14
Arrived as youth	.04	.02	−.59**	.20	−.18	.31
Arrived as adult	.11***	.02	.35*	.17	.70*	.29
General interest × youth	−.02	.03	.98**	.32	.12	.58
General interest × adult	−.15***	.03	−.78**	.25	−1.77***	.46
N	9,241		9,453		7,051	
Civic duty	.21***	.01	.81***	.05	1.80***	.08
Arrived as youth	.04	.03	−.16	.18	.09	.26
Arrived as adult	.13***	.03	.43**	.17	−.01	.24
Civic duty × youth	.03	.03	.31	.21	−.09	.34
Civic duty × adult	−.07*	.03	−.51**	.18	−.21	.29
N	9,371		9,443		7,053	
Cynicism	−.35***	.02	−1.58***	.11	−2.25***	.19
Arrived as youth	−.02	.04	−.32	.30	−.03	.55
Arrived as adult	−.03	.04	−.50*	.26	−.85*	.42
Cynicism × youth	.15**	.07	.65	.48	.12	.81
Cynicism × adult	.20***	.06	1.08**	.40	1.30*	.63
N	6,661		6,689		6,685	
Partisan strength	.25***	.01	.85***	.06	1.49***	.12
Arrived as youth	.08***	.02	.05	.14	.09	.23
Arrived as adult	.12***	.02	.28*	.12	.19	.21
Partisan strength × youth	−.05	.04	−.01	.24	−.05	.46
Partisan strength × adult	−.08**	.03	−.46*	.19	−.39	.38
N	8,653		8,712		6,543	

Source: CES (2004–08).
[a] Unstandardized OLS regression coefficients.
[b] Ordered logit coefficients.
[c] Binary logit coefficients.
* $p < .05$, ** $p < .01$, *** $p < .001$

differences are between the Canadian-born population and immigrants who arrived in Canada as adults. For example, the predicted probability of knowing at least three party leaders is 36 points lower among domestic-born Canadians with the highest level of political cynicism compared to those with the lowest level of cynicism; the corresponding difference among immigrants who arrived in Canada as adults is only 12 points. In fact, in nearly every other case, the impact of predispositions is much smaller among immigrants who arrived as adults than among their domestic-born counterparts. In six instances, the effect is half the size or less. For instance, the predicted probability of voting is 36 points higher among domestic-born Canadians with the highest levels of general political interest compared with those with the lowest levels of interest, whereas the difference among immigrants who arrived as adults is only 16 points.

There are no signs of a comparable dynamic among immigrants who arrived in Canada before adulthood, however. Consistent with the second expectation, about the ease with which immigrants who arrive at a younger age adapt to Canadian politics, the evidence in Table 9.3 indicates that immigrants who arrive in Canada before reaching adulthood are virtually indistinguishable from domestic-born Canadians. With only two exceptions, there are no discernible differences between the two groups. Moreover, one of these exceptions suggests that the effect of general political interest on leader knowledge is actually *stronger* among immigrants who arrived before adulthood.

It is clear that orientations are related to electoral engagement in the expected ways. But among those whose formative years were spent elsewhere, the relationships are weaker – and consistently so. This evidence supports the persistence hypothesis: the link between electoral engagement and predispositions is systematically weaker among immigrants who spent their "impressionable years" in a different political environment. At the same time, the evidence with respect to immigrants who arrived before adulthood supports the adaptation hypothesis: like domestic-born Canadians, the impact of political predispositions on responses to election campaigns remains strong among this group of immigrants.

The final question is whether, in addition to age at arrival, the origins of immigrant Canadians also matter. Recall the expectation that the relationship between predispositions and electoral behaviour ought to be weaker among immigrants who arrive as adults, but only from countries with political systems that are markedly different from Canada's. To explore this possibility, two groups of adult immigrants are compared to domestic-born Canadians. The first group includes immigrants who arrived from Anglo-American or Western European countries – those with typically long democratic traditions. The second group consists of all other countries, including those from which the vast majority of contemporary immigrants are drawn. The same estimation methods employed in the previous analysis are applied here.

The relevant information from this analysis is presented in Table 9.4 below. As it turns out, the same fundamental pattern that emerged in

Table 9.4. Electoral Engagement by Predisposition and Source Country Type, 2004–08 (Pooled Data)

Predisposition	Election interest[a]		Leader knowledge[b]		Turnout[c]	
	B	RSE	B	RSE	B	RSE
General interest	.80***	.01	2.50***	.08	3.12***	.14
General interest × adult (West)	−.20***	.04	−1.03*	.41	−2.99***	.94
General interest × adult (non-West)	−.13***	.03	−.74*	.31	−1.44**	.54
Civic duty	.21***	.01	.81***	.05	1.80***	.08
Civic duty × adult (West)	−.07	.05	−.77**	.31	−.03	.53
Civic duty × adult (non-West)	−.07	.03	−.38	.22	−.21	.35
Cynicism	−.35***	.02	−1.58***	.11	−2.25***	.19
Cynicism × adult (West)	.25**	.08	1.11	.60	−.09	1.22
Cynicism × adult (non-West)	.17*	.07	1.09*	.52	1.83*	.74
Partisan strength	.25***	.01	.85***	.06	1.49***	.12
Partisan strength × adult (West)	−.09	.05	−.11	.34	.84	.77
Partisan strength × adult (non-West)	−.08	.04	−.70**	.23	−.93	.43

Source: CES (2004–08).
[a] Unstandardized OLS regression coefficients.
[b] Ordered logit coefficients.
[c] Binary logit coefficients.
* p < .05, **p < .01, ***p < .001

the previous analysis also appears when immigrants who arrived as adults are divided into these two country-related groupings. Although the standard errors are larger and the estimates are somewhat less reliable, there are no indications of any systematic difference among immigrants from different countries of origin. In some instances, the effects of predispositions are weaker among immigrants who arrived as adults from non-Western countries, but in other instances the effects are, in fact, weaker among those from Anglo-American or Western European countries. In short, the degree of discontinuity between political systems in the country of origin and the host country does not seem to be an important factor here.

Conclusion

Voting in general elections is a central component of democratic citizenship. And to take full advantage of opportunities to participate in politics, citizens must be able to identify and pursue their own political interests.

They need to vote, but, first and foremost, they need to become aware of what is at stake in elections by paying attention to them and acquiring information about the issues, policies, and personalities involved.

Although foreign-born Canadians are just as involved in elections as their domestically born co-citizens, the intriguing finding presented here is that electoral engagement is not geared to precisely the same factors for all immigrants. The focus of this analysis was on how the age at which immigrants arrive conditions the effects of one particular set of determinants: political predispositions. These general political outlooks, it turns out, are consistently less likely to affect the short-run attitudes and behaviour of immigrants who arrived in Canada as adults and whose predispositions were shaped initially in their country of origin. Age at the time of migration has thus far received little attention in studies of immigrant political behaviour as researchers have given greater thought to how migrants' origins might influence their thoughts and actions. However, whereas *levels* of electoral engagement are affected by *where* immigrants arrive from (Bueker 2005; Bilodeau 2008), these results suggest that the *determinants* of engagement depend on *when* immigrants arrive in their host country.

These findings also have important implications for political socialization research more generally. Immigrant populations are unique testing grounds for some of the fundamental precepts of theories of political socialization, precisely because of the cultural discontinuities they experience. There is clear evidence presented here that early political socialization matters: immigrants with the greatest amount of exposure to political environments outside Canada – those who arrived as adults – are systematically different from other citizens.

What remains to be answered is why immigrants who arrived as adults are nevertheless just as engaged in Canadian elections as their domestic-born counterparts. One possibility is that other factors push both domestic and foreign-born Canadians to similar levels of engagement. Although core political beliefs, norms, and values can be important determinants of electoral engagement, a variety of other factors also influence how people react to political events like election campaigns. These include free time, education, civic skills, and mobilization (see Norris 2002; Blais 2000; Verba, Schlozman, and Brady 1995; Rosenstone and Hansen 1993). Unfortunately, the limited number of cases available for analysis in this study makes it virtually impossible to reliably estimate the effects of these many other factors.

Another possibility, however, is that immigrants have two separate and distinct sets of political outlooks that guide their behaviour: those shaped by politics in the source country and those shaped by politics in the host country. The kinds of questions typically asked in national surveys – questions about political interest, cynicism, and norms, for example – do not give immigrant respondents the opportunity to distinguish between these sets of outlooks. But it is quite conceivable that immigrants do make such a distinction and that outlooks shaped in the host country are the primary drivers of political behaviour.

NOTES

1 My analysis of CES data distinguishes between immigrants who arrived in Canada before and after 18 years of age. This differs from categories in the Canadian census.
2 Further analyses show that differences in demographics and socio-economic status do not explain the gaps in levels of interest.

10 What Accounts for the Local Diversity Gap? Supply and Demand of Visible Minority Candidates in Ontario Municipal Politics

KAREN BIRD

As this chapter will show, the integration of ethnic diversity into local councils and at the level of municipal electoral politics has lagged far behind developments in Canadian national politics (see also Andrew et al. 2008; Siemiatycki 2011a, 2011b). Yet inclusion is no less important at the local level. The failure to achieve diverse representation in local government is problematic, in terms of both the signal it sends to local residents about accessibility and inclusivity at city hall and the equality of opportunity to shape ideas in the policy domain. And it is clear that the municipal-policy domain is one of increasing relevance to immigrants and ethnic minorities. Today more than ever before, municipalities are directly involved in the elaboration of local immigrant-settlement strategies, and they work closely with local settlement agencies to deliver a whole range of basic and specialized services to newcomers (Good 2009; Tolley and Young 2011; Andrew et al. 2012).

While in Chapter 8 Gidengil and Roy examined the political engagement of visible minorities, this chapter examines the scope of under-representation of visible minorities in local politics and assesses some of its causes. It takes municipal politics in Ontario cities as the site for analysis, focusing on the political representation of visible minorities in larger cities throughout the province. The chapter considers both "supply-side" and "demand-side" factors that may contribute to disparities in representation. On the supply side, it asks whether visible minorities' under-representation on city councils occurs because the members of these groups are disproportionately reluctant to come forth as candidates or because these candidates enjoy fewer resources and have less political experience than their opponents. On the demand side, the chapter assesses whether voters are less likely to favour visible minority candidates. To provide a better assessment of visible minorities' under-representation and its potential cause, the chapter relies on a comparative strategy, comparing the situation of visible minorities with that of women and foreign-born Canadians.

Under-Representation of Visible Minorities in Ontario Municipalities: The Scope of the Problem

Despite the overall success of multiculturalism in urban governance in some of Canada's largest cities (Good 2009), visible minorities appear less likely to be elected municipally than at the provincial or federal level. For example, the Greater Toronto Area (GTA) is Canada's largest and one of its most ethnically diverse urban agglomerations, where over 40 per cent of residents identify as belonging to a visible minority. Yet Siemiatycki (2011a) found that across the GTA's 25 municipalities, visible minorities held a mere 18 of 253 (7.1 per cent) municipal council positions. Why do visible minorities find it so difficult to become elected to council in some of Canada's most diverse and cosmopolitan cities? We have few, if any, conclusive answers to this question, owing to the sparse amount of research on municipal elections in Canada generally (Cutler and Matthews 2005, 359; Kushner, Siegel, and Stanwick 1997, 539) and the lack of attention to immigrants and visible minorities in local politics more specifically. There has been some analysis of the geography of voting in Canadian cities – for example, correlating the concentrations of immigrants and visible minorities with turnout across wards (Hicks 2006; Siemiatycki and Marshall 2014) and with the ethnic background of winning councillors (Smith and Walks 2013). But no research has yet examined the role of individual voter and candidate socio-demographics in local elections. This is in sharp contrast to the United States, where there has been far-reaching examination of how political institutions combine with racial and ethnic divisions in local contexts to shape municipal voting patterns and policy outcomes (e.g., Kaufmann 2004; Hajnal and Trounstine 2005; Hajnal 2009; Trounstine 2010; Vedlitz and Johnson 1982).

The first step in this study is to assess the scope of the numerical under-representation of visible minorities in local politics across Ontario's larger municipalities. To do this, I conducted an online Municipal Candidates Survey of candidates for the October 2010 municipal elections in Ontario.[1] An invitation to participate in the survey was sent to the approximately 1,500 declared candidates across the 23 largest cities in the province (cities of at least 100,000 inhabitants). Candidates were asked a series of questions regarding their personal background, including age, country of birth, and ethnic origin. In addition to these demographic questions, the survey asked candidates about their political experience and campaign resources, including whether they had run for election before, whether they had a paid campaign manager, and whether they had volunteers from a political or party organization. This invitation to participate, along with follow-up telephone calls, produced 702 completed surveys, a response of about 47 per cent. For non-respondents, data on background characteristics were drawn from candidates' websites and local newspaper articles. Using these two approaches, data were collected on visible minority status, gender, incumbency, and electoral outcome for 1,340 of almost 1,500 municipal candidates.

The first row of Table 10.1 below presents a summary of the survey data, focusing on diversity among candidates and elected members of council across these 23 cities for the 2010 municipal elections in Ontario. The second and third rows present comparable data for candidates and elected members at the provincial and federal levels, respectively.[2] As explained above, the data for visible minorities are compared with those for women and foreign-born Canadians to provide a better relative assessment of the scope of their representation.

Looking first at the municipal level, we see that visible minorities held only 7.6 per cent of council seats in these 23 municipalities, despite comprising over 32 per cent of the general population across these cities. Expressed as a ratio of proportionality in representation, visible minorities across these cities hold less than one-quarter (0.23) of the council seats that would be expected if their representation mirrored their population share. For women and the foreign-born, the level of under-representation is also notable, although less extreme: 28 per cent of all council seats were held by women, while 19 per cent were held by citizens born outside Canada. Each of these latter two groups has slightly more than half of the seats that would be expected given their presence in the population (women's ratio of proportionality in local councils is 0.55, while for the foreign-born, it is 0.52.)

It is also noteworthy that visible minorities are more likely than women to run for municipal office, relative to each group's population share. Visible minorities comprised 18 per cent of all local candidates (proportionality ratio 0.55), while women made up just 19.6 per cent of candidates (proportionality ratio 0.39). Foreign-born citizens, for their part, comprised 25 per cent of the candidate pool (proportionality ratio 0.68). Thus, women come closer to proportionality as we move from

Table 10.1. Statistical Representation of Ontario's Diverse Groups: Municipal Councils, Provincial and Federal Legislatures, 2010–11[a]

	Visible minorities	Women	Foreign-born
2010 municipal elections, 23 largest Ontario cities			
Population[b]	32.4%	50.6%	36.9%
Elected to city council (ratio of	7.6%	27.9%	19.3%
proportionality)[c]	(0.23)	(0.55)	(0.52)
Candidates for city council (ratio	18.0%	19.6%	25.0%
of proportionality)	(0.55)	(0.39)	(0.68)
2011 provincial election, 107 Ontario ridings			
Population	22.8%	51.2%	–
Elected to legislature (ratio of	12.1%	28.0%	–
proportionality)	(0.53)	(0.55)	–
Candidates for legislature (ratio	17.8%	24.9%	–
of proportionality)	(0.78)	(0.49)	–
2011 federal election, 106 Ontario ridings			
Population	22.8%	51.2%	36.9%
Elected to Parliament (ratio of	8.5%	18.9%	17.0%
proportionality)	(0.37)	(0.37)	(0.46)
Candidates for Parliament (ratio	12.6%	31.8%	–
of proportionality)	(0.55)	(0.58)	–

a Data on visible minority candidates and elected councillors are drawn from the author's survey. See note 4 for data on provincial and federal elections.
b All population figures are based on 2006 census data.
c Ratio of proportionality is calculated as a group's proportion in an elected assembly (or its proportion among electoral candidates) divided by its proportion in the population. A score of 1.0 indicates a perfect ratio of representation, a score above 1 indicates that a group is over-represented, while a score below 1 indicates that a group is numerically under-represented relative to its share of the population.

municipal candidate share to seat share (from proportionality ratio 0.39 to 0.55), while the foreign-born and, even more dramatically, visible minorities fall further away (from 0.55 to 0.23).[3] Furthermore, the lower rows of Table 10.1 above suggest that the decline from visible minority candidate share to seat share is far more precipitous at the municipal level compared to the federal and provincial levels.

There is no denying that visible minorities, women, and the foreign-born are vastly under-represented in electoral politics in Ontario's largest cities. Relatively few members of these groups contest elections, and none comes close to achieving a level of representation that their populations in the electorate might warrant. While the groups have this much in common, there appear to be important differences in the nature and mechanisms behind their under-representation. Though few female candidates contest elections, those who do run are significantly more successful than are visible minorities. Female council representation outpaces candidate share, while the opposite is true for visible minorities. Such a finding suggests that one way to achieve higher levels of female representation on council is to have more candidates run. The story for visible minorities, however, may not be so straightforward.

Assessing the Supply Side of Visible Minority Under-Representation

What are the causes of the extraordinary under-representation of visible minorities at the municipal level? The "supply-and-demand" analytical framework distinguishes between factors influencing the supply of candidates who come forward and those influencing the judgments and decisions of voters in choosing among available candidates. On first glance, it seems that there is no exceptional supply-side deficit of visible minority candidacies. As was shown in Table 10.1 above, visible minorities are certainly under-represented among candidates (ratio of proportionality 0.55), yet they are more likely than women (proportionality ratio 0.39) to run for municipal office, relative to their population share.

There may, however, be more subtle factors that constrain the supply of viable visible minority candidates. One possible factor is incumbency. Research points to significant structural advantages that incumbents enjoy over challengers, including name recognition, media exposure, a record of constituency service, networks with community leaders, and the ability to raise more campaign funds (Krebs 1998; Kushner, Siegel, and Stanwick 1997; Marland 1998; MacDermid 2009). These factors appear to be exacerbated in Ontario municipal politics, given the absence of political parties, which would otherwise assist in levelling the playing field between incumbents and challengers. For example, Kushner, Siegel, and Stanwick (1997, 544) show that the re-election rate of incumbents in municipal elections in Ontario cities over 100,000 was over 88 per cent, on average, across three electoral periods from 1982 to 1994. They also show that the incumbency advantage becomes more important as community size increases. There is further evidence that the incumbency advantage in Ontario municipalities grew as a result of municipal amalgamation under the Ontario Progressive Conservative

Table 10.2. Electoral Success Rate of Municipal Candidates in Ontario's 23 Largest Cities (%)

	Incumbents	Non-incumbents
Men	79.3	8.7
Women	78.3	15.5
Canadian-born	79.1	11.0
Foreign-born	77.8	9.2
Non-minorities	79.5	11.9
Visible minorities	70.0	0.9
Overall	79.0	9.2

government of the late 1990s and that this may have been especially detrimental to minorities (Andrew et al. 2008, 263; Hicks 2006).

The incumbency factor in municipal politics may help explain the particularly wide representational deficit facing visible minorities, who are overwhelmingly running as non-incumbents. Yet the results shown in Table 10.2 above indicate that the rate of electoral success of visible minority candidates, after controlling for incumbency, remains dramatically lower than the success rate of other groups. In 2010 municipal elections, across the 23 cities examined in this study, 79 per cent of incumbents who ran for re-election were successful. Yet where the incumbent was from a visible minority, the rate of re-election was just 70 per cent. Non-incumbents overall had a very low success rate, with just 9.2 per cent winning election. But it was lower still for challengers who were from visible minorities: less than 1 per cent of these non-incumbents were elected.

Another possible supply-side explanation for the lack of electoral success among visible minority candidates is that there may be a tendency for such candidates to become "packed" into wards with greater immigrant and visible minority populations. Where this occurs, we would find a persistent pattern of visible minority candidates competing against each other for a single seat; this may reduce the probability of victory for any single candidate. Simply put, the low electoral success of visible minority candidates might be the result of their tendency to all run in the same few wards in any given city. This explanation could also account for why the trend among visible minorities is different than that among women as there is no evidence that women are more likely to run against each other than to run against men.

While it is not possible here to investigate empirically the validity of this hypothesis, two caveats can be mentioned. First, the fact that all cities in this study use ward-level elections to elect members of council should provide an electoral edge to geographically concentrated groups. In at-large elections, by contrast, the entire city forms an electoral arena, thereby diluting potential minority voting strength when groups are spatially segregated. Scholars have therefore found that concentrated minority groups are more likely to elect one of their own in single-seat, ward-level elections than they are in at-large contests (Engstrom and McDonald 1986; Marschall, Ruhil, and Shah 2010; Trounstine and Valdini 2008). Second, this hypothesis of crowding of visible minority candidates into ethnically segregated electoral districts can hardly provide an explanation as to why the electoral success of visible minority candidates would be lower at the municipal than at the provincial and federal levels. Further work needs to be done to assess whether there is a more pronounced tendency towards packing minority candidates into so-called "colour coded" wards at the local level compared to provincial and federal electoral districts.

To sum up, while the data point to candidacy as a major barrier for visible minorities and other groups to be elected municipally, there is evidence that visible minorities may face *additional* obstacles once they become candidates. Even when visible minorities run as candidates in municipal elections, something limits their capacity to be elected (more so than for other groups). Our initial investigations do not point towards supply-side explanations. The remainder of this chapter looks at demand-side explanations – specifically, voter bias – as a possible explanation for the relative absence of visible minorities on Ontario city councils.

Assessing the Demand Side of Visible Minority Under-Representation

Turning to demand-side explanations related to voter preferences, there is considerable evidence in the United States that white voters prefer white candidates, while minorities prefer minority candidates (Wolfinger 1965; Bobo and Gilliam 1990; Terkildsen 1993; Sigelman et al. 1995; Hutchings and Valentino 2004; Collet 2005; Barreto 2007; Philpot and Walton 2007). There is also modest evidence of co-ethnic "affinity" voting in Britain (Fisher et al. 2014) and France (Brouard and Tiberj 2011). There has been less research in Canada on whether minority candidates are disadvantaged due to voter bias. Black and Erickson (2006) find no significant difference in the vote share received by visible minority compared to non-minority candidates in Canadian federal elections. They also find no evidence of compensation effects among visible minority candidates – that is, the possibility that parties might choose exceptionally well-qualified visible minority candidates to offset potential voter bias. While there appear to be no aggregate effects of candidate ethnicity on vote share in the context of Canadian federal elections, it is nevertheless possible that voter bias does operate at the individual level. Specifically, if ethnic minority candidates encounter negative bias from non-minority voters, but positive bias from same-ethnicity voters, we may fail to detect any effect at the aggregate level. It is also possible that bias may be more manifest in local elections, where the level of information is typically low and voters cannot rely on leader or party cues (Matson and Fine 2006; McDermott 1998).

Here we use a unique voter experiment to examine the possibility that voters are more disposed to support candidates who share their ethnic background and less inclined to support those from a different ethnic background. This experiment was deployed using an online survey of voting-age citizens resident in Ontario, during the municipal elections of October 2010.[4] The non-partisan nature of these elections allows us to parse out the confounding factors of party leaders and partisan cues that tend to supersede candidate characteristics in elections at other levels of government.

The study sample included 910 participants, of whom one-third self-identified as white/Caucasian, one-third as South Asian, and one-third as "other" (non–South Asian) visible minorities.[5] The sample also included approximately equal numbers of male and female respondents within each ethnic group. Each participant in this experiment viewed a single photograph and read a brief biography and platform of an individual the participant was told was a first-time candidate running for municipal election. Participants were asked to rate the candidate on a number of competency and trait-stereotype dimensions as well as to indicate how likely it was that they would vote for such a candidate were he or she running for council in their ward. The ethnicity (South Asian or white), sex (male or female), and biography/platform statement (business development–focused versus social service–focused) of the fictional candidate were systematically varied, thereby producing eight distinctive candidate conditions. These various stimuli – candidate photos, names, and platform statements – were carefully developed and tested to ensure similarity and authenticity across all treatments. For example,

photos were selected from a larger pool of stock headshots of British parliamentary candidates and then pretested for similarity in age, attractiveness, and ethnic group membership. The names assigned to candidates
were also vetted to ensure that they effectively signalled to both minority
and non-minority respondents the intended ethnic origin of each candidate.[6] (These candidate statements are presented in Appendix D.)

Respondents were randomly assigned to one of these eight candidate conditions, thus allowing us to assess how responses vary across
different voter-candidate combinations. While the study design permits
a wide range of analyses, the main goal of this chapter will be to test
for ethnic affinity effects, or the degree of preference that voters show
towards a candidate from their own ethnic group and corollary bias
against a candidate from another ethnic group. We also look briefly at
sex affinity and ideological affinity effects.

Respondents evaluated the presented candidate on a number of dimensions, thus producing several independent variables for analysis. We
consider four dimensions here, each measured along a 0-to-10-point scale.
These questions are as follows: "How qualified do you think [candidate
name] is to serve as a municipal councillor?" "If elected, do you think
that [candidate name] would tend to work for narrow interests within the
city or would tend to work for the broad interests of the entire city?" "If
elected to your Municipal Council, how likely is it that [candidate name]
would speak on behalf of you and your concerns?" and "If [candidate
name] were a candidate in your ward, would you vote for (him/her)?"

Before moving to the analysis, it is important to note that voter experiments do have certain weaknesses, especially with respect to ex-
ternal validity. It is doubtful whether respondent impressions and
evaluations formed under a set of contrived and artificial conditions
can be generalized to the context of a real election. In this experiment,
the main weakness is that respondents are not presented with a choice
among competing candidates, as they would in an actual election. I
have strived to compensate for this by implementing the study in the
context of an actual election and by presenting the hypothetical candidate as much as possible as a real candidate running for municipal
office in their city. Municipal elections are generally low-interest, low-
information events, and it is thus reasonable to think that the informational context of this experiment and the kind of evaluations that
respondents are asked to make are not entirely unrealistic, especially
as voters generally have little familiarity with or knowledge about the
various candidates competing across multiple wards in their city.

Table 10.3. Candidate Characteristic Effects on Candidate Evaluation

Candidate	Mean difference when candidate is		
	South Asian vs. white	Female vs. male	Service- vs. business- focused
Is well qualified	−.02	.11	.09
Would work for broad interests of entire city	−.18	.02	.19
Would speak on behalf of me and my concerns	.12	.16	.31*
Respondent would vote for candidate	−.13	.23	.04
N = 910			

Note: All candidate evaluation measures are based on a 0–10 scale.
* $p < .01$

We begin the analysis by examining the aggregate effects of the candidate's ethnicity, sex, and ideological orientation. Because we are looking at results across the whole sample of respondents, we will not pick up affinity effects in this analysis. Rather, the analysis is intended simply to show whether, overall, voters tend to form different impressions of a candidate's particular strengths or weaknesses based on the candidate's ethnicity, sex, and ideological orientation. Table 10.3 above presents mean differences on each of the four key dependent variables.

Neither the ethnicity nor the sex of the candidate generates systematically more positive or negative reaction across the whole sample of voters. As seen in the table, these socio-demographic characteristics of the candidate had no significant impact on any of the four main dependent variables related to voter choice. There is only one difference that achieves statistical significance, and it relates to the candidate's ideological positioning. Voters who evaluated the left-leaning, service-oriented candidate were significantly ($p < .05$) more likely to find him or her to be someone who "would speak on behalf of me and my concerns" compared to those who evaluated the right-leaning, business-oriented candidate. That some candidate characteristics do not generate systematically positive or negative reaction across the whole sample of voters does not mean, however, that there are not particular bias or affinity effects among the different subsamples of respondents. It is still possible that, for instance, white voters react negatively to South Asian candidates or that South Asian voters react positively to them.

Table 10.4 below reveals the nature of these voter affinity effects. A few features stand out. First, the overall ethnic affinity effect is positive,

Table 10.4. Sex, Ethnicity, and Ideological Affinity Effects on Candidate Evaluations

Candidate	Mean difference when candidate and respondent are of		
	Same ethnicity vs. different	Same sex vs. different	Same ideology vs. different
Is well qualified	.24***	−.23*	.10
Would work for broad interests of entire city	.32***	−.25*	.22
Would speak on behalf of me and my concerns	.48**	−.31***	.21
Respondent would vote for candidate	.55**	−.40**	.03
N = 910			

Note: All candidate evaluation measures are based on a 0–10 scale.
* p < .10, **p < .05, ***p < .01

whereas the overall sex affinity effect is negative. That is, the general trend among respondents is towards *more favourable* ratings of same-ethnicity candidates compared to different-ethnic candidates and *more negative* ratings of same-sex candidates compared to different-sex candidates. A second finding is that there is no significant ideological affinity effect. Or if ideological affinity is operating, it appears to be overwhelmed by the previous two effects.

The findings in Table 10.4 are quite interesting because they suggest that voter choice is generally unaffected by the degree of match or mismatch between voter and candidate ideology; on the other hand, the socio-demographic characteristics of candidate sex and ethnicity do matter – albeit in different ways for different groups of voters. Nevertheless, we should be cautious in applying these experimental findings to voter choice in real electoral contests. Although sex and ethnicity may be more salient in the experimental design, it would be wrong to assume that an actual candidate's ideology and platform matter less to real voters than the candidate's sex and ethnicity. The differences between ideological approaches and candidate platforms may become more apparent, and also may come to matter more in terms of voter choice, when voters have the opportunity (as they do in real elections) to assess more than one candidate.

Table 10.4 also masks the more detailed nature of these ethnic and sex affinity effects. With respect to ethnic affinity, we know that, overall, voters evaluate candidates who share their ethnic background more

Figure 10.1. Predicted Values of Ethnic Affinity Effect on Candidate Evaluation

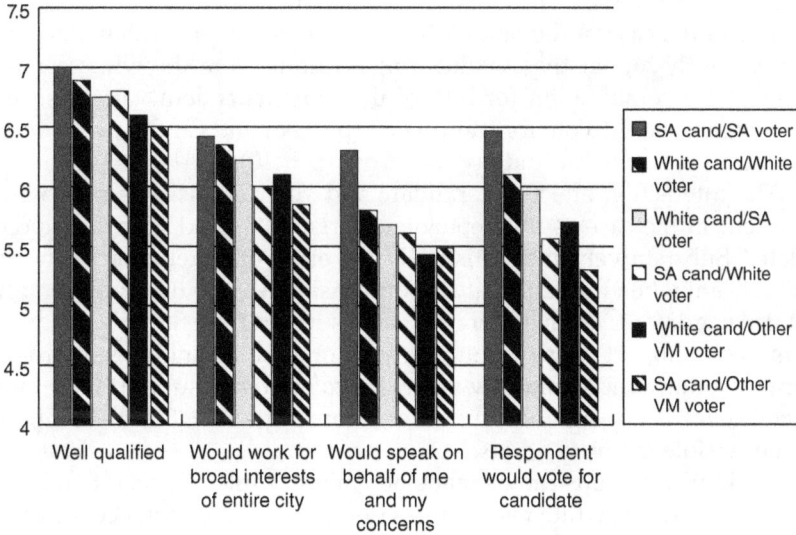

positively compared to candidates of a different ethnic background. The table does not tell us whether this aggregate effect is composed of a particularly strong or weak ethnic affinity effect among distinctive respondent subsamples. For example, it could be that South Asian voters are especially prone to supporting a same-ethnicity candidate, while the response of white voters towards candidates of various ethnic backgrounds is more neutral.[7] To examine subsample differences, it is necessary to regress all voter ethnicity by candidate ethnicity combinations (interactions) on the dependent variable, then calculate predicted values for each combination. The results of this procedure for ethnic affinity effects are summarized in Figure 10.1 above.

Figure 10.1 shows that the ethnic affinity effect is consistently more positive for the South Asian candidate–voter combination than for the white candidate–voter combination. The bar heights represent average predicted values, resulting from regressing a set of dummy variables representing all candidate-voter combinations, onto each of the four dependent variables. The ordinary least squares (OLS) regression results also produce significance tests of the relative effect of each candidate-voter combination on the dependent variable. These are not presented in the figure, but they can be understood as testing whether the difference in height between each pair of bars is beyond what we might see by chance. These tests reveal that predicted candidate evaluations in the case of the South Asian candidate–voter combination are significantly higher than evaluations resulting from the white candidate–voter combination for two of the four dependent variables: respondent "would vote for candidate" (p < .06) and candidate "would speak on behalf of me and my concerns" (p < .10).

The interaction effect of candidate and voter ethnicity is especially evident in the case of the dependent variable "would vote for candidate." Substantively and statistically, the effect on voter choice is most significant when the candidate is South Asian. We see that while South Asian candidates receive a large boost in support from South Asian voters, their support drops significantly among white, and even more so among other visible minority voters. In comparison, support for white candidates is not significantly different among white, South Asian, or other visible minority voters.

Two further points can be made here. First, while it is clear that both South Asian and white respondents demonstrate a preference for candidates of their own ethnicity over those of a different ethnicity, the ethnic affinity effect is significantly stronger for the South Asian voter–candidate combination than for the white voter–candidate combination. Second, this predominant South Asian ethnic affinity effect is strongest (and statistically significant) on two of the four dependent variables: whether the respondent would vote for the candidate and whether the respondent thought that the candidate would, if elected, "speak on behalf of me and my concerns." We still know little about the underlying causes and manifestations of ethnic affinity in the political sphere. However, these findings suggest that a same-ethnic voting preference may work through anticipation that one's views and interests will thereby be more fairly represented. This may also help explain why the effect is observed most vividly among a group (South Asian) that has been historically under-represented in comparison to the majority, or reference, group (whites).

This brings us to our "other" (non-South Asian) visible minority respondents. Moving along each set of bars in Figure 10.1, we find that the South Asian candidate–other visible minority voter condition produces the consistently lowest predicted candidate evaluations. For all four dependent variables, the average candidate evaluations observed within the South Asian candidate–other visible minority voter condition are significantly lower (p < .05) than candidate evaluations in each of the same-ethnicity candidate–voter conditions. On all but one of the dependent variables ("Would speak on behalf of me and my concerns"), other visible minority voters also evaluated South Asian candidates more negatively than they did white candidates. These findings point to a possible malaise in relations among minority groups, who may live side by side in the same ethnically diverse neighbourhoods. Such tensions have rarely been explored in Canada (but see Besco 2014), although they have been amply demonstrated by studies in the United States (Casellas 2008; Kaufmann 2003; Ramakrishnan et al. 2009; but see Collet 2005). Resistance among racialized minorities in the United States to candidates from other minority groups, over white candidates, may reflect inter-group hostility and prejudice as well as crucial differences in language, ideology, residential location, and historical experiences of different groups. The evidence from the present study suggests that "other" racialized minorities in Ontario may likewise feel resentful of their relatively well-mobilized and better-represented South Asian neighbours. This interpretation remains highly speculative insofar as we cannot estimate the degree or direction of bias that these "other" visible minorities might express towards a same-ethnicity candidate.

The final step in this analysis explores the full effects of the experimental design with respect to candidate and voter ethnicity and sex.[8] As in the previous steps, the procedure for examining subsample differences involves regressing all voter ethnicity/sex by candidate ethnicity/sex combinations (interactions) on the dependent variable, then calculating predicted values for each combination. This required creating a full set of dummy variables to represent every candidate-voter combination. In the interests of brevity, I will focus my remarks on the results for the most pivotal measure of candidate support: "respondent would vote for candidate." Figure 10.2 below plots the predicted values on this measure.[9]

There are a few substantive findings that stand out as especially noteworthy. First, looking at the overall levels of predicted support for different candidates, it appears that white female candidates are somewhat advantaged relative to others. They receive relatively high levels of support – well above the 5.0 midpoint on the 0–10 scale – among voters across all socio-demographic categories. Support is notably strongest among white men. These findings suggest that white female candidates may be relatively successful because they are least likely to incite strong reactions of voter affinity or bias along socio-demographic lines. Certainly the strong support for white female candidates among white male voters contradicts the prediction that female voters are more likely than men to support female candidates, all else being equal

Figure 10.2. Effects of Candidate and Voter Ethnicity and Gender
on Candidate Evaluations (Predicted Values)

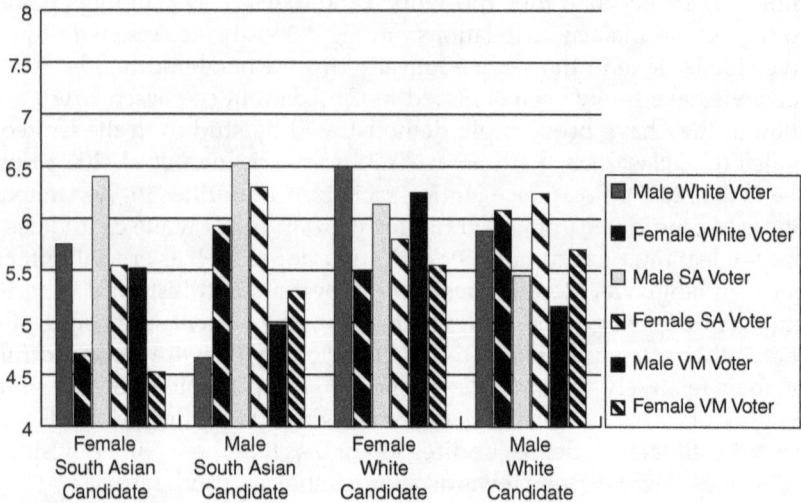

(Dolan 2008; King and Matland 2003; Sanbonmatsu 2002). Indeed, there
is scant evidence of gender affinity voting in Canadian federal elections (Goodyear-Grant and Croskill 2011). Looking at aggregate results
for municipal elections in Ontario, Kushner and his colleagues likewise
found that female candidates enjoyed a slightly higher rate of electoral success than male candidates, especially in larger municipalities.
However they could only speculate as to whether this was a result of
women engaging in "block voting in favour of women in order to support their own" or an effect of both men and women voting "disproportionately for the limited number of women on the ballot in a conscious
effort to even the gender balance on council" (Kushner et al. 1997, 547).
Our results suggest that there is rather an opposite-sex affinity effect at
work in this study.[10]

White male candidates also receive relatively steady levels of support
among voters across all socio-demographic categories. With the notable
exception of other visible minority male respondents, support for white
male candidates remains safely above the 5.0 midpoint among all other
voter groups. Support for South Asian candidates varies much more
widely depending on respondents' sex and ethnicity. South Asian male

candidates receive strong support from South Asian male and female voters, but their support plummets among white and visible minority male respondents. Similarly, South Asian female candidates receive strong support from South Asian male voters. However, their support among co-ethnic females is considerably weaker. Support falls even further among white female and other visible minority voters. Overall, it appears that female voters (among all ethnic groups, including co-ethnics) are less likely to vote for the South Asian female candidate than for any other candidate.

From the perspective of different voter socio-demographics, white male voter support for a presented candidate varies considerably depending on that candidate's sex and ethnicity. Predicted scores among white male voters range almost 2 full points, from a low of 4.8 for the South Asian male candidate to a high of 6.6 for the white female candidate. White female voters are also somewhat fickle in who receives their support, with predicted scores ranging from 4.8 for the South Asian female candidate to 6.2 for the white male candidate. In contrast, South Asian voters appear to discriminate less on the grounds of a candidate's sex and ethnicity; the predicted levels of support for different candidates among South Asian male and female voters never vary by more than 1 point.

Conclusion

Visible minorities are severely under-represented on municipal councils in Ontario's large and medium-sized cities. While other groups – notably women – are also under-represented, the magnitude and the causes of the problem facing visible minorities appear to be quite different. This chapter has considered factors that might explain the exceptional deficit in visible minority representation at this level. Part of the problem appears to begin with a deficit in candidacies, a factor relating to the supply side. However, this cannot explain why visible minorities are less likely than women and other under-represented groups to be elected when they do run. Nor can it explain why the representation gap among visible minorities is so pronounced at the local level compared to the provincial and national levels.

The chapter then explored the role of demand-side explanations. More specifically, the main hypothesis investigated here is whether voter bias might be a factor; that is, do voters tend to favour candidates with the same ethnic background as them and reject candidates of a different ethnic background? The results of the experiment show rather clearly that there is a significant ethnic affinity bias, with voters preferring same-ethnicity over different-ethnicity candidates.

This effect is most powerful for the question "Would you vote for this person?" The response we are seeing, therefore, suggests a preference to *elect to city council* someone who is ethnically similar to oneself. The results, in other words, suggest that respondents (and South Asians, in particular) want descriptive and/or symbolic *political representation* and, relatedly, are less enthusiastic about having people of other ethnic backgrounds represent them.

It is important to ask whether the effects we find reflect ethnic "pride or prejudice" or both. That is, to what extent is the preference for a same-ethnicity candidate over a different-ethnicity candidate a reflection of pride in one's own group versus prejudice against other groups? In the current social context, one in which Ontario's municipal councils remain almost exclusively white, I suggest that there should be greater cause for concern that white male and female voters are so strongly inclined to vote for a white candidate and so disinclined to vote for a South Asian. In the case of South Asian voters, it seems normatively less problematic – more like pride than prejudice – to demonstrate a strong preference to elect one of their own, thereby finding a voice or at least a symbolic measure of political inclusion in the political affairs of their city. In the current circumstances, this may be the only reasonable strategy available for visible minorities seeking inclusion in the arena of municipal electoral politics.

Finally, what are the mechanisms through which the ethnic affinity effect, which we have observed in this study, can become relevant to the actual outcomes of municipal elections? One important factor to consider is the demographic distribution of ethnic minority and majority voters within a city. The results of the voter experiment suggest that the ethnic affinity bias operates in a roughly similar way across all ethnic groups. That is, members of ethnic groups (whatever their background) tend to be more positively disposed towards a same-ethnicity candidate and more negatively disposed towards a candidate of a different ethnic origin. From ward to ward, then, outcomes for visible minority candidates will depend on the proportion of co-ethnics among the voting population and on voter turnout among different ethnic groups. If South Asian voters were evenly distributed across wards, then the additional support that a South Asian candidate might generate from co-ethnic voters would be offset – indeed, overwhelmed – by the negative dispositions manifested in the much larger population of non-co-ethnic voters. Of course, minority groups are not dispersed evenly across ward boundaries, but rather tend to live clustered in certain neighbourhoods and relatively sparsely in others.

Thus, to the extent that an ethnic affinity bias is a factor in municipal voter choice, it is rational for visible minority candidates to run in wards with higher proportions of same-ethnicity voters. The ethnic affinity bias will therefore contribute to the ghettoization of visible minority candidates. What is more, this tendency towards ghettoization may become part of a self-fulfilling prophesy, validating the presumption that candidates are more attentive and responsive to the interests of their own ethnic groups and leading voters to feel more justified in invoking stereotypes and ethnic preferences when choosing among them. Furthermore, this hypothesized mechanism suggests that visible minority electoral representation will rise quite slowly, at a rate consistent with "tipping point" demographics. That is, visible minorities will tend to be elected only when wards tip from majority white to "majority-minority" populations. Minority representation will thus lag behind overall increases in population diversity and will lag even more as a function of lower turnout among the minority population.

Another crucial mechanism linking the ethnic affinity bias to the observed diversity gap on municipal councils is the low informational context of local politics. As mentioned briefly above, these elections take place without the formal party organizations that otherwise serve to aggregate and articulate interests and to socialize, educate, and mobilize citizens into participating in politics and political decision making. Typically, there is also fairly limited media coverage of candidates who are not incumbent councillors or the front-runners for a mayoral election. Thus, voters' knowledge of candidates' names and platforms tends to be very limited. This exceptionally low-information context has at least two important consequences. First, turnout tends to be lower, and lower-turnout elections have been shown in several contexts to produce electorates that are less representative with regard to race, education, age, income, and employment of city populations (Hajnal 2009; Trounstine 2010). Second, the lack of partisan electoral cues likely enhances the power of other kinds of heuristics, such as race and ethnicity (Conover and Feldman 1989; McDermott 1998; Matsubayashi and Ueda 2011). In low-information contexts, where voters have little else by which to form an evaluation of candidates, voter biases resulting from ethnic affinity and sex affinity effects will tend to play a much greater role in voter choice. In contrast, these biases may be readily overridden in the partisan and generally richer informational context of elections at the national and provincial levels.

Finally, without political parties as a mobilizing and informational vehicle, candidates must rely heavily on local news coverage to disseminate their message. Local media are thus especially crucial in choosing the type of information that they broadcast about municipal candidates. To a significant degree, therefore, media play the role of "selectorate" in communicating to the voter who is a serious or worthy candidate and who is not. There is emerging evidence that race structures the media's reporting on candidates in Canadian national elections, positioning visible minorities in terms of their socio-demographics, novelty, and interest in more marginal policy issues (Tolley 2011). In my own exploratory interviews with a number of local visible minority candidates, the role of the media and the overall lack of coverage afforded to these candidates is a theme that has consistently emerged. The tendency of local media to exclude from coverage all but a few high-profile incumbent and front-runner municipal candidates has been shown to have detrimental effects on female candidates (Wagner 2011). It is reasonable to hypothesize that such selectivity in local media coverage has similarly negative effects for visible minority candidates – and that these serve to compound the informational deficit and voter bias against visible minority candidates. It is worth exploring, in future research, whether (and how) biases regarding visible minority candidates might be manifested through local media.

NOTES

1 Support for undertaking this survey was generously provided by the Social Sciences and Humanities Research Council of Canada (SSHRC) and the Welcoming Communities Initiative.
2 Data on the sex and visible minority status of provincial and federal candidates and elected members are based on the author's comprehensive review of candidates' websites, supplemented by information drawn from the Parliament of Canada website. The latter source also includes information on the sex and place of birth for members of Parliament. Note that the analysis includes only candidates for the three main parties (Liberal, Conservative/Progressive Conservative, and New Democrat). Data have been double checked for accuracy using two independent coders.

3 In light of the influx of newcomers into many large and mid-sized Ontario cities, both the visible minority and the foreign-born populations include a substantial portion of non-citizens. As non-voters, these people contribute to a lower ratio of proportionality of elected members among both groups. Nevertheless, the fact that the foreign-born perform relatively well, compared to visible minorities, suggests that the extraordinary representational deficit suffered by visible minorities is not simply a function of electoral ineligibility.

4 The Municipal Voter Survey was administered during the two weeks preceding the municipal elections, which were held across Ontario on 25 October 2011. Participants were recruited by Environics Analytics, which uses online ads and co-offers as well as random-digit dialing to maintain a bank of potential survey respondents. These individuals are contacted periodically and asked whether they would like to receive nominal compensation to participate in a survey. Screening questions helped to ensure that sufficient numbers of white and visible minority participants were included in this study. Funding for this survey came from SSHRC and McMaster University's Arts Research Board.

5 The category of South Asian was chosen for theoretical reasons. Both Siemiatycki (2011a) and Matheson (2005) report that while South Asians are numerically under-represented relative to their numbers in the population, they are nevertheless the best represented among all visible minority groups across all levels of government within the GTA. Introducing a South Asian candidate within the experimental design should thus present a more conservative estimate of negative voter bias towards candidates from an ethnic group other than one's own, given that there will be greater familiarity with South Asian elected officials.

6 An initial set of 12 photos (six South Asian and six white men and women) was drawn from a base of visually similar candidate headshots from a political party website. These 12 photos were presented to a small panel ($n=8$) of South Asian and white testers, each of whom was asked to identify the ethnicity (visible minority or white), estimate the age, and score the physical attractiveness (from 1 to 10) of each candidate. Any photo that did not receive unanimous scores on ethnic identity was eliminated; among the remainder, the four candidates (South Asian male, South Asian female, white male, white female) with the closest mean age and mean attractiveness scores were selected for use in the experiment.

7 Such a strong ethnic affinity effect could result from stronger in-group identification among members of some communities or from an awareness that one's group is less well represented politically than another group.

8 Recall that Table 10.4 shows significant ethnic affinity and sex affinity effects, but no effects of ideological affinity (that is, the interaction between candidate and voter ideology) on any of the four dependent variables.

9 OLS regression results are available on request.

10 Further analysis of the experimental data (not shown here) suggests that male and female voters are both more likely to support an ideologically left-wing female candidate (compared to a comparable male candidate). But female voter support for the female candidate dips, while male voter support remains high, when the female candidate has a more right-wing/pro-business platform.

11 Who Represents Minorities? Question Period, Minority MPs, and Constituency Influence in the Canadian Parliament

JEROME H. BLACK

In the same vein as the preceding chapter, this chapter addresses questions of representation among immigrants and ethnic minorities in Canada. But rather than focusing on the representation of elected officials at the municipal level, it examines the representation of the minority agenda in the federal Parliament. This chapter focuses on Question Period in the Canadian House of Commons to consider hypotheses about the representation of the minority agenda – understood here as policy matters that are of disproportionate concern to minority ethno-racial and immigrant-based communities. This agenda includes a range of issues and themes touching on immigration and refugee affairs, citizenship rights, multiculturalism, social acceptance and discrimination, and the socio-economic and political status of minorities and immigrants in Canada. The extent to which members of Parliament (MPs) pose questions that reference such topics is assumed to reflect the representation of minority interests, and it forms the basis of hypotheses about the impact of two types of diversity on that representation: the minority/immigrant heterogeneity of the constituencies that MPs represent and the ethno-racial origins of the legislators themselves. The key questions examined here are whether MPs from diverse constituencies pose more questions bearing on the minority agenda than parliamentarians representing less diverse districts and whether MPs with minority origins are more likely to ask minority-focused questions compared to their non-minority counterparts.

One broad justification for this inquiry is the promise of further insights into the vital research area of newcomer and minority political integration. Current research, as demonstrated by most chapters in this volume, is heavily preoccupied, and understandably so, with the extent of the engagement of newcomers and minorities in ordinary or mass-level political activities and, further, with what may account for the variations seen. However, attention to their involvement in more demanding, elite-level political roles, not least as office seekers and office holders, would yield a more complete picture of political integration. Moreover, if studies of political integration are ultimately to have relevance, the consequences of both mass-level and elite-level activism must be understood, including how effectively minority-linked policy concerns are transmitted to, and represented in, the political system.

Studying minority-interest representation also ties into the extensive general comparative literature aimed at understanding what it means when historically disadvantaged groups (such as women and minorities) begin to establish a presence in legislative chambers. There is widespread agreement that these group-based, or "descriptive," representatives (e.g., Mansbridge 1999) have a symbolic impact, providing significant psychological benefits, and a sense of inclusion, for the group. Uncertainty continues, however, with respect to how readily increased numbers of descriptive representatives enhance attention to a group's more concrete concerns – that is, the extent to which such growth brings about responsive or substantive representation (Pitkin 1967). Somewhat mixed empirical results relating numbers and responsiveness have contributed to this doubt, although diverse findings probably reflect the varied testing situations and methodologies ranging across groups, countries, and indicators of substantive impact. In the women's representation literature, for example, the lack of a consistent effect by female legislators has helped give impetus to assertions that women's interests can be promoted in alternative ways, including by key groups of (sympathetic) men. Thus, there has been a corresponding shift in the questions posed. Rather than ask whether women represent women or whether women make a difference, the newer and broader question is "How does the substantive representation of women occur?" (Celis et al. 2008). Such an agnostic approach looks for the possible impact of group-based representatives, while acknowledging the potential influence of other legislators. This expanded view comports with the now widely accepted idea that representation is best understood as a multiform activity (e.g., Mansbridge 2003).

Reflecting this, this chapter examines hypotheses pertaining not only to minority MPs asking minority-oriented questions but also to nonminority MPs responding to their diverse constituencies. Altogether, four hypotheses are examined, and, as seen below, each is introduced in the context of the particular strands of representation theory that are most appropriate for its consideration. In this way, the findings promise to add, even if only modestly so, to an understanding of contemporary theorizing in the area of representation.

These considerations provide justifications that have cross-national reach, but this study is also compelling from a Canadianist perspective. It makes an incidental contribution by bolstering the value of Question Period as a focal point for the study of representation in Canada – which, as noted below, has only recently been examined on a rigorous, empirical basis. More fundamental is that it adds to the sparse empirical literature on the substantive representation of the minority agenda in Canada.

The next section notes very briefly the benefits of focusing on Question Period and then justifies and contextualizes the four hypotheses relating constituency diversity and MP origins to the propensity to ask minority-oriented questions. Also spelled out are some countervailing factors that likely operate to diminish the expected effects. Next there is a review of a few selected studies that are pertinent to the focus here. The following two sections form the heart of the empirical analysis; the first introduces the data set, explains its organization, discusses the operationalization of the main variables, and then presents preliminary bivariate results. These findings, in turn, point to the need for a more extended, multivariate analysis, which is set up and carried out in the follow-up section. The conclusion provides an opportunity for discussing the implications of the findings.

Four Hypotheses

In Canada, as in most parliamentary regimes, Question Period has long been recognized and commented on as a key feature of the democratic process, one that helps ensure executive accountability (for Canada, see Franks 1987; for selected other countries, see the references in Martin 2011). Question Period is also well understood to serve other significant purposes (e.g., showcasing talent on both government and opposition sides) and has a high profile in the game of parliamentary politics because of the very visible and often-newsworthy perspectives it provides. More recently, it has been increasingly understood that investigating Question Period also affords special opportunities to discern the true interests and preferences of individual legislators because they are

Table 11.1. Four Hypotheses about Representing the Minority Agenda

---

1. *Ceteris paribus*, MPs elected in diverse constituencies are more likely to represent the minority agenda (ask minority-oriented questions) than MPs elected in less diverse ridings.
2. The impact of constituency diversity on the representation of the minority agenda will be greater in competitive constituencies (where MPs have narrower margins of victory).
3. *Ceteris paribus*, minority MPs are more likely than non-minority MPs to represent the minority agenda.
4. The impact of constituency diversity on the representation of the minority agenda:
   a. Will be greater among minority MPs than non-minority MPs.
   b. Will be greater among non-minority MPs than minority MPs.

---

less subject to the constraints of party discipline. MPs' questions can be scrutinized for a more meaningful indication of their content and geographical orientation.[1]

Table 11.1 above displays the four hypotheses. The first two highlight the potential impact of constituency diversity on the representation of the minority agenda in Question Period. The first hypothesis asserts that, *ceteris paribus*, MPs elected in more diverse ridings (e.g., those with larger immigrant populations) are more likely to ask minority-oriented questions. The phrase *"ceteris paribus"* is admittedly redundant – since proper hypothesis tests assume the statistical correction of other relevant factors – but is nevertheless made explicit to emphasize that MPs' ethno-racial origins are taken into account. Indeed, the adjustment is a practical necessity given that minority parliamentarians are more likely to be elected in diverse constituencies.[2] Support for the hypothesis would mean, therefore, that MPs, independent of their origins, pose more minority-oriented questions as a function of representing diverse districts. The second hypothesis is related – and indeed might even be regarded as a corollary – since it identifies electoral pressures as conditioning the degree to which legislators pay attention to constituency interests. The expectation is that MPs with narrower margins of victory are more responsive.

These two hypotheses are intimately associated with the classical *dyadic*, or principal-agent, model of representation, which depicts legislators as acting as instructed constituency "delegates" and which is regarded as typical of legislative representation in the United States, where legislators are able to act fairly independently. In Canada, however, the dyadic model is generally considered to have less relevance precisely because of the strong exercise of party discipline and control by party leaders (Docherty 1997; Malloy 2003b). Nonetheless, this may be too narrow a view. As Soroka, Penner, and Blidook (2009) point out, when all is said and done, MPs have incentives to respond to constituency priorities to enhance their re-election chances, even in the face of party-wide defeat. This fits with the perspective that legislators are mindful of the possibility of developing a "personal vote." More fundamental is that most Canadian MPs claim that the constituency is their primary focus (Heitshusen, Young, and Wood 2005).[3]

Research by Koop (2012) on the role of party constituency associations adds further support to the idea that "constituency matters" to MPs. Based on interview and observation methods, he concluded that MPs often endeavour to have local "sector" representatives on their riding executives to help learn of their constituents' needs and preferences (and communicate the legislators' accomplishments back to them). Defined as "any group of citizens with a common characteristic within a given constituency that is recognized by the MP," sectors can entail any kind of demographic or values-oriented grouping, and, of direct relevance here, Koop specifically includes "language and cultural communities" (ibid., 362).

Still, not all MPs invest similarly in their constituencies. Some regard themselves more as party delegates than as constituency delegates, while others place more emphasis on national- or international-level issues (Shane 2010).[4] These offsetting factors likely diminish the strength of the connection between constituency diversity and minority-oriented representation. Other confounding effects may stem from the focus here on the legislator's "policy responsiveness" vis-à-vis the constituency when, in fact, responsiveness can also entail "service," "allocation," and "symbolic" aspects (Eulau and Karps 1977; for the Canadian case, see Price and Mancuso 1995; Koop 2012). Future research would do well to incorporate the correspondingly appropriate measures (such as role orientation and geographic focus) directly into the analysis. Here the relationships in the two hypotheses must overcome these countervailing effects, so, in this sense, any positive results might be viewed conservatively.

The third hypothesis attaches a substantive component to descriptive representation by asserting that MPs with minority origins ask more questions related to the minority agenda than their non-minority counterparts. It is underpinned by perspectives in the "politics of presence" literature (e.g., Phillips 1995), which argue that group-connected legislators advance group interests in concrete ways. The general argument is that they provide group members with a more effective kind of representation as a result of intimate and personal knowledge of group concerns – qualities that translate into insight, empathy, and commitment.

For critics with a particularly strong individualist orientation, this hypothesis stands in opposition to the first two, which are rooted in more traditionally liberal representative perspectives. Such opponents regard the very idea of group-connected representation as problematic and are particularly apprehensive about proactive measures that would "artificially" enhance the number of descriptive representatives. Such "distortions" are deemed unnecessary because appropriate mechanisms of authorization and accountability ensure that non-group legislators strive to represent the diverse elements in their constituencies.[5] However, those who see fundamental value in the presence of descriptive representatives view these concerns as deriving from a conceptualization of representation that is overly monolithic, procedural, and individualist (Williams 1998) and correspondingly indifferent to, or dismissive of, the idea that groups have distinctive interests. For advocates, then, descriptive representatives compensate for the fundamental unfairness of traditionally liberal-based systems of representation.

The perspective adopted in this chapter is that representation can occur in various guises and that both constituency diversity and MP origin can drive responsiveness. Indicative of this, empirical support for the third hypothesis (with district effects separated out) would imply that minority MPs provide representational benefits outside of (or in addition to) any constituency context and that part of what passes for minority representation results from minority MP input into the general policy-making process. Such system-level contributions, as part of a broader process of "collective representation" (Weisberg 1978), can be understood as complementing the dyadic approach in the representation of minority interests.

Representation at the system level is also implicated by key parts of Mansbridge's (2003) work on contemporary democratic representation. She identifies and explicates several models that have become part of the present-day reality of democratic representation but that deviate from the traditional constituency-legislator power relationship. One form, "surrogate representation," appears to further justify the current hypothesis that minority origins matter as it emphasizes that group-based legislators can feel "a particular responsibility for representing [group] interests and perspectives ... even when members of these groups do not constitute a large fraction of their constituents" (ibid., 523); this orientation, in turn, advances otherwise marginal viewpoints. While the extra-geographical (representation) relationship can involve any number of groups, Mansbridge specifically mentions historically disadvantaged groups and, furthermore, suggests that the surrogate representative's commitment is likely to be stronger when he or she "shares experiences with surrogate constituents in a way that a majority of the legislature does not" (ibid.). Surrogate representation, then, squares with the general idea that minority MPs are inherently receptive to the minority agenda; in the present context, it would presumably characterize those minority MPs who represent relatively homogeneous constituencies.

Mitigating factors may also diminish the potential strength of the connection between origins and minority-agenda representation. Since most minority MPs represent fairly diverse districts, this implies a constraint on the overall effect associated with surrogate representation. As well, some minority MPs see themselves principally as strong party adherents and thus may be less inclined to represent minority concerns. What is more fundamental, in practice not all minorities see themselves as *minority* representatives. Some do not regard their origins as a major component of their self-definition; for others who do, they believe that their background has no bearing on the public sphere or politics (Black and Lakhani 1997). In other words, the hypothesis assumes an innate sensitivity to minority concerns that is in reality less than universal; again, this implies that any positive results generated here might be regarded conservatively.

The fourth hypothesis connects constituency diversity and MP origin in an interaction relationship, with two possible versions. One asserts that constituency heterogeneity is more consequential for minority representation among minority MPs than among their non-minority colleagues, while the other version affirms the opposite. A possible justification for the former follows on from the general idea behind the third hypothesis – namely, that minority MPs are already predisposed to represent the minority agenda and that district diversity simply amplifies this tendency. This notion might also be underpinned by what Koop (2012) notes are variations in the way legislators subjectively perceive sectors in their ridings. The implication is that minority MPs objectively facing the same constituency diversity as non-minority MPs are more prone to emphasize that heterogeneity because of their sensibilities. Alternatively, it might be maintained that minority legislators are already so attuned to the minority agenda that diversity adds only marginally to their responsiveness, thus implying that it may be more important for their non-minority counterparts. Surrogate representation might also (modestly) attenuate the impact of constituency diversity for minority MPs as some of them address minority concerns even while representing homogeneous constituencies. This variant of the hypothesis also finds support in the instrumental idea that non-minority MPs attend to minority concerns largely because of electoral realities and pressures in their ridings.

Some Relevant Studies

Four studies help to further frame expectations about these hypotheses, although in different ways. Two studies that deal specifically with Question Period in the Canadian Parliament have relevance for the first two hypotheses. Both used a large data set compiled under the supervision of Stuart Soroka, which includes information on over 43,000 oral questions from mid-1983 to 2004. While neither study focused specifically on the minority agenda, together they found ample evidence that the questions posed by MPs accord with appropriate characteristics of their constituencies. In the first study, Soroka, Penner, and Blidook (2009) determined that MPs with military bases in their constituencies ask more defence-related questions and that those representing right- and left-leaning constituencies are more prone to reference debt and tax matters and welfare issues, respectively. Moreover, they reported some modest evidence for the idea that competitiveness bolsters MPs' responsiveness to constituency interests.[6]

Using the same database, Blidook and Kerby (2011) investigated a wider range of Question Period themes – specifically, eight topic areas – and discovered that, in most cases, but not all, the measure employed to capture constituency interest (e.g., proportion in agriculture) is associated with the number of questions asked (e.g., questions on agriculture). The variation in results, they suggest, probably reflects the heightened constituency focus by MPs when "the issue aligns with a clearly articulated (such as organized or economic) interest, not simply where there is diffuse or unorganized interest within the constituency" (ibid., 330). For example, links were discerned between questions and constituency interest in the case of agriculture or fishing but not for intergovernmental affairs or constitutional and national unity topics.[7]

Overall, the two studies point to the importance of Question Period as a significant feature of the representational process in the Canadian Parliament. They are also helpful for emphasizing the employment of multivariate methodology suitable for analysing Question Period data, which is emulated in the current analysis.

A third study, by Bird (2010), deals directly with representational possibilities associated with visible minority MPs but has only suggestive status because it did not incorporate the necessary methodological aspects.[8] Further, her focus was not exclusively on Question Period but all parliamentary speeches during a fairly limited period of time (covering the first session of the 39th Parliament, February 2006 to September 2007). Nevertheless, she found that visible minority MPs are more likely to address minority concerns compared to non-visible minority MPs, a finding that is suggestive evidence on behalf of the third hypothesis. Furthermore, she found that constituency diversity makes a difference, and modestly so, only for non-visible minority MPs.

A fourth study by Saalfeld (2011), although focused on the British case, applies the relevant methodology and is the closest to the present analysis in the four hypotheses explored. The author studied questions tabled by visible minority and non-visible minority MPs during the course of the 2005–10 parliaments, focusing on "cost of immigration" and "promoting ethnic diversity" as indicators of minority representation. Visible minority MPs did indeed ask more questions in these areas (with constituency diversity held constant). For its part, district heterogeneity also makes a difference in the case of immigration, but not in connection with ethnic-diversity issues; this provides partial support for the first hypothesis. However, Saalfeld found no statistically significant interaction effect between MP origins and constituency diversity (akin to the fourth hypothesis here). While it is unclear how much national differences between Canada and Britain play a role, including the fact that questions are typically oral in the former and tabled in the latter, his results indicate that origins matter and constituency diversity partially so.

The Minority Agenda in Numbers

The database used here originates from several sources and employs the individual MP as the unit of analysis. Information on oral questions, including their subject matter and the inquiring MPs, has been taken from Soroka's study and incorporated into the author's data set, which contains information on MPs' ethno-racial origins as well as relevant constituency and census characteristics. For practical reasons, only questions associated with the period from 1993 to 2004 were used,[9] although the scope of the analysis is still quite extensive, involving three

Table 11.2. Subject Matter of Oral Questions, 35th to 37th Parliaments

	Number	Per cent	Average number of questions per MP	
			All MPs	Minority MPs
Economics	5,438	23.7	13.0	6.1
Foreign policy	4,428	19.3	10.6	7.3
Intergovernmental	4,100	17.8	9.8	3.1
Natural resources	3,259	14.2	7.8	4.6
Civil rights	2,309	10.1	5.5	2.4
Social welfare	2,036	8.9	4.9	4.4
Minority agenda	696	3.0	1.6	1.9
Immigration and refugee affairs[a]	*582*	*2.5*	*1.4*	*1.3*
Ethnic and racial groups[b]	*75*	*0.3*	*0.2*	*0.5*
Multiculturalism[c]	*39*	*0.2*	*0.1*	*0.2*
Aboriginal	572	2.5	1.4	0.7
Gender	133	0.6	0.3	0.4
N	*22,971*		*419*	*69*

[a] Immigration to Canada, resettlement expenditures, immigration and public health, expenditures and policies related to the Immigration and Refugee Board and Citizenship and Immigration Canada, Immigration and Refugee Protection Act, enforcement of immigration laws, legalization procedures, visas, political refugees, deportation, expedition, migrant and seasonal workers, migrant farm workers.

[b] Race-based crimes, hate crimes, investigation of racist individuals and/or organizations, appointment of minorities to judgeships, government and/or bureaucracy hiring and promotion, minority set-aside programs.

[c] Discussion of multiculturalism, multicultural programs.

full parliaments and 22,971 oral questions. The working data set consists of 419 parliamentarians, who asked at least one question in one or more parliaments. On average, they posed 54.8 oral questions each.

Table 11.2 above presents the author's reclassification of the categories available in Soroka's codebook.[10] The questions were grouped into eight non-minority topics and a summary minority one, which itself is composed of three subsets: questions on immigration and refugee affairs, ethnic and racial groups, and multiculturalism.[11] (The listings in the table have been taken directly from the original codebook.)

As is plain, most questions do not deal with minority-oriented concerns. It is not surprising, then, that economics-related topics head the list. Altogether, in the three parliaments, the 419 MPs asked 5,438 questions involving economic themes, representing 23.7 per cent of all the questions posed. They also asked a large number of questions dealing with foreign policy (4,428, or 19.3 per cent of all questions), intergovernmental affairs (4,100, or 17.8 per cent), and natural resources (3,259, or 14.2 per cent); somewhat further down the list are questions pertaining to civil rights (2,309, or 10.1 per cent) and social welfare matters (2,036, or 8.9 per cent). In contrast, the MPs asked 696 questions relating to the three minority topics; this constitutes only 3 per cent of all questions directed towards the government.

That fewer questions pertained to minority-related subject matter is not entirely unanticipated. To a large extent, this reflects the more encompassing and multi-sided nature of most, if not all, of the non-minority topics. Minority topics, while themselves quite multifaceted and complex, are less wide-ranging and involve a more limited number of themes and issues. The imbalance is also, no doubt, a product of the fact that minority concerns are precisely that, and they are of less interest to most MPs and Canadians, who are preoccupied with more "mainstream" subject matter. At the same time, arguably, this makes it even more imperative to understand the traces of minority representation that do occur.

The separate counts for the three minority topics also reveal unevenness. Over 80 per cent of all minority-related questions (582 of 696) deal with immigration and refugee affairs, reflecting its central importance on the minority agenda and, as emphasized below, its consuming nature as an ongoing preoccupation for urban MPs. Origin group–related questions and those involving multiculturalism number 75 and 39, respectively.

The third column of the table reports the mean number of questions posed by the MPs for the various topics and provides another perspective on the disparity between minority and non-minority topics. Thus, the top figure of 13 signifies the average number of questions that each of the 419 MPs asked on economic matters. By contrast, they directed an average of 1.6 questions related to the minority agenda (means of 1.4, .2, and .1 for immigration and refugee affairs, origin groups, and multiculturalism, respectively).

The fourth column displays these mean scores for the subset of 69 MPs who are identified here as having minority origins. Naturally, they include visible minority MPs,[12] but also represented are groups whom the author in previous work (e.g., Black 2009) has labelled the "distinctive Europeans" – those with Southern European, Eastern European, or Jewish origins. Their history of out-group status in Canadian society and politics justifies their inclusion; furthermore, there is evidence that in the contemporary period, many MPs with such backgrounds still regard themselves as having marginal status in Parliament.[13]

The results themselves, however, do not indicate that MP origin and asking minority-oriented questions are particularly related. Minorities asked on average 1.9 such questions, while the mean for all MPs is 1.6. For immigration and refugee matters, the figures are virtually identical (1.3 questions for minority MPs, 1.4 for all MPs). For topics having a bearing on origin groups, the corresponding differences are .5 versus .2 and, for multiculturalism, .2 versus .1. Still, it would be premature to draw any firm conclusion that MP background has no effect, a caution suggested by another pattern evident in the data – namely, the tendency of minority MPs to ask fewer questions in general. In nearly every case, their mean scores are lower than those for MPs taken as a whole, and, in fact, globally, minority MPs posed an average of only 30.9 questions (versus an overall mean of 54.8). What explains this gap is the disproportionate association of minority MPs with the Liberal Party, which governed throughout the study period, and thus their fewer opportunities to ask questions compared with opposition MPs. Nearly three of every four minority MPs caucused with the Liberals compared with a little less than half of all MPs who did so. This means that to reach reliable inferences about the effects of MP origin, party affiliation must be controlled for. Other variables, to be noted below, also suggest themselves as candidates for statistical correction. The next section discusses these requirements in light of what is clearly called for: a multivariate model.

Multivariate Analysis

The model of choice is negative binomial regression. Employed by Soroka, Penner, and Blidook (2009) as well as by Saalfeld (2011) in his British study, it is more appropriate for analysing dependent variables in count form (here, the number of questions asked) and specifically characterized by positive integers only, many zeros, positive skews, and over-dispersion (observed variance greater than the mean). Further, count data are often analysed with an exposure measure, a logged variable that adjusts for the opportunity of event occurrence. Soroka, Penner, and Blidook (2009) used the length of each parliament to take into account that longer parliaments provide greater opportunities for questions than shorter ones. Here the log of the number of sitting days for the three parliaments was employed.

The core independent variables in this study are constituency diversity, constituency competitiveness, and MP origin. For the first hypothesis, constituency diversity was measured using census data on the percentage of immigrants or visible minorities in each MP's riding.[14] The second hypothesis considers an MP's margin of victory (in the previous election),[15] including its product with district diversity as an interaction term. Origin is a binary variable dividing non-minority and minority legislators (based on the already-noted ethno-racial categories). An interaction term multiplying MP origin and constituency diversity provides the basis for assessing the fourth hypothesis – that is, whether diversity has a different impact for minority and non-minority MPs.

Six other measures were incorporated as controls. Party affiliation was included to adjust for the connection between minority MPs and the governing Liberals, but more generally to capture any unspecified residual cross-party effects, such as a disproportionate preoccupation with minority-oriented questions by one or more parties. Dummy variables were crafted for MPs affiliated with the Bloc Québécois (BQ), the New Democratic Party (NDP), and parties of the right (combining Progressive Conservative, Reform, Alliance, and Conservative party affiliations), thus leaving the Liberals as the reference category.

However, one party-related aspect – namely, the relative size of opposition parties – was explicitly measured to allow for the fact that larger opposition parties have more opportunities to ask questions. Following Soroka and his colleagues (2009), two measures were incorporated: one, the relative size of each opposition party; and the other, the same measure squared to capture a curvilinear effect (Soroka, Penner, and Blidook 2009, 573).

Two additional dummy variables handled possible broader contextual differences in the expression of the minority-oriented issues across the three parliaments. The fact that some opposition MPs asked more minority-oriented questions because of minority-related portfolio responsibilities was also addressed. An examination of parliamentary websites led to the identification of 20 opposition MPs with responsibilities typically defined as citizenship and immigration, multiculturalism, and – for BQ MPs – cultural communities. The number of parliamentary sessions that individuals served as such critics was employed to index the "degree" of their involvement; the maximum number of sessions was seven.[16] Another metric worked into the analysis is the total number of questions asked by each MP since parliamentarians who generally ask more questions can be expected to pose more questions on any given topic, minority-oriented matters included. Finally, a variable specifying whether an MP was foreign-born or not was also included.[17]

Table 11.3 below displays the relevant negative binomial regression results, beginning with the dependent variable: the number of questions related to immigration and refugee affairs. Robust standard errors are reported, and some of the variables, including constituency diversity (here measured by percentage of immigrants), have been centred. The first set of columns, excluding interaction terms, addresses the first and third hypotheses. The coefficient for constituency diversity (2.46) is statistically significant at the .01 level, and it thus supports the hypothesis linking greater heterogeneity with more oral questions about immigration matters. The coefficient is interpreted as meaning that a one-standard deviation shift in immigrant composition (14 per cent) leads to an increase of about 2.5 in the expected log count of immigration questions. A clearer sense of the impact of constituency diversity is available from post-estimation prediction or expected count analysis:[18] with other variables set at their means, MPs representing constituencies with an immigrant make-up of 10 per cent can be expected to ask .51 questions; for those with immigrant compositions of 30 per cent, 50 per cent, and 70 per cent, the counts are .83, 1.36, and 2.22, respectively. MPs do indeed respond to the heterogeneity in their districts by posing more questions touching on immigration and refugee matters.

For its part, a statistically significant coefficient of .62 for MP origins indicates support for the third hypothesis: constituency diversity being equal, MPs with minority origins direct more immigration-oriented questions towards government than do their non-minority colleagues. In prediction terms, the former have an expected count of .94 questions, nearly twice as many as the latter (.51).

As for the other variables, nativity has no effect whatsoever, nor are the measures of party, parliament, and party proportion statistically significant. Similarly, the degree of competitiveness in the constituency does not by itself make a difference in the number of questions asked. At the same time, critic status and the total number of questions asked do have significant effects.

In sum, the core results signify that immigration matters are represented both by MPs responding to their constituency interests and by minority MPs whose backgrounds appear to make them more sensitive to such interests. For this dominant component of the minority agenda,

Table 11.3. Antecedents of Oral Questions Involving Immigration and Refugee Affairs and Ethnic and Racial Groups/Multiculturalism

	Immigration and refugee affairs				Ethnic and racial groups/ multiculturalism			
	B	SE	B	SE	B	SE	B	SE
Constituency diversity (CD)[a,b]	2.46***	.74	3.80***	1.00	1.14	1.01	.94	1.42
Minority origin (MO)	.62**	.31	.80**	.34	.88**	.36	.86**	.39
Constituency competitiveness (CC)	.89	.67	.68	.64	−.65	.89	−.78	.91
MO x CD	–		−2.99*	1.54	–		.55	2.03
CD x CC	–		5.21*	3.03	–		2.03	4.52
Party – BQ	−.53	1.62	−.47	1.74	−.20	2.34	−.24	2.24
Party – NDP	−.76	1.14	−.91	1.23	.84	1.50	.85	1.52
Party – Right	.08	1.23	.08	1.32	−.39	1.79	−.41	1.78
36th Parliament	.14	.29	.14	.28	.85*	.47	.85*	.47
37th Parliament	.37	.28	.38	.28	−.04	.36	−.03	.36
Opposition critic	.96***	.21	.90***	.21	.43*	.21	.43*	0.22
Party proportion[b]	3.58	4.47	3.66	4.76	−.37	6.72	−.26	6.67
Party proportion squared	−4.35	18.36	−6.93	19.26	27.58	27.50	26.88	2.03
Total questions asked	.01***	.00	.01***	.00	.00	.21	.00	.00
Foreign-born	.11	.28	.14	.28	.14	.38	.09	.40
Constant	−3.31		−3.11		−5.67		−5.58	
Log likelihood	−478.59		−476.34		−229.83		−299.74	
N = 419								

[a] Percentage of immigrants for immigration and refugee affairs, percentage of visible minorities for ethnic and racial groups/multiculturalism.
[b] Centred variable.
* p < .10, **p < .05, ***p < .01

then, both dyadic and descriptive forms of substantive representation take place concurrently.

The next set of columns addresses the second hypothesis with its focus on constituency diversity, competitiveness, and their interaction and its expectation that MPs are more responsive to district heterogeneity if they face greater electoral pressures – i.e., have smaller win margins. Competitiveness, by itself, continues to have no impact on the number of immigration questions asked, but the coefficient for constituency diversity strengthens in this extended model (from 2.46 to 3.80), and the interaction term is both positive (5.21) and statistically significant.

Figure 11.1. Constituency Diversity, Win Margin, and Questions on Immigration

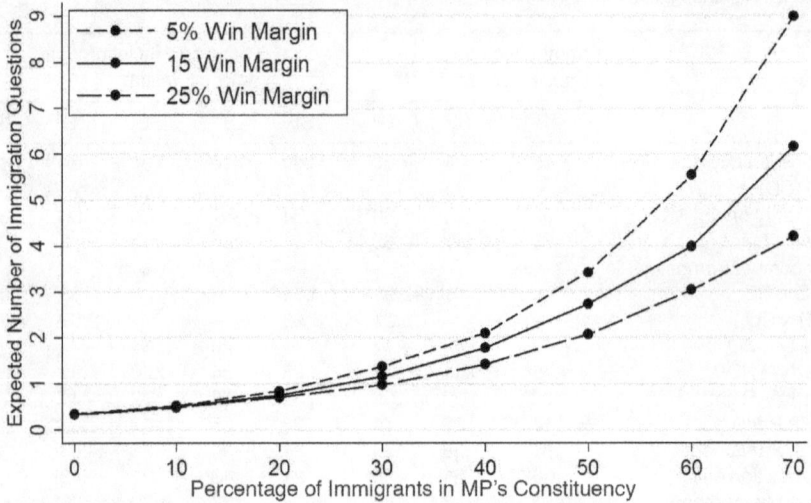

Figure 11.1 above provides a visual interpretation of the combined results, with three plots of competitiveness – for MPs with win margins of 5 per cent, 15 per cent, and 25 per cent. The general effect of diversity is quite evident. Also unmistakable is its enhanced impact, along with the strengthening influence of competitiveness, as immigrant constituency composition ranges beyond 30 per cent. In particular, as the incidence of immigrants in MPs' districts increases from 30 per cent to 70 per cent, the expected question counts for those with a 25 per cent vote margin rise substantially, from .97 to 4.20. For parliamentarians with win margins of 15 per cent, the counts increase even more, from 1.15 to 6.15, and, finally, for MPs in the most competitive situations, with win margins of only 5 per cent, the counts climb even more steeply, from 1.37 to 8.99. This is, then, strong evidence of the effect of competitiveness in mediating the constituency-immigration-question relationship – a result that fits well with dyadic representation as an integral part of the way that immigration matters are taken up in Parliament.

This second set of columns also addresses the fourth hypothesis with its two alternatives involving MP origin, constituency diversity, and their interaction. All the relevant coefficients in this model are statistically significant: .80 for MP origin, 3.80 for constituency diversity, and –2.99 for the interaction term. As coded, and as translated into the plots

Figure 11.2. Constituency Diversity, MP Origin, and Questions about Immigration

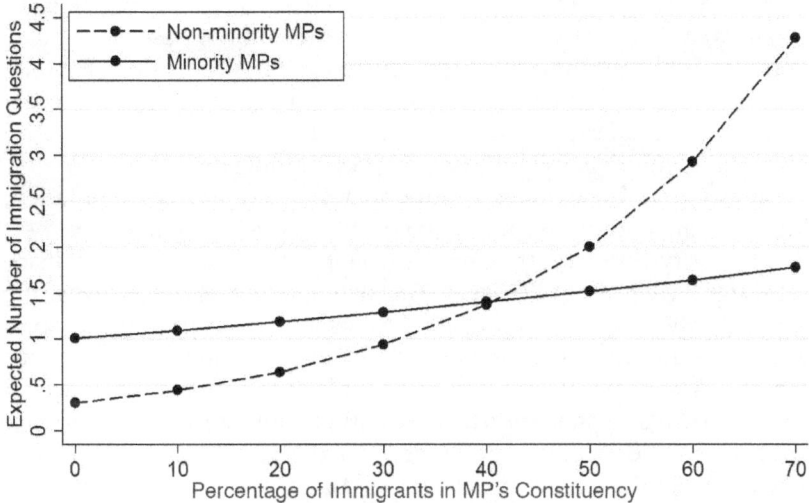

of predicted immigration question counts in Figure 11.2 above, these results unequivocally signify that district heterogeneity matters more for non-minority MPs. To be sure, diversity does make some difference for minority parliamentarians, but the effect is modest; their expected question counts barely double (from 1.01 to 1.78) over the full range of constituency diversity percentages. For non-minority MPs, the question counts increase from .30 to .94 as constituency diversity ranges up to 30 per cent, but then they surge, from 1.37 to 4.28 over the remaining immigrant composition interval of 40 per cent to 70 per cent. It is unmistakably MPs with non-minority backgrounds who respond more sharply to the heterogeneity in their constituencies.[19] It is noteworthy, however, that non-minority MPs match the question counts of minority MPs only in constituencies where immigrants reach 40 per cent – the point where the two lines cross; in other words, it takes a substantial amount of constituency diversity before non-minority MPs make up the gap that results from differences in MP origin.

The next column sets present parallel results for oral questions dealing with ethnic and racial groups and multiculturalism, combined,[20] and with constituency diversity measured by the percentages of visible minorities. The overall representation picture is less faceted. There is little, if any, support for the two hypotheses centred around constituency diversity. The coefficient is positive (1.14) but is not statistically significant, and the same is true of the interaction term involving diversity and competitiveness. Simply put, MPs do not pose more questions dealing with ethnic and racial groups and multiculturalism if they represent more diverse districts. At least with regard to this part of the minority agenda, the dyadic approach and constituency influence do not seem to figure in the process of representation.

On the other hand, there is support for descriptive representation. Minority MPs are more preoccupied with these topics than are their non-minority counterparts. The coefficient is positive (.88) and statistically significant at the .05 level. Translated into prediction terms, the expected question count for origin groups and multiculturalism topics is .37 for minority MPs, compared to .15 for their non-minority counterparts. Altogether, there are only a couple of factors that help explain why some MPs pay attention to these particular minority concerns; only critic status and the dummy variable for the 36th Parliament achieve statistical significance. Nor does the addition of the interaction terms alter this conclusion. The coefficient for the product of origin and constituency diversity (.55) is not statistically significant, and this means that neither version of the fourth hypothesis is supported by the test results. It would appear, then, that minority MPs are not necessarily reacting to the diversity in their constituencies when they ask questions that deal with the status of ethnic and racial groups and multiculturalism. Descriptive representation is what seems to matter in these instances.

Conclusion

A variety of implications and conclusions flow from this study of the relationship between Question Period in the Canadian Parliament and representation of the minority agenda. One substantive conclusion is that Question Period is a noteworthy venue for the agenda to be addressed. Even if MPs tend to ask questions that reference "mainstream" topics, matters that are of disproportionate interest to minorities are nevertheless raised. Here the available information allowed for a consideration of themes and issues involving immigration and refugee affairs – which formed the bulk of the minority-oriented questions – as well as origin groups and multiculturalism.[21]

Another substantive conclusion is that both constituency influence and MP origins help explain which MPs pose minority-oriented questions. That parliamentarians who represent immigrant-dense districts ask more immigration-related questions is evidence of the relevance of constituency, as is its heightened effect for MPs elected with narrower margins of victory. Furthermore, minority MPs, by virtue of their origins, bring about an *additional* measure of minority representation. Their queries also include themes associated with ethno-racial groups and multiculturalism, whereas constituency diversity has little relevance for this subject matter.

From a Canadian perspective, this study sustains recent work on Question Period and representation. Even with strong party discipline, a responsive link between constituents and MPs can occur. Moreover, the findings here reveal some of the different ways that minority politics play out in Canada. Minority interests are addressed to some extent in Parliament, and non-minority legislators assist in the process of representing those concerns. And, of further importance, diversity in the House of Commons does translate into substantive representation: minority MPs are particularly responsive to the minority agenda.

There are also implications for the broader literature on representation, including the work on group-based representation. Some are plainly evident, others perhaps less so. An obvious conclusion is that the findings here accord with current thinking that emphasizes representation as a dynamic process with multiple forms. For its part, evidence that the constituency context has a bearing on legislator behaviour supports the cornerstone notion of dyadic representation. The augmenting effect of competitiveness further enhances understanding of this process of representation as involving a principal-agent relationship between constituents and legislators.

The current analysis also supports the wisdom of modifying the approach to group representation studies. In the present context, it seems highly appropriate to expand the question from "Do minorities represent minorities?" to "How are minorities represented?" Minority representation does not depend exclusively on the presence of minority MPs. Non-minority MPs also provide a degree of representation (at least in connection with immigration and refugee affairs) if they are elected to districts that comprise a substantial number of immigrants.

Another important conclusion is that descriptive representation matters in ways that go beyond symbolism. The responsiveness of minority MPs squares with the tenet that descriptive legislators are inherently more sensitive to the concerns of "their" groups and that the groups are better off for their presence. Minority MPs, compared to their non-minority counterparts, have a more broadly based approach to representation. Their advancement of the minority agenda does not depend solely on the constituency context; riding diversity makes much less of a difference for them than it does for their non-minority counterparts. Further study would be needed to determine how much of this extra-constituency representation is of a "collective" or "surrogate" form, but these system-level processes are at least suggested by the present evidence. Also, minority parliamentarians alone raise questions dealing with topics about ethno-racial groups and multiculturalism. Taken together, the data paint a picture of minority MPs with a more robust commitment to the minority agenda.

The finding that dyadic representation has virtually no relevance for origin groups and multiculturalism topics has its own implications. At first glance, this result fits with Blidook and Kerby's (2011) proposition, noted above, that MPs respond to "clearly articulated" and "organized" constituency interests and not those that are "diffuse or unorganized." Applied here, this suggests that immigration-related themes fall into the former category, while origin groups and multiculturalism belong to the latter category. Immigration concerns are no doubt strongly articulated in urban districts; the wrinkle is that they are mostly voiced not by organized groups, but rather by individuals and their families seeking the assistance of MPs on separate immigration and refugee files (e.g., matters touching on family reunification, visitor's visas, passports, and citizenship acquisition). In dealing with such demands, MPs engage in "service responsiveness" (Eulau and Karps 1977), but there is likely a linkage effect – immigration-related demands made on MPs (and their staff) induce them to be more mindful of immigration concerns, and, consequently, to raise such matters in Question Period.

What is truly striking, however, is the scale of the demands. According to one observer, metropolitan constituencies "routinely report spending upwards of 85 per cent of their time on immigration files" (MacLeod 2006, 11). Another reference suggests that "in some ridings in Toronto, Vancouver and Montreal, immigration may comprise 60 per cent to 80 per cent of all constituency casework, and the annual number of all immigration inquiries is over forty thousand" (Malloy 2003a, 47–8). In turn, MPs understand the associated electoral imperatives. Interviewed about constituency casework and immigration, Pat Martin (NDP, Winnipeg Centre) declared, "You can't turn somebody down; there's a political price to pay if you're unsuccessful. And I suppose there's a political reward if you do manage to get somebody what they wanted, to have their mother come to a family wedding" (Shane 2010, 15).

The notion that the volume of demands, organized or not, can also drive MP response might be behind Saalfeld's (2011) British-based finding that constituency diversity makes a difference only for immigration-related questions. Beyond this, the revelation in the British and Canadian cases that minority MPs additionally address non-immigration questions is noteworthy. This pattern adds some comparative heft to the characterization of minority legislators as more innately in tune with minority needs and, therefore, more broadly responsive – and, again, not necessarily in reaction to constituency-based pressures. Examining minorities at this level provides not only a means of indexing the extent to which they are able to gain access to the top tiers of the political system but also a way to appreciate their role in substantively representing the minority agenda.

NOTES

1 To be sure, institutional factors also play a role in determining what questions are asked and by which MPs in Question Period. Clearly, the party leadership in its pre–Question Period meetings will prioritize and frame questions that are sharply critical of the government and that draw maximum media attention – by reflecting the day's headlines, creating tomorrow's headlines, or, less often but more strategically, by laying the groundwork for future headlines. Typically, senior party leaders will ask such questions. However, the balance of the questions, more often than not, is the result of a backbench MP's own initiative and will require him or her to convince the party leadership that the question is meritorious. That means expending political capital both to add oneself to the list of questioners and to use up what might be a limited number of opportunities to ask a question in the life of a parliamentary session. Further, with regard to the focus here, questions about immigration and minority communities are likely not generated in Question Period planning meetings as they will rarely generate the wanted immediate news coverage. In short, it would be extremely unusual for an MP to pose a question on immigration unless doing so had a clear benefit to either personal interest or political return.
2 Minority MPs in this study (see below) were elected in constituencies that are about two-and-a-half times as diverse as those won by non-minority MPs. For instance, visible minorities averaged about 16 per cent of the constituencies represented by minority MPs compared to 7 per cent for non-minority MPs.

3 In their sample of Canadian MPs, the authors found that 57 per cent of the parliamentarians ranked constituency as their primary focus, and another 23 per cent responded that it was tied with another priority.

4 Of course, in reality, legislators move back and forth among different roles and even attempt to play them simultaneously. Similarly, they alter their focus among constituency, national, and international levels depending on the issue. Minority MPs might also be regarded as party delegates if their party *instructs* them to specifically represent minority interests (Saalfeld 2011). Moreover, depending on electoral considerations (tied, in large measure, to constituency demographics), minority legislators may engage in a sophisticated strategy of "toggling" (Collet 2008): playing up or down minority concerns as they send different "signals to voters and observers in different arenas and media" (Saalfeld 2011, 273).

5 See, for instance, the discussion in Mansbridge (1999).

6 All of the relevant coefficients had the appropriate signs, but only one was statistically significant.

7 Nor is a relationship found for questions potentially focusing on minority concerns – a cluster that the authors labelled "civil rights and multiculturalism" (with the percentage of non-English, non-French language as the constituency interest measure). While the lack of an association might be due to the diffuse nature of the subject matter, the codebook also makes it clear that only a small percentage, about 5 per cent, of the questions in fact involve minority concerns. Most questions deal with topics on discrimination on the basis of gender, sexual, age, and handicap status as well as with voting rights and freedom of speech.

8 More specifically, it did not include control variables that, as pointed out below, very much suggest themselves for inclusion.

9 Specifically, the information on the ethno-racial origins of MPs before 1993 is not as reliable as one would like. See Black and Lakhani (1997).

10 See Soroka, Penner, and Blidook (2009, 15); the authors indicate that the codebook is available on request.

11 Although the codebook is detailed, not all relevant minority-related topics are listed (e.g., the status of minorities and immigrants in Canadian politics, citizenship-related themes). Furthermore, passport matters were unavailable for separate analysis as they had been coded into a larger category dealing mostly with Canadian diplomats, embassies, and citizens abroad. It should also be noted that the codebook does not indicate the *direction* of the questions, but it is assumed here that MPs pose their minority-oriented questions in a sympathetic manner. Does this mean that questions that are antithetical to minority interests are being included with potentially confounding implications? Probably not. It is very likely that

questions about minority themes are overwhelmingly on the positive side. Bird (2010), in her analysis (of the 39th Parliament), found no interventions (including questions) that "could be clearly categorized as antagonistic to ethnic minorities" (330). Still, it is well known that during the first session of the 35th Parliament, the new Reform Party, led by its immigration critic, Art Hanger, did engage in anti-immigration rhetoric (Anderson and Black 1998). The inclusion of controls in the multivariate analysis for Parliament, party, and, also important, opposition-critic positions in the areas of citizenship and immigration as well as multiculturalism should help minimize any distortions in interpreting the test results.

12 Of these 69 MPs, 20 have visible minority origins.

13 See Stasiulis and Abu-Laban (1991) for an indication that many non–visible minority candidates and politicians find that the dominant "bicultural" (French-English) discourse in Canadian politics, including in Parliament, limits their efforts and ambitions. The author's own interviews with dozens of non-visible minority MPs in the mid-1990s also revealed a felt status gap between themselves and "majority" MPs.

14 These measures were taken from the 1996 and 2001 censuses and were, in some cases, averaged for MPs elected more than once (and who asked questions in the associated parliaments).

15 The competitiveness measure is the MP's percentage vote margin over the runner-up, averaged over the particular elections (one, two, or three) that the MP contested – but only if the parliamentarian asked a question in the associated parliament.

16 There were two sessions in both the 35th and 36th parliaments and three in the 37th.

17 While potentially bearing on minority status, nativity is not synonymous with MP ethno-racial origin. Indeed, of the 54 foreign-born MPs in the current data set, over 40 per cent have non-minority roots. More to the point, MP origin is taken as the more relevant "background" marker. Among other reasons, topics dealing with integration, social acceptance, and multiculturalism are of interest to Canadian-born minorities as well as to immigrants.

18 Estimates were determined using Stata's margin routine.

19 Compare with Saalfeld (2011, 280).

20 Separate analyses were undertaken for questions on multiculturalism and on ethnic and racial groups, but standard convergence criteria were not met for the former; thus, multiculturalism and origin questions were combined.

21 Again, this does not exhaust the full range of issues and themes that comprise the minority agenda.

Conclusion: The Political Immigrant – Just an Ordinary Citizen?

ANTOINE BILODEAU

Are immigrants just ordinary citizens? It is a simple question, but the answer may not be quite so simple. Immigrant political integration is a complex phenomenon. In many ways, the comparative evidence gathered in this volume suggests that, yes, the political immigrant appears to be an ordinary citizen like any other, but this does not mean that the political immigrant is similar to the rest of the population in every way. Most important, perhaps, the comparative evidence presented proposes a diversity of political immigrants. We might want to refer to the "political immigrant," as we did in the title of this volume, but, in fact, there is no single one. There are many different kinds, just as there are many different kinds of other citizens. This Conclusion provides a synthesis of some of the core findings of this volume and discusses them in the context of other research in the field.

Describing the Political Immigrant

A Political Voice for Immigrants?

As the chapters and the review of the field demonstrate, scholars studying immigrant political integration have devoted a substantial amount of energy to trying to understand immigrant *electoral participation*. We have discussed in the review the reasons why this might be the case, including relying on surveys and theoretical frameworks constructed around election studies more generally. In many ways, such a focus has helped answer one of the two major questions that has driven the growth of research in the field since the end of the 1990s – namely, can immigrants articulate a political voice of their own?

Whether immigrants vote in national or local elections is often one of the first questions asked by scholars when discussing whether immigrants integrate successfully. The evidence from the Netherlands, Belgium, the United Kingdom, and Canada points to a lower propensity to vote among immigrants than among the local population – with considerable variations, however, across groups of immigrants. This seems to hold both for national- and for local-level elections as well as for other forms of political engagement, such as being a member of a political party, discussing politics, signing petitions, and demonstrating in the streets (see Gidengil and Roy in Chapter 8).

The second dimension of immigrant political integration often examined concerns their partisan preferences. When voting, immigrants seem to have a preference for centre-left parties. Our contributors observed this pattern of preference in the Netherlands, Belgium, and the United Kingdom, and other scholars have observed a similar tendency in immigrant partisan preferences in Canada (Blais 2005; Bilodeau and Kanji 2010) as well as Australia and New Zealand (White and Bilodeau 2014).

The third dimension relates to the representation of immigrants in political institutions. All of the chapters that examined the political representation of immigrants and ethnic minorities (the Netherlands, Belgium, the United Kingdom, and Canada) point to a common trend: immigrants and ethnic minorities appear under-represented in the ranks of elected public officials in local and national institutions. Here as well, the evidence is consistent with research in other countries (see Bird, Saalfeld, and Wüst 2011). Thus, achieving descriptive representation appears to be a challenge for immigrants and ethnic minorities in many Western democracies.

Until a larger number of immigrants and ethnic minorities are elected as political representatives, Black in Chapter 11 provides very important evidence indicating that even without descriptive political representation, immigrants and ethnic minorities can nevertheless have their voice heard in Parliament, at least in Canada. His study indicates that members of Parliament are sensitive to the size of the immigrant population in their constituency and that their propensity to ask questions in Question Period in relation to the "minority agenda" increases as the size of the immigrant population increases, especially when the previous electoral contest was won by a small margin. Black does not claim that immigrants' interests can simply be circumscribed to issues relating to immigration, refugees, and multiculturalism or that these issues attract a lot of attention during Question Period; rather, his important contribution in this volume is to provide evidence that the political representation of immigrants – or at least some form of it – can occur even when public officials are not members of immigrant or ethnic communities.

To conclude on the matter of political representation, the preference of immigrants in many countries for centre-left parties suggests that they have identified one party or one type of party that stands up for them. The fact that immigrants in each country tend to rally behind this type of party suggests that these parties speak up on behalf of immigrants or at least that they defend an agenda in which immigrants recognize themselves. If this were not the case, we might suppose that the immigrant vote would be more scattered across different parties than it seems to be at the moment. This raises the question of what it is that immigrants find appealing in the programs of these centre-left parties. Saggar in Chapter 3 discusses various possibilities that might account for such an attraction. One appealing possibility is that of issue ownership. Not only is it possible that centre-left parties in many Western democracies are perceived as the most open to the minority agenda, but it is also possible that they are perceived by immigrants as the most devoted and competent parties to push forward this agenda and to respond to the specific needs and preferences of immigrants and ethnic minorities. (On this question, see also Bilodeau and Kanji 2010.) The discussions in Black's and Saggar's chapters highlight the multidimensionality of the phenomenon of immigrant political representation. Descriptive representation is critical, but political representation cannot be evaluated solely on the basis of the number of immigrants and ethnic minorities elected to Parliament or other institutions. Whether parties and elected representatives speak on behalf of immigrants and ethnic minorities, and whether immigrants and ethnic minorities recognize themselves in the discourse and policy platforms of parties and candidates (substantive representation), are also important dimensions of immigrant political representation to consider.

Immigrants: Good Democratic Citizens?

This volume demonstrates that the field has produced a more limited set of evidence in answering the second question – namely, how well do immigrants fit into liberal democracies? Are they good democratic citizens? Whether immigrants participate in the political process is part of the answer to this second question, but, to provide a complete answer, research must move beyond the study of immigrant political participation. The task is more sensitive because this second question is partly associated with the growth of a backlash against immigration. It also requires a more normative discussion as to what is expected from immigrants (and other citizens), a discussion in which scholars and public officials rarely engage. This question is also complicated given that citizens born and socialized in liberal democracies do not themselves often meet what is thought to be expected from democratic citizens – that is, to be at least minimally informed, to vote in elections, and even to be strong patriots. Yet, even if this is a sensitive topic – or because it is a sensitive topic – it is of the utmost importance to answer this second question, if only to help allay the popular concerns that immigrants might not be as good or loyal democratic citizens as others. To answer this question, therefore, the field needs to move beyond the strict study of political participation and examine the values held by immigrants (at least with regard to democracy and liberal values); the kind of relationships that immigrants entertain with political authorities and institutions; and the strength of attachment, loyalty, and sense of civic duty that they express for the host country.

The field has not neglected these questions, but it has been more timid in addressing them. One of the chapters in this volume has begun such investigations: Pietsch and McAllister (Chapter 5) examine levels of confidence in political institutions in Australia, and they find few differences between immigrants and other Australians. If not overwhelmingly represented in this volume, other studies provide some evidence to answer the question of how immigrants fit into liberal democracies. These studies indicate a strong support for democracy and its underlying principles among newcomers. Immigrants are as supportive of democracy (if not more) as the rest of the population, believe democracy is the best form of government, and understand democracy in similar terms as the rest of the population (Bilodeau 2014). However, among a minority of immigrants from politically repressive countries, there appears to be some lasting authoritarian imprints, expressed by a stronger support for non-democratic forms of government than found among the rest of the population (McAllister and Makkai 1992; Bilodeau, McAllister, and Kanji 2010; Bilodeau 2014).

Being good democratic citizens entails more than adhering to the fundamental values on which democracy rests; it also entails loyalty and attachment to the (host) country. On these questions, Canadian research has made an invaluable contribution. Recent studies by White, Bilodeau, and Nevitte (2015), Kazemipur and Nakhaie (2014), and Bilodeau and

White (2015) find a strong attachment to Canada among immigrants and a high level of trust in fellow citizens of the host country. What is perhaps most important, these three studies indicate that the strength of immigrants' attachment to the host country and the level of trust in other members of the host country largely depend on whether immigrants achieve the level of economic prosperity they expected, the ways immigrants perceive they are treated in the host country, and whether they generally feel accepted by the host country. In short, these three studies indicate that the host country has a critical role to play in building ties between newcomers and their new country. Whether immigrants become loyal citizens like any others is not solely their own responsibility but also a collective responsibility of the state and all members of society. (See the discussion below under contextual-level variation.)

Not One but Many Political Immigrants

This volume is not only descriptive in its contribution. In drawing a portrait of the political immigrant, it highlights that there is not one, but rather many, political immigrants. Individual immigrants do not all undergo the same experiences in the process of political integration. Different communities also face different challenges; and, finally, immigrants also face different sets of policies and broader contexts in the process of integration. This volume provides an assessment of the range of factors that structure the expression of the political immigrant.

Individual-Level Variation

That immigrant political integration varies at the individual level is not really a surprise. As indicated in the review presented in the Introduction, the most common way of trying to understand immigrant political integration has been to focus on individual-level characteristics, either through individual socio-economic characteristics or acculturation variables such as acquiring the language of the host country. Quite often, then, the process of immigrant political integration is conceived as an individual experience. In effect, almost all chapters in this volume and most studies in the field integrate an individual-level perspective into understanding immigrant political integration. Haynes and Ramakrishnan (Chapter 6) provide one such example with their investigation of the relationship between ethnic-media news consumption and knowledge of American politics, but it is probably best described, and in the most innovative way, by White (Chapter 9).

The age at which immigrants arrive in the host country is one such individual-level characteristic, and we do not yet have a clear understanding of the extent of its importance in the process of integration. The impact of age at migration arguably depends on many things, including the specific set of attitudes examined and the origins of newcomers. White, however, demonstrates that the impact of age at migration is not reflected in the level of certain attitudes (for instance, more or less politically engaged or more or less trustful of politicians). Instead, he observes that the effect of age at migration structures the strength of the relationships between political predispositions and political engagement. For instance, general interest in politics, a sense of civic duty, and the strength of party identification are all positively associated with a greater propensity to vote, but the relationships are stronger among Canadian-born respondents and immigrants who arrived at a younger age than among immigrants who arrived at an older age. Such evidence suggests that those immigrants who arrive at a younger age tend to develop an understanding of politics through a similar prism as the rest of the population, more so than other immigrants.

Community-Level Variation

If immigrant political integration varies at the individual level, it also varies substantially across communities of immigrants. Which communities are more likely to participate? It is difficult to provide a simple answer to this question, but the evidence in this volume suggests at least three complementary answers. First, Gidengil and Roy in Chapter 8 suggest that immigrants of visible minority background in Canada – those of non-Caucasian ethnic background – tend to engage less than other immigrants and the rest of the population in a wide range of political activities, a finding that echoes other Canadian research (Tossutti 2007; Bilodeau and Turgeon 2015). Ethnic background could well be a determining factor in identifying immigrant communities that experience greater difficulties during the process of political integration. This finding is not completely unexpected. That political inequalities are often rooted in social and economic inequalities is well documented (Verba, Schlozman, and Brady 1995), and it is also well documented that immigrants of visible minority background struggle more than others to find employment and decent housing (Plante 2010; Skuterud 2010, 878). With the economic and social dimensions of integration more challenging for visible minority immigrants, greater difficulty on the political dimension could be seen as a predictable extension. Moreover, members of visible minority groups are likely to suffer from discriminatory experiences of many sorts, and existing research draws a link between such negative experiences and weaker trust in political institutions among immigrants (Michelson 2003; Maxwell 2010b).

Second, variations across immigrant communities can also be potentially explained by the varying density and organization of ethnic networks in the host country. Van Heelsum and her colleagues in the Netherlands (Chapter 1) raise the hypothesis that communities that are most engaged with politics in the host country are those that can rely on a dense and vibrant ethnic network. This echoes important contributions made by research in the field that highlights the critical role that ethnic networks play in facilitating the acquisition of political knowledge (Gidengil and Stolle 2009) and in the political mobilization of immigrants in the host country (Tillie 2004). Such a possibility is quite important as it directly challenges the fear of the "parallel societies" that immigrant communities would build. Indeed, some of the findings discussed in Chapter 1 suggest that strong immigrant communities do not result in "parallel societies," but instead in a better political integration.

Third, the evidence is not always conclusive, but at least some of it suggests that the variation across immigrant communities can also partly be explained by the pre-migration experiences of newcomers. Jones-Correa's findings in Chapter 4 lend support for this perspective; they highlight the fact that Mexican immigrants' political participation in the United States varies with the extent of their democratic experiences acquired before migration. Such a conclusion is consistent with other research in the field that makes a link between the degree of political repression experienced by immigrants in the country of origin and their reluctance to engage in protest activities, especially signing petitions (Bilodeau 2008), and their support for democracy and authoritarianism (Bilodeau 2014; Bilodeau, McAllister, and Kanji 2010; McAllister and Makkai 1992). In short, immigrants are not a blank slate upon arrival in the host country; they bring with them a host of political experiences that appear to have an enduring effect on their relationship with politics, even with politics in the host country.

Contextual Variation

Political integration also varies across contexts. This is somewhat evident from the different case studies presented in this volume, but Helbling et al. in Chapter 7 most systematically document some cross-national variation. Research on immigrant political integration has only recently started investigating the role of policies in structuring immigrant political experiences in the host country, and Helbling and his colleagues suggest that such policies are indeed an important component in structuring, positively or negatively, the political experiences of immigrants in the host country.

In this line of reasoning, Irene Bloemraad's book *Becoming a Citizen* (2006) was acclaimed not only because of its capacity to explain the gap in naturalization rates between Canada and the United States, but also because it drew attention to the role of policies in fostering a welcoming environment that is conductive to a positive integration of immigrants. Bloemraad's rationale is straightforward: in part because Canada's multiculturalism policy helps immigrants feel accepted, they are more likely to formally join the country's political community. In the Canadian context, White, Bilodeau, and Nevitte (2015) observe that the feeling of being accepted is a powerful correlate of feelings towards Canada among recent immigrants; and in the context of Quebec, Bilodeau (2013) observes that weak feelings of being accepted by that province have similar consequences for the bond developed with it. More specifically, immigrants with weak feelings of being accepted by Quebec exhibit less satisfaction with democracy in that province and a weaker attachment to it. Such research further suggests that the context in which immigrants settle plays an important role in structuring the quality and depth of immigrant political integration and the extent to which immigrants become the "good citizens" the population expects them to be.

Albeit indirectly, Chapter 10 by Bird also speaks to the variation in immigrant political integration across different contexts. Her analysis demonstrates that the local population's opinions of candidates in local elections are in part influenced by their ethnic background, thereby highlighting one of the barriers to the election of political representatives of ethnic-minority groups. Such a finding is important as it points to the tolerance and openness of the local population as a key factor to consider when accounting for variation in immigrant political integration across contexts.

Beyond immigration policies and the general acceptance of immigration in host countries, research on immigrant political integration needs to pay closer attention to the role of electoral systems in structuring the political voice of immigrants. Is it easier for immigrants to articulate a political voice and have their voice heard in certain types of electoral systems than in others? In Triadafilopoulos's narrative (2013), the first-past-the-post electoral system in Canada has helped to crystallize new Canadians' political influence because of the importance played by regional concentration. The heavy concentration of immigrants in the urban ridings of Toronto, Montreal, and Vancouver, Triadafilopoulos argues, has given them the political weight to have their voices heard and to influence the policy process that has contributed to reforming immigration policies in Canada. The argument is appealing, and it highlights the need for more of such investigations to understand the factors that structure cross-national variations in immigrant political integration. As Freeman (2004) argues, the institutional factors structuring immigrant political integration go beyond strict immigration policies or integration regimes.

It is also clear that more cross-national research on immigrant political integration is needed as very few such accounts are available, as explained earlier. But comparative research in the field also needs to be performed at the sub-national level; political participation and belonging are not only matters of national politics. In this regard, local-level politics may represent a unique opportunity for studying immigrant political integration; not only are local governments closest to citizens, but immigrants are also often concentrated in a few cities in a country, and local governments are often on the front line of service delivery in the day-to-day lives of immigrants. On this front, European cities might be especially interesting to investigate, as some of the contributors in this volume do, given that many European countries have granted voting rights at the local level to non-citizens.

Between national and local governments lie regional governments in many countries, and, in the case of the European Union, immigrants are also presented with a supranational government. These are also areas of investigation that we need to pursue to provide a more complete portrait of the political immigrant. We need to know not only how immigrants relate to these multi-level governments but also whether and how their relationship with each level of government varies and what explains any such variations. At the moment, the majority of the work on immigrant political integration is limited to national politics.

Taking Research beyond Comparisons with the Local Population

The chapters in this volume and all other studies in the field make a significant contribution to drawing a comparative portrait of the political immigrant, but there are still important dimensions that are missing before we can paint a complete picture of how strongly the political voice of immigrants is heard and in which channels it is more likely to be expressed. Research on political participation over the past decades has extended its investigations to a wider range of activities, to consider non-institutional activities such as political consumerism (Stolle and Micheletti 2013). Research on immigrant political participation, aside from a few exceptions, has yet to investigate whether immigrant populations are taking part in these new forms of participation. More important, when investigating immigrant political participation, in newer or more traditional forms, our efforts have been devoted to comparing immigrants to the local population, and by doing so we have considered what the political voice of immigrants has in common with the rest of population. Using the local population as a benchmark for comparison is a major help and an essential point of reference; but, by always relying on comparisons with the local population, we have neglected to investigate immigrants' unique forms of political participation, ones that we cannot compare with the local population.

One such missing dimension concerns transnational engagement. How strongly oriented is immigrants' political voice towards what happens in the country of origin? In a related vein, are immigrants involved in diaspora politics or in the politics of ethnic associations? And what about imported conflicts? These are questions for which we possess very few accounts, especially when considering the political-behaviour perspective that this book has taken. Yet these are questions that will become increasingly salient with sustained flows of immigration and means of communication, which facilitate contacts with the country of origin and with the diaspora all over the world.

Even though the field has covered a wide range of possible explanatory factors to account for variations in immigrant political integration (at individual, community, and contextual levels), it has provided a more limited account of how experiences unique to immigrants structure their political integration. Such investigations are not absent. For instance, a large body of research examines the role of acculturation in the process of political integration. Moreover, a certain number of studies have begun paying closer attention to pre-migration experiences. More could be done, however, to extend and refine this range of investigation. For instance, scholars interested in the impact of pre-migration experiences often look at the characteristics of countries of origin, but they also need to examine immigrants' *personal* experiences and how they feel about them. Another example concerns the process of migration that newcomers experienced when moving from the country of origin to the host country. How easy or difficult was it for immigrants to arrive in the host country? Under what status were they admitted? What kinds of support have they received during their settlement? Beyond what experiences immigrants accumulate before and after migration, it is the process itself and its impact on political integration that deserves greater attention by immigration scholars.

As discussed in the review of the field, the limited number of studies paying attention to immigrants' unique political experiences (either in the expression of a political voice or the factors that structure that political voice) is not surprising. A large proportion of existing studies have relied on databases and surveys that were not designed to study immigrants and hence often do not store information about immigrants' unique experiences, even such basic information as citizenship status, language proficiency, ethnic networks, and sometimes length of residence or country of birth. Survey instruments that capture these unique immigrant experiences are needed to raise the level of our understanding of immigrant political integration a notch.

Moreover, these studies often suffer from a clear selection bias towards better-integrated immigrants because of the selection criteria to be included in the study (naturalized citizens) or because of practical considerations that lead to such biases (required good proficiency in language of host country). We need to better understand the potential biases inherent in many of the studies that we conduct as experts in the field and how they might reveal a distorted (and possibly rosier) portrait of the political immigrant. Indeed, the field seems to have reached a certain level of maturity necessary to proceed with such a reflection. Joan Font and Monica Méndez published an edited volume in 2013 entitled *Surveying Ethnic Minorities and Immigrant Populations*, which is entirely devoted to discussing such questions. As the authors rightfully indicate, given the (growing) importance of these issues over the last two decades, the need to produce data and evidence was so great that scholars' efforts were focused on making sense of this newly collected evidence at the expense of discussing how it was produced and how reliable it was (Font and Méndez 2013, 16).

Another related set of considerations concerns the expression of socially desirable responses by immigrants to survey questions or the existence of taboos in relation to certain topics. Many immigrants – especially those who are not yet citizens or who have experienced different forms of repression in the country of origin – may be hesitant to share their genuine opinions on a certain number of issues. For instance, when asked to provide an opinion on the government of the host country, does someone who has experienced political repression feel comfortable doing so? In such situations, can we trust the answer provided? Are immigrants just telling us what we want to hear out of fear of negative consequences? Of course, socially desirable responses are a problem well documented in the field of public opinion (see, for instance, Karp and Brockington 2005); it is not just an issue for immigrant populations. Given the vulnerability status of some groups of immigrants and their pre-migration experiences, however, it would be appropriate to investigate whether immigrants (or some groups of immigrants) are more likely to express what they believe the interviewer wants to hear.

The possibility that some type of questions might lead to high levels of discomfort among certain immigrant communities should also be considered. Taboos exist in most societies. When designing questionnaires, scholars usually know how to navigate such taboos in the context of a given society. The challenge is that those taboos might be more distinct among some immigrant communities than among the rest of the population. For instance, while questions relating to views on homosexuality are usually not considered to be too sensitive in Western democracies, in some countries these questions cannot even be asked. How do immigrant populations from those countries react when questioned on such topics? Do they stop participating in the survey? We possess very little or no evidence at all to answer these questions.

Bilodeau (2015) further highlights the need for such discussions through his study of immigrant women participating in the Canadian Election Study (CES). He indicates that retention biases across the different waves of the survey vary across immigrant communities and, most important, between men and women of the same communities. Hence, the difficulty in retaining immigrant women in comparison to immigrant men increases with the level of gender inequalities in the country they come from. Because the CES was not designed to study immigrants, it is very difficult to identify the reasons why these immigrant women from countries with large gender inequalities drop out of the survey; the tools are simply not built into the study.

In his 1981 survey of immigrants in the Greater Toronto Area, Jerome H. Black provided an example of how to try to address these issues. He inserted an item at the end of the survey for the interviewer to code his or her general impression of the respondent's level of comfort during the interview. Have other initiatives like this one been put in place? If so, what do they teach us? Immigration scholars need to start thinking about methodologies to better measure these possible socially desirable effects and discomfort among immigrant populations participating in political survey research. The variance in cultural backgrounds and pre-migration experiences, as well as the sense of vulnerability that some immigrants might feel, necessitate that we start examining these questions.

These are only a handful of the issues that research in the field of immigrant political integration should consider addressing in the future. The link among them – whether we look at the dimensions of political integration to be examined, the structural factors of political integration, or the tools and methodologies to use – is a need to start looking at realities that are often unique to immigrants and that have often been neglected, or that have been very difficult or impossible to study so far, given the tools that were available. These are important issues as they raise concerns about the reliability and validity of the conclusions that existing research provides. This volume and previous research provide a comparative portrait of the political immigrant, but what if the shades of "colours" are off? What if some parts of the portrait reveal too much or not enough "light" compared to the reality? There are no reasons to believe that our portrait critically misrepresents the political immigrant, but the field of immigrant political integration appears to have reached a stage of growth and intellectual maturity that allows us, even invites us, to begin asking those questions more systematically than we have done so far.

Appendices

INTRODUCTION: BILODEAU, "JUST ORDINARY CITIZENS?"

Appendix A: Methodology for Literature Review: Immigrant Political Integration

For the present literature review, we opted for a content analysis of peer-reviewed journals, requiring the analysis of a specific journal's entire publication history. This approach allowed for a more exhaustive and systematic account of publications on the topic than the keyword search. Based on prior findings that confirmed the relative immaturity of the sub-field, the content review of each journal was limited to volumes published between 1955 and 2011, inclusively. Once again, all book reviews were omitted from the analysis.

A list of relevant peer-reviewed journals was established, and a database created, using the American Political Science Association's table of "Various Impact Scores by Political Science Journal" as a guideline; this initial list was composed of approximately 44 English-language political science and multidisciplinary journals. When we recognized the regional bias favouring the case of Latinos in the United States, we targeted additional journals with a European or international focus. In short, this literature-review approach allowed us to better correct and account for regional bias. This later addition of journals to the database was then also expanded to comprise those explicitly in the field of sociology. The final number of journals included in this literature review was 55. (See Table A1 below for the complete list.)

Table A1. List of Peer-Reviewed Journals Included in Database

1. *International Migration Review (formerly International Migration Digest)*	28. *International Political Science Review*
2. *Journal of Ethnic and Migration Studies (formerly New Community)*	29. *Latin American Research Review*
3. *Journal of International Migration and Integration*	30. *Australian Journal of Political Science (formerly Politics)*
4. *Ethnic and Racial Studies*	31. *PS: Political Science and Politics (formerly P.S.)*
5. *International Migration*	32. *American Politics Research*
6. *Canadian Ethnic Studies*	33. *Political Quarterly*
7. *American Political Science Review*	34. *International Social Science Journal*
8. *American Journal of Political Science (formerly Midwest Journal of Political Science)*	35. *Canadian Journal of Political Science*
9. *Public Opinion Quarterly*	36. *Social Science Journal (formerly Rocky Mountain Social Science Journal)*
10. *Politics and Society*	37. *Political Science*
11. *Urban Studies*	38. *Perspectives on Politics*
12. *Comparative Political Studies*	39. *German Politics*
13. *Journal of Politics*	40. *Social Science Research*
14. *British Journal of Political Science*	41. *Comparative European Politics*
15. *Comparative Politics*	42. *Party Politics*
16. *Political Psychology*	43. *Scandinavian Political Studies*
17. *American Behavioral Scientist*	44. *Swiss Political Science Review*
18. *European Journal of Political Research*	45. *Journal of Sociology (formerly Australian and New Zealand Journal of Sociology)*
19. *Urban Affairs Review (formerly Urban Affairs Quarterly)*	46. *European Sociological Review*
20. *Political Research Quarterly (formerly Western Political Quarterly)*	47. *Turkish Studies*
	48. *Acta Politica*
21. *Social Science Quarterly (formerly Southwestern Social Science Quarterly)*	49. *European Political Science*
22. *Political Behavior*	50. *Citizenship Studies*
23. *Political Science Quarterly*	51. *West European Politics*
24. *Electoral Studies*	52. *Ethnicities*
25. *Political Studies*	53. *Journal on Ethnopolitics and Minority Issues in Europe*
26. *Annals of American Academy*	54. *Diversities (formerly International Journal on Multicultural Societies)*
27. *Journal of Latin American Studies*	55. *International Review of Sociology*

Defining the Search Criteria

The subsequent step involved identifying relevant articles in each of the selected journals. Here the primary focus was on identifying all potential articles on the theme of immigrant political integration, regardless of the nature of the article (for example, a critical review).

Political integration. Given the expansive nature of the term *political integration*, a guideline was created to identify the various sub-themes it comprises. This guideline drew from a preliminary review of the

Table A2. Sub-themes Used to Identify Articles on Immigrant Political Integration

Political participation of immigrants	Conventional political participation (formal, direct): voting, campaigning, contacting official, participation in political party, attend public meeting, donating money to political cause, etc. Unconventional political participation (informal, indirect): protesting, signing petitions, boycotting, wearing buttons, contacting media, community activities, etc.
Ethnic political activities	Membership in ethnic organization Ethnic mobilization Group-interested policy preferences
Relation or attachment to host political system	Political trust Political efficacy Satisfaction with government Self-identification with host country Perception of civic duty Support for democratic/political institutions
Political interest; Political knowledge	
Partisan preferences	Partisanship Party support level
Political attitudes	Political ideology Authoritarianism Tolerance of minorities
Attitudes towards integration	Citizenship acquisition (naturalization) Attitudes on assimilation
Political representation	
Transnationalism	Transnational political participation Dual citizenship

literature's topology of dependent variables. Equipped with this guideline, one researcher was charged with identifying all potentially relevant articles by examining their title or abstract (for ambiguous cases). This researcher was explicitly instructed to document all false-positive articles. Table A2 above presents the list of all sub-themes that were searched for.

Immigrant. Defining the search criteria for articles using this term was a second challenge because of the expansive and ambiguous terms used to refer to immigrants – for example, the case of articles on visible minorities, ethnic minorities, and religious minorities. As a result, the researcher was instructed to include all articles on political integration that may refer to immigrants directly or indirectly. As a general rule, we excluded the case of African Americans because of their distinct circumstance in the United States. As a general rule, an article concerned with religious minorities (for example, Muslim, Jewish, Christian) was included only when it was implied or understood that the group was primarily a migrant community.

For each journal included in the literature review, a document (titled "Article List") was created to record all possible articles of relevance. This inventory provided information on the following:

- All articles from a given journal included in the database (coded).
- All articles from a given journal excluded from the database and the reason for its elimination.
- The peer-reviewed journal in question. This includes the journal's years of publication; whether the journal was published under a former name; where access to the journal is available (e.g., CU library, McGill library, online); and, in rare cases, whether we were unable to gain access to certain volumes.

For each article identified, a PDF file or paper copy was kept on file.

Criteria for Relevant Articles

The review established strict criteria for relevant articles. Articles had to meet the following criteria:

1. First, we narrowed the search to articles whose *primary* unit of analysis was the individual. More precisely, we focused on studies concerned with *migrant behaviour and attitudes*. As a result, we excluded articles whose primary unit of analysis was rights and benefits regimes, newspapers or media (content analysis of), laws, political party policies, political party responses, political ads, websites, etc.
2. Second, we limited the literature review to qualitative and quantitative studies of migrant behaviour and attitudes. As a result, we excluded historical examinations, critical reviews, theoretical articles, literature reviews, and introductions to special issues.

The complete list of articles retained for the analysis is available on request.

Coding Relevant Cases

The coding of each relevant case required a closer reading of the article, particularly the introduction, methodology, and hypotheses. This scheme provided all outcome variables studied in the field of immigrant political integration. For each case, we coded all relevant outcome variables examined; hence, the categories are not mutually exclusive. The coding scheme also lists the broad groupings of independent variables used to explain political integration. For each study, we coded the explanatory variables of primary interest – more precisely, the independent variables included in the studies' hypotheses. Again, the categories are not mutually exclusive as, often, many explanatory variables were the object of study. The breakdown of the all items and variables coded is available on request.

CHAPTER 6: HAYNES AND RAMAKRISHNAN, "HOW MUCH DO THEY HELP?"

Appendix B: Survey Questions

Political knowledge questions

Collaborative Multi-racial Post-election Study, 2008

> *Do you happen to know which political party currently has the most seats in the United States House of Representatives in Washington, D.C.?*
> *And do you know what political office is currently held by John Roberts?*

American National Election Study, 2008

> *Now we have a set of questions concerning various public figures. We want to see how much information about them gets out to the public from television, newspapers, and the like.*
> > *The first is Nancy Pelosi: What job or political office does she NOW hold?*
> > *Dick Cheney: What job or political office does he NOW hold?*
> > *John Roberts: What job or political office does he NOW hold?*

Media utilization

Collaborative Multi-racial Post-election Study, 2008

People rely on different sources for political information. Do you read newspapers for information about politics?
[If yes and Asian interview] Is that Asian-language or Asian-oriented newspapers, English-language, or both?
[If yes and Latino interview] Is that Spanish-language newspapers, English-language, or both?
[If yes and black interview] Is that Black-oriented papers, mainstream papers, or both?

Do you listen to the radio for political information?
[If yes and Asian interview] Is that Asian-language or Asian-oriented radio, English-language, or both?
[If yes and Latino interview] Is that Spanish-language radio, English-language, or both?
[If yes and black interview] Is that Black-oriented radio, mainstream radio, or both?

Do you watch television for political information?
[If yes and Asian interview] Is that Asian-language TV or Asian-oriented, English-language, or both?
[If yes and Latino interview] Is that Spanish-language TV, English-language, or both?
[If yes and black interview] Is that black-oriented TV, mainstream TV, or both?

American National Election Study, 2008

Ethnic media:
V085279: For information about politics, would you say you get the most information from Spanish-language television, radio, and newspapers, or from English-language TV, radio, and newspapers?

Radio news: (Split sample between two versions)
V083022: How many days in the PAST WEEK did you listen to news on the radio?
V083026: During a typical week, how many days do you listen to news on the radio, not including sports?

Television news: (Split sample between two versions)
V083019: How many days in the PAST WEEK did you watch the NATIONAL network news on TV?
V083024: During a typical week, how many days do you watch news on TV, not including sports?

Internet news: (Split sample between two versions)
V083023: During a typical week, how many days do you watch, read, or listen to news on the Internet, not including sports?
V083021b: How many days in the PAST WEEK did you read a daily newspaper on the internet?

Newspapers: (Split sample between two versions)
V083025: During a typical week, how many days do you read news in a printed newspaper, not including sports?
V083021a: How many days in the PAST WEEK did you read a daily newspaper?

CHAPTER 9: WHITE, "DO YOUNGER AND OLDER IMMIGRANTS ADAPT DIFFERENTLY?"

Appendix C: Variable Construction

Variable	Item wording	Coding
Leader knowledge (0–3 scale)	Four questions: – Do you happen to recall the name of the leader of the federal NDP/ – Conservative Party/ – Liberal Party/ – Bloc Québécois? (Quebec only)	4-pt index: 0 – No leaders correctly named 1 – One leader correctly named 2 – Two leaders correctly named 3 – Three or four leaders correctly named
Election interest (0–1 scale)	Using the same scale (0 to 10), how interested are you in the FEDERAL election? Zero means no interest at all, and ten means extremely interested.	Re-scaled from: 0 – (no interest) to 1 – (extremely interested)
Turnout (dichotomous)	Did YOU vote in the election?	0 – Did not vote 1 – Voted
Civic duty (dichotomous)	It is EVERY citizen's duty to vote in federal elections. Do you strongly agree, somewhat agree, somewhat disagree, or strongly disagree?	0 – Somewhat agree to strongly disagree 1 – Strongly agree
Cynicism (0–1 scale)	Do you strongly agree, somewhat agree, somewhat disagree, or strongly disagree?: – All federal parties are basically the same; there isn't really a choice. – Politicians are ready to lie to get elected. – I don't think the government cares much what people like me think.	1-pt index: 0 – low cynicism 1 – high cynicism
General interest (0–1 scale)	And your interest in POLITICS GENERALLY? Using the same scale (from 0 to 10), how interested are you in politics generally? Zero means no interest at all, and ten means extremely interested.	Re-scaled from: 0 – (no interest) to 1 – (extremely interested)
	Two questions: – In federal politics, do you usually think of yourself as a: [list of parties] – How strongly [party name] do you feel: very strongly, fairly strongly, or not very strongly?	0 – does not identify with a party .33 – identifies "not very strongly" with a party .66 – identifies "fairly strongly" with a party 1 – identifies "very strongly" with a party

CHAPTER 10: BIRD, "WHAT ACCOUNTS FOR THE LOCAL DIVERSITY GAP?"

Appendix D: Candidate Manipulations (Statements)

Candidate Statement 1: Sex/Ethnicity/Ideology

(**Jim Stevenson/Farida Khan**) is a first-time candidate for municipal council. (**Jim/Farida**) has lived in the community since moving here with (**his/her**) family at the age of 10. (**He/She**) completed (**his/her**) elementary and secondary education here before earning a BA in economics. (**Jim/Farida**) has strong connections to the city and its residents. (**He/She**) has worked for 15 years as a local (**community organizer/business owner**). (**He/She**) has been an active participant in the local Collaborative Partnership for Economic and Cultural Development. (**Jim/Farida**) also started up an innovative youth (**leaders/entrepreneurs**) program to equip young people with (**civic and leadership/business and financial**) skills and encourage them to create their own (**social responsibility and democratic engagement/job opportunities**). (**Jim/Farida**)'s many contributions were recognized recently when (**he/she**) was honoured with a nomination for a local (**civic/business**) leadership award. (**Jim/Farida**) promises to bring a fresh perspective to local council. (**His/Her**) first priority, if elected to office, is to (**improve public services so that all residents can share in the best quality of life the municipality can offer/control spending and promote greater fiscal responsibility in local government**). (**Jim and his wife, Sandra/Farida and her husband, Imran**) have been married 14 years and have three children.

References

Abrajano, Marisa. 2010. *Campaigning to the New American Electorate: Advertising to Latino Voters*. Stanford, CA: Stanford University Press.

Ajinkya, Julie, and Michael Jones-Correa. 2007. "Gender, Immigration and Political Socialization." Paper presented at the annual meeting of the American Political Science Association, Chicago.

Aleksynska, Mariya. 2008. "Quantitative Assessment of Immigrants' Civic Activities: Exploring the European Social Survey." In *Highly Active Immigrants: A Resource for European Civil Societies*, edited by Dita Vogel, 59–74. Frankfurt: Peter Lang.

Almond, Gabriel A., and Sidney Verba. 1963. *The Civic Culture: Political Attitudes and Democracy in Five Nations*. Princeton: Princeton University Press.

Anderson, Christopher G., and Jerome H. Black. 1998. "Navigating a New Course: Liberal Immigration and Refugee Policy in the 1990s." In *How Ottawa Spends, 1998–99: Balancing Act – The Post-Deficit Mandate*, edited by Leslie A. Pal, 191–216. Don Mills: Oxford University Press.

André, Stéfanie, Jaap Dronkers, and Ariana Need. 2009. "To Vote or Not to Vote? Electoral Participation of Immigrants from Different Countries of Origin in 24 European Countries of Destination." Paper presented at the ECSR conference "Changing Societies in the Context of the European Union Enlargement," Sciences Po-CNRS, Paris, 11–12 December.

Andrew, Caroline, John Biles, Meyer Burstein, Vicki Esses, and Erin Tolley, eds. 2012. *Immigration, Integration and Inclusion in Ontario Cities*. Montreal and Kingston: McGill-Queen's University Press.

Andrew, Caroline, John Biles, Myer Siemiatycki, and Erin Tolley, eds. 2008. *Electing a Diverse Canada: The Representation of Immigrants, Minorities and Women*. Vancouver: University of British Columbia Press.

Arvizu, John R., and F. Chris Garcia. 1996. "Latino Voting Participation: Explaining and Differentiating Latino Voting Turnout." *Hispanic Journal of Behavioral Sciences* 18 (2): 104–28.

Ashcroft, Lord. 2012. *"Degrees of Separation: Ethnic Minority Voters and the Conservative Party."* London: Biteback. http://lordashcroftpolls.com/wp-content/uploads/2012/04/DEGREES-OF-SEPARATION.pdf.

Bacon, Jacqueline. 2007. *Freedom's Journal: The First African-American Newspaper.* Lanham, MD: Lexington Books.

Barlow, William. 1999. *Voice Over: The Making of Black Radio.* Philadelphia, PA: Temple University Press.

Barreto, Matt A. 2007. "¡Si Se Puede! Latino Candidates and the Mobilization of Latino Voters." *American Political Science Review* 101 (3): 425–41.

Barreto, Matt A., and José A. Muñoz. 2003. "Reexamining the 'Politics of In-Between': Political Participation among Mexican Immigrants in the United States." *Hispanic Journal of Behavioral Sciences* 25 (4): 427–47.

Bartels, Larry M. 1996. "Uninformed Votes: Information Effects in Presidential Elections." *American Journal of Political Science* 40 (1): 194–230.

Bauböck, Rainer. 2006. "Migration und Politische Beteiligung: Wahlrechte jenseits von Staatsgebiet und Staatsangehörigkeit." In *Die Missglückte Integration? Wege und Irrwege in Europa*, edited by Manfred Oberlechner, 115–29. Vienna: Braumüller.

Beck, Paul Allen, and M. Kent Jennings. 1991. "Family Traditions, Political Periods, and the Development of Partisan Orientations." *Journal of Politics* 53 (3): 742–63.

Beer, Caroline, and Neil J. Mitchell. 2004. "Democracy and Human Rights in the Mexican States: Elections or Social Capital?" *International Studies Quarterly* 48 (2): 293–312.

Bell, Laurie, and Jo Casebourne. 2008. *Increasing Employment for Ethnic Minorities: A Summary of Research Findings.* Prepared by the Centre for Economic & Social Inclusion for a National Audit Office Study on Increasing Employment for Ethnic Minorities. London: National Audit Office.

Bennett, Stephen Earl. 1994. "The Persian Gulf War's Impact on Americans' Political Information." *Political Behavior* 16 (2): 179–201.

– 1995. "Comparing Americans' Political Information in 1988 and 1992." *Journal of Politics* 57 (2): 521–32.

Berger, Maria, Meindert Fennema, Anja van Heelsum, Jean Tillie, and Rick Wolff. 2001. *Politieke participatie van etnische minderheden in vier steden: Een onderzoek in opdracht van het Ministerie van Binnenlandse Zaken en Koninkrijksrelaties.* Amsterdam: IMES.

Berger, Maria, Christian Galonska, and Ruud Koopmans. 2004. "Political Integration by a Detour? Ethnic Communities and Social Capital of Migrants in Berlin." *Journal of Ethnic and Migration Studies* 30 (3): 491–507.

BES (British Election Study). 2010. "The 2009–10 BES." http://www.bes2009-10.org/.

Besco, Randy. 2014. "Rainbow Coalitions or Inter-minority Conflict? Racial Affinity and Diverse Minority Voters." Paper presented at the Canadian Political Science Association Annual Conference, Brock University, St. Catharines.

Bevelander, Pieter, and Ravi Pendakur. 2009. "Social Capital and Voting Participation of Immigrants and Minorities in Canada." *Ethnic and Racial Studies* 32 (8): 1406–30.

Biles, John, Meyer Burstein, and James Frideres. 2008. *Immigration and Integration in Canada in the Twenty-First Century*. McGill-Queen's University Press.

Bilodeau, Antoine. 2008. "Immigrants' Voice through Protest Politics in Canada and Australia: Assessing the Impact of Pre-migration Political Repression." *Journal of Ethnic and Migration Studies* 34 (6): 975–1002.

– 2009. "Residential Segregation and the Electoral Participation of Immigrants in Australia." *International Migration Review* 43 (1): 134–59.

– 2013. "The Importance of Feeling Accepted by the Host Society: Political Consequences among Visible Minorities in Quebec." Paper presented at the "Democratic Deficits? Equality and Representation in Canadian Politics" workshop, Montreal, 20 November.

– 2014. "Is Democracy the Only Game in Town? Tension between Immigrants' Democratic Desires and Authoritarian Imprints." *Democratization* 21 (2): 359–81.

– 2015. "Migrating Gender Inequalities? Immigrant Women's Participation in Political Survey Research." *International Migration Review*. (Available through Early View.) DOI: 10.1111/imre.12194.

Bilodeau, Antoine, and Mebs Kanji. 2006. "Political Engagement among Immigrants in Four Anglo-Democracies." *Electoral Insight* 8 (2): 43–9.

– 2010. "The New Immigrant Voter, 1965–2004: The Emergence of a New Liberal Partisan?" In *Voting Behaviour in Canada*, edited by Cameron D. Anderson and Laura B. Stephenson, 65–85. Vancouver: University of British Columbia Press.

Bilodeau, Antoine, Ian McAllister, and Mebs Kanji. 2010. "Adaptation to Democracy among Immigrants in Australia." *International Political Science Review* 31 (2): 141–66.

Bilodeau, Antoine, and Neil Nevitte. 2003. "Political Trust for a New Regime: The Case of Immigrants from Non-Democratic Countries in Canada." Paper prepared for the annual meeting of the Canadian Political Science Association, Halifax, 30 May.

Bilodeau, Antoine, and Luc Turgeon. 2015. "Voter Turnout among Younger Canadians and Visible Minority Canadians: Evidence from the Provincial Diversity Project." Ottawa: Elections Canada.

Bilodeau, Antoine, and Stephen E. White. 2015. "Trust among Recent Immigrants in Canada: Levels, Origins, and Implications for Integration." *Journal of Ethnic and Migration Studies.* DOI: 10.1080/1369183X.2015.1093411.

Bird, Karen. 2010. "Patterns of Substantive Representation among Visible Minority MPs: Evidence from Canada's House of Commons." In *The Political Representation of Immigrants and Minorities: Voters, Parties and Parliaments in Liberal Democracies,* edited by Karen Bird, Thomas Saalfeld, and Andreas M. Wüst, 25–65. New York: Routledge.

Bird, Karen, Thomas Saalfeld, and Andreas M. Wüst, eds. 2011. *The Political Representation of Immigrants and Minorities: Voters, Parties and Parliaments in Liberal Democracies.* New York: Routledge.

Black, Jerome H. 1982. "Immigrant Political Adaptation in Canada: Some Tentative Findings." *Canadian Journal of Political Science* 15 (1): 3–28.

– 1987. "The Practice of Politics in Two Settings: Political Transferability among Recent Immigrants to Canada." *Canadian Journal of Political Science* 20 (4): 731–53.

– 2009. "The 2006 and 2008 Canadian Federal Elections and Minority MPs." *Canadian Ethnic Studies* 41 (1/2): 69–93.

– 2011. "Immigrant and Minority Political Incorporation in Canada: A Review with Some Reflections on Canadian-American Comparison Possibilities." *American Behavioral Scientist* 55 (9): 1160–88.

Black, Jerome H., and Lynda Erickson. 2006. "Ethno-racial Origins of Candidates and Electoral Performance. Evidence from Canada." *Party Politics* 12 (4): 541–61.

Black, Jerome H., and Aleem S. Lakhani. 1997. "Ethnoracial Diversity in the House of Commons: An Analysis of Numerical Representation in the 35th Parliament." *Canadian Ethnic Studies* Canada 29 (1): 1–21.

Black, Jerome H., Richard G. Niemi, and G. Bingham Powell Jr. 1987. "Age, Resistance, and Political Learning in a New Environment: The Case of Canadian Immigrants." *Comparative Politics* 20 (1): 73–84.

Blais, André. 2000. *To Vote or Not to Vote? The Merits and Limits of Rational Choice Theory.* Pittsburgh: University of Pittsburgh Press.

– 2005. "Accounting for the Electoral Success of the Liberal Party in Canada." *Canadian Journal of Political Science* 38 (4): 821–40.

Blais, André, Elisabeth Gidengil, Richard Nadeau, and Neil Nevitte. 2002. *Anatomy of a Liberal Victory: Making Sense of the 2000 Canadian Election.* Toronto: Broadview Press.

Blais, André, Elisabeth Gidengil, Neil Nevitte, Patrick Fournier, and Joanna Everitt. 2007. *The 2004 and 2006 Canadian Election Surveys.* Toronto: Institute for Social Research.

Blidook, Kelly. 2012. *Constituency Influence in Parliament: Countering the Centre.* Vancouver: University of British Columbia Press.

Blidook, Kelly, and Mathew Kerby. 2011. "Constituency Influence on 'Constituency Members': The Adaptability of Roles to Electoral Realities in the Canadian Case." *Journal of Legislative Studies* 17 (3): 327–39.

Bloemraad, Irene. 2000. "Citizenship and Immigration: A Current Review." *Journal of International Migration and Integration* 1 (1): 9–38.

– 2006. *Becoming a Citizen: Incorporating Immigrants and Refugees in the United States and Canada.* Berkeley: University of California Press.

Bobo, Lawrence, and Franklin D. Gilliam, Jr. 1990. "Race, Sociopolitical Participation, and Black Empowerment." *American Political Science Review* 84 (2): 377–93.

Bousetta, Hassan, Sonia Gsir, and Dirk Jacobs. 2005. *Active Civic Participation of Immigrants in Belgium.* Oldenburg: POLITIS.

Brim, Orville, and Jerome Kagan, eds. 1980. *Constancy and Change in Human Development.* Cambridge, MA: Harvard University Press.

Brouard, Sylvain, and Vincent Tiberj. 2011. "Yes They Can: An Experimental Approach to the Eligibility of Ethnic Minority Candidates in France." In *The Political Representation of Immigrants and Minorities,* edited by Karen Bird, Thomas Saalfeld, and Andreas M. Wüst, 164–80. New York: Routledge.

Bueker, Catherine Simpson. 2005. "Political Incorporation among Immigrants from Ten Areas of Origin: The Persistence of Source Country Effects." *International Migration Review* 39 (1): 103–40.

Cain, E. Bruce, D. Roderick Kiewiet, and Carole J. Uhlaner. 1991. "The Acquisition of Partisanship by Latinos and Asian Americans." *American Journal of Political Science* 35 (2): 390–422.

Campbell, Angus, Philip Converse, Warren E. Miller, and Donald E. Stokes. 1960. *The American Voter.* Chicago: University of Chicago Press.

Casellas, Jason P. 2008. "Coalitions in the House? The Election of Minorities to State Legislatures and Congress." *Political Research Quarterly* 62: 120–31.

CBS (Centraal Bureau voor de Statistiek). 2010. "StatLine." http://statline.cbs.nl.

Celis, Karen, Sarah Childs, Johanna Kantola, and Mona Lena Krook. 2008. "Rethinking Women's Substantive Representation." *Representation* 44 (2): 99–110.

Chaffee, Steven, and Stacey Frank. 1996. "How Americans Get Political Information: Print versus Broadcast News." *Annals of the American Academy of Political and Social Science* 546 (1): 48–58.

Childs, Sarah, and Paul Webb. 2011. *Sex, Gender and the Conservative Party: From Iron Lady to Kitten Heels.* Oxford: Palgrave Macmillan.

Cho, Wendy K. Tam. 1999. "Naturalization, Socialization, Participation: Immigrants and (Non-)Voting." *Journal of Politics* 61 (4): 1140–55.

Cho, Wendy K. Tam, James G. Gimpel, and Joshua J. Dyck. 2006. "Residential Concentration, Political Socialization and Voter Turnout." *Journal of Politics* 68 (1): 156–67.

Chui, Tina, Kelly Tran, and Hélène Maheux. 2007. *Immigration in Canada: A Portrait of the Foreign-Born Population, 2006 Census*: Statistics Canada, catalogue no. 97–557–XWE2006001.

Clark, Ken, and Stephen Drinkwater. 2007. *Ethnic Minorities in the Labour Market: Dynamics and Diversity.* Bristol: Policy Press.

Cleary, Matthew R., and Susan C. Stokes. 2006. *Democracy and the Culture of Skepticism: Political Trust in Argentina and Mexico.* New York: Russell Sage Foundation.

CMPS (Collaborative Multi-racial Post-election Study). 2008. http://www.cmpstudy.com/.

Collet, Christian. 2005. "Bloc Voting, Polarization, and the Panethnic Hypothesis: The Case of Little Saigon." *Journal of Politics* 67 (3):907–33.

– 2008. "Minority Candidates, Alternative Media, and Multiethnic America: Deracialization or Toggling?" *Perspectives on Politics* 6 (4): 707–28.

Conover, Pamela Johnston, and Stanley Feldman. 1989. "Candidate Perception in an Ambiguous World: Campaigns, Cues, and Inference Processes." *American Journal of Political Science* 33 (4): 912–40.

Cracknall, Richard. 2012. *Ethnic Minorities in Politics, Government and Public Life.* SN01156. House of Commons Library Research Papers 08/12, 10/36.

Crepaz, Markus M.L. 2008. *Trust beyond Borders: Immigration, the Welfare State and Identity in Modern Societies.* Ann Arbor: University of Michigan Press.

Cutler, Fred, and J. Scott Matthews. 2005. "The Challenge of Municipal Voting: Vancouver 2002." *Canadian Journal of Political Science* 38 (2): 359–82.

Dawson, Michael C. 1994. *Behind the Mule: Race and Class in African-American Politics.* Princeton: Princeton University Press.

Dekker, Lisette. 2006. *Vrouwen en allochtonen in de nieuw gekozen Tweede Kamer 2006.* Amsterdam: IPP.

– 2010. *Dossier: Allochtonen in de politiek.* Amsterdam: Instituut voor Publiek en Politiek.

de la Garza, Rodolfo O., Louis DeSipio., F. Chris Garcia, John Garcia, and Angelo Falcon. 1992. *Latino Voices: Mexican, Puerto Rican, and Cuban Perspectives on American Politics*. Boulder, CO: Westview Press.

Delli Carpini, Michael X., and Scott Keeter. 1997. *What Americans Know about Politics and Why It Matters*. New Haven, CT: Yale University Press.

DeSipio, Louis. 1996. *Counting on the Latino Vote: Latinos as a New Electorate*. Charlottesville: University Press of Virginia.

– 2011. "Immigrant Incorporation in an Era of Weak Civic Institutions: Immigrant Civic and Political Participation in the United States." *American Behavioral Scientist* 55 (9): 1189–213.

de Wit, Thom Duyvené, and Ruud Koopmans. 2005. "The Integration of Ethnic Minorities into Political Culture: The Netherlands, Germany and Great Britain Compared." *Acta Politica* 40 (4): 50–73.

Dinesen, Peter, and Marc Hooghe. 2010. "When in Rome, Do as the Romans Do: The Acculturation of Generalized Trust among Immigrants in Europe." *International Migration Review* 44 (3): 697–727.

Docherty, David C. 1997. *Mr. Smith Goes to Ottawa*. Vancouver: University of British Columbia Press.

Dolan, Kathleen. 2008. "Is There a 'Gender Affinity Effect' in American Politics? Information, Affect, and Candidate Sex in the U.S. House Elections." *Political Research Quarterly* 61 (1): 79–89.

Drobnič, Sonja. 2006. "Political Participation of Yugoslav Immigrants in Sweden." *European Journal of Political Research* 16 (6): 645–58.

Dronkers, Jaap, and Maarten Peter Vink. 2012. "Explaining Access to Citizenship in Europe: How Citizenship Policies Affect Naturalization Rates." *European Union Politics* 13 (3): 390–412.

Easton, David. 1975. "A Re-assessment of the Concept of Political Support." *British Journal of Political Science* 5 (4): 435–57.

Easton, David, Jack Dennis, and Sylvia Easton. 1969. *Children in the Political System: Origins of Political Legitimacy*. New York: McGraw-Hill.

Eckstein, Harry. 1988. "A Culturalist Theory of Political Change." *American Political Science Review* 82 (3): 789–804.

Economist. 2012. "David Cameron's race problem." 3 March, 38.

EMBES (Ethnic Minority British Election Study). 2010. "The British Election Study Ethnic Minority Survey 2010." http://discover.ukdataservice.ac.uk/catalogue/?sn=6970&type=Data%20catalogue.

Engstrom, Richard L., and Michael D. McDonald. 1986. "The Effect of At-Large versus District Elections on Racial Representation in U.S. Municipalities." In *Electoral Laws and Their Political Consequences*, edited by Bernard Grofman and Arend Lijphart. New York: Agathon Press.

Entzinger, Hans, and Renske Biezeveld. 2003. *Benchmarking in Immigrant Integration*. European Research Centre on Migration and Ethnic Relations. Rotterdam: Erasmus University.

Ersanilli, Evelyn, and Ruud Koopmans. 2010. "Rewarding Integration? Citizenship Regulations and the Socio-cultural Integration of Immigrants in the Netherlands, France and Germany." *Journal of Ethnic and Migration Studies* 36 (5): 773–91.

Eulau, Heinz, and Paul D. Karps. 1977. "The Puzzle of Representation: Specifying the Components of Responsiveness." *Legislative Studies Quarterly* 2 (4): 233–54.

Fennema, Meindert, and Jean Tillie. 1999. "Political Participation and Political Trust in Amsterdam: Civic Communities and Ethnic Networks." *Journal of Ethnic and Migration Studies* 25 (4): 703–26.

Finifter, Ada W., and Bernard M. Finifter. 1989. "Party Identification and Political Adaptation of American Migrants in Australia." *Journal of Politics* 51 (3): 599–630.

Fisher, Stephen D., Anthony F. Heath, David Sanders, and Maria Sobolewska. 2014. "Candidate Ethnicity and Vote Choice in Britain." *British Journal of Political Science*: 1–23.

Fleischmann, Fenella, and Jaap Dronkers. 2010. "Unemployment among Immigrants in European Labour Markets: An Analysis of Origin and Destination Effects." *Work, Employment and Society* 24 (2): 337–54.

Font, Joan, and Monica Méndez, eds. 2013. *Surveying Ethnic Minorities and Immigrant Populations: Methodological Challenges and Research Strategies*. Amsterdam: Amsterdam University Press.

Foquz EtnoMarketing. 2006. "Allochtonen bepalen door hoge opkomst 13 kamerzetels, bijna allemaal gaan naar links: Foquz." Persbericht, 22 November.

Forsander, Annika. 2004. "Social Capital in the Context of Immigration and Diversity: Economic Participation in the Nordic Welfare States." *Journal of International Migration and Integration* 5 (2): 207–27.

Fossati, Flavia. 2011. "The Effect of Integration and Social Democratic Welfare States on Immigrants' Educational Attainment: A Multilevel Estimate." *Journal of European Social Policy* 21 (5): 391–412.

Fraga, Luis, John Garcia, Rodney Hero, Michael Jones-Correa, Valerie Martinez-Ebers, and Gary Segura. 2012. *Latinos in the New Millennium*. Cambridge: Cambridge University Press.

Franks, C.E.S. 1987. *The Parliament of Canada*. Toronto: University of Toronto Press.

Freeman, Gary. 2004. "Immigrant Integration in Western Democracies." *International Migration Review* 38 (3): 945–69.

Galston, William A. 2001. "Political Knowledge, Political Engagement, and Civic Education." *Annual Review of Political Science* 4 (1): 217–34.

Gamson, William A. 1968. *Power and Discontent*. Homewood, IL: Dorsey Press.

Garcea, Joseph. 2006. "Provincial Multiculturalism Policies in Canada, 1974–2004: A Content Analysis." *Canadian Ethnic Studies* 38 (3): 1–20.

Garcia, John A. 1987. "The Political Integration of Mexican Immigrants: Examining Some Political Integration." *International Migration Review* 21 (2): 372–89.

Gidengil, Elisabeth, André Blais, Neil Nevitte, and Richard Nadeau. 2004. *Citizens*. Vancouver: University of British Columbia Press.

Gidengil, Elizabeth, Joanna Everitt, Patrick Fournier, and Neil Nevitte. 2009. *Canadian Election Study, 2008*. Toronto: York University, Institute for Social Research (ISR) / Montréal: Université de Montréal.

Gidengil, Elisabeth, and Dietlind Stolle. 2009. "The Role of Social Networks in Immigrant Women's Political Incorporation." *International Migration Review* 43 (4): 727–63.

Gitelman, Zvi. 1982. *Becoming Israelis: The Political Resocialization of Soviet and American Immigrants*. New York: Praeger.

Glick Schiller, Nina, Linda Basch, and Cristina Szanton Blanc. 1995. "From Immigrant to Transmigrant: Theorizing Transnational Migration." *Anthropological Quarterly* 68 (1): 48–63.

Good, Kristin. 2009. *Municipalities and Multiculturalism: The Politics of Immigration in Toronto and Vancouver*. Toronto: University of Toronto Press.

Goodyear-Grant, Elizabeth, and Julie Croskill. 2011. "Gender Affinity Effects in Vote Choice in Westminster Systems: Assessing 'Flexible' Voters in Canada." *Politics & Gender* 7 (2): 223–50.

Greenwell, Lisa R., Burciaga Valdez, and Julie Da Vanzo. 1997. "Social Ties, Wages, and Gender in a Study of Salvadorean and Pilipino Immigrants in Los Angeles." *Social Science Quarterly* 78 (2): 559–77.

Hajnal, Zoltan. 2009. *America's Uneven Democracy: Race, Turnout, and Representation in City Politics*. New York: Cambridge University Press.

Hajnal, Zoltan, and Jessica Trounstine. 2005. "Where Turnout Matters: The Consequences of Uneven Turnout in City Politics." *Journal of Politics* 67 (2): 515–35.

Harris-Perry, Melissa V. 2004. *Barbershops, Bibles, and Bet: Everyday Talk and Black Political Thought*. Princeton: Princeton University Press.

Heath, Anthony, and Omar Khan. 2012. *Ethnic Minority British Election Study – Key Findings*. London: Runnymede Trust.

Heitshusen, Valerie, Garry Young, and David M. Wood. 2005. "Electoral Context and MP Constituency Focus in Australia, Canada, Ireland, New Zealand, and the United Kingdom." *American Journal of Political Science* 49 (1): 32–45.

Hicks, Bruce M. 2006. "Are Marginalized Communities Disenfranchised? Voter Turnout and Representation in Post-merger Toronto." IRPP Working Paper Series no. 2006-03. Montreal: Institute for Research on Public Policy. http://irpp.org/wp-content/uploads/assets/research/strengthening-canadian-democracy/are-marginalized-communities-disenfranchised/wp2006-03.pdf.

Hoskin, Marilyn. 1989. "Socialization and Antisocialization: The Case of Immigrants." In *Political Learning in Adulthood: A Sourcebook of Theory and Research*, edited by Roberta S. Sigel, 340–76. Chicago: University of Chicago Press.

Howard, Marc. 2009. *The Politics of Citizenship in Europe*. New York: Cambridge University Press.

Huddleston, Thomas, Jan Niessen, Eadaoin Ni Chaoimh, and Emilie White. 2011. *Migrant Integration Policy Index III*. Brussels: British Council and Migration Policy Group.

Huddy, Leonie, and Nadia Khatib. 2007. "American Patriotism, National Identity, and Political Involvement." *American Journal of Political Science* 51 (1): 63–77.

Hutchings, Vincent L., and Nicholas A. Valentino. 2004. "The Centrality of Race in American Politics." *Annual Review of Political Science* 7:383–408.

Hyman, Herbert H. 1959. *Political Socialization*. New York: Free Press.

Ichilov, Orit, ed. 1990. *Political Socialization, Citizenship Education, and Democracy*. New York: Teachers College Press.

IfG (Institute for Government). 2011. *Party People: How Do – and How Should – British Political Parties Select Their Parliamentary Candidates?* London: IfG.

IPP (Instituut voor Publiek en Politiek). 2006. "Meer diversiteit in de gemeenteraden." 7–10. The Hague: IPP.

ISP (Informatie Service Punt). 2002. "Informatie Service Punt Nieuwsbrief." Amsterdam: Instituut voor Publiek en Politiek.

Jacobs, Dirk. 1998. *Nieuwkomers in de politiek: Het parlementaire debat omtrent kiesrecht voor vreemdelingen in Nederland en België (1970–1997)*. Gent: Academia Press.

Jacobs, Dirk, Hassan Bousetta, Andrea Rea, Marco Martiniello, and Marc Swyngedouw. 2006. "Qui sont les candidats aux élections bruxelloises? Le profil des candidats à l'élection au parlement de la Région de Bruxelles-Capitale du 13 Juin 2004." *Cahiers Migrations* 37. Bruxelles: Academia Bruylant.

Jacobs, Dirk, Marco Martiniello, and Andrea Rea. 2002. "Changing Patterns of Political Participation of Citizens of Immigrant Origin in the Brussels Capital Region: The October 2000 Election." *Journal of International Migration and Integration* 3 (2): 201–21.

Jacobs, Dirk, Karen Phalet, and Marc Swyngedouw. 2004. "Associational Membership and Political Involvement among Ethnic Minority Groups in Brussels." *Journal of Ethnic and Migration Studies* 30 (3): 543–59.

Jacobs, Dirk, and Andrea Rea. 2009. "Allochthones in the Netherlands and Belgium." *International Migration* 50 (6): 42–57.

Jacobs, Larry, and Robert Shapiro. 2000. *Politicians Don't Ponder: Political Manipulation and the Loss of Democratic Responsiveness*. Chicago: University of Chicago Press.

Jedwab, Jack. 2006. "The 'Roots' of Immigrant and Ethnic Voter Participation in Canada." *Electoral Insight* 8 (2): 3–9.

Jennings, M. Kent. 1987. "Residues of a Movement: The Aging of the American Protest Generation." *American Political Science Review* 81 (2): 367–82.

– 2002. "Generation Units and the Student Protest Movement in the United States: An Intra- and Intergenerational Analysis." *Political Psychology* 23 (2): 303–24.

Jones, Felecia G. 1990. "The Black Audience and the Bet Channel." *Journal of Broadcasting & Electronic Media* 34 (4): 477–86.

Jones-Correa, Michael. 1998. *Between Two Nations: The Political Predicament of Latinos in New York City*. Ithaca, NY: Cornell University Press.

– 2001. "Institutional and Contextual Factors in Immigrant Naturalization and Voting." *Citizenship Studies* 5 (1): 41–56.

Jones-Correa, Michael, and David Leal. 2001. "Political Participation: Does Religion Matter?" *Political Research Quarterly* 54 (4): 751–70.

Joppke, Christian. 2007. "Immigrants and Civic Integration in Western Europe." In *Belonging? Diversity, Recognition and Shared Citizenship in Canada*, edited by Keith G. Banting, Thomas J. Courchene, and F. Leslie Seidle, 321–50. Montreal: Institute for Research on Public Policy.

– 2010. *Citizenship and Immigration*. Cambridge: Polity Press.

Junn, Jane. 1997. "Assimilating or Coloring Participation? Gender, Race and Democratic Political Participation." In *Women Transforming Politics: An Alternative Reader*, edited by Cathy Cohen, Kathleen B. Jones, and Joan Tronto, 387–97. New York: New York University Press.

Karp, Jeffrey A., and David Brockington. 2005. "Social Desirability and Response Validity: A Comparative Analysis of Overreporting Voter Turnout in Five Countries." *Journal of Politics* 67 (3): 825–40.

Kaufmann, Karen M. 2003. "Cracks in the Rainbow: Group Commonality as a Basis for Latino and African-American Political Coalitions." *Political Research Quarterly* 56 (2): 199–210.

– 2004. *The Urban Voter: Group Conflict and Mayoral Voting Behavior in American Cities*. Ann Arbor: University of Michigan Press.

Kaufman, Robert L., and Paul G. Schervish. 1986. "Using Adjusted Cross-tabulations to Interpret Log-Linear Relationships." *American Sociological Review* 51 (5): 717–33.

Kazemipur, Abdolmohammad, and M. Reza Nakhaie. 2014. "The Economics of Attachment: Making a Case for a Relational Approach to Immigrants' Integration in Canada." *Journal of International Migration and Integration* 15 (4): 609–32.

King, David C., and Richard E. Matland. 2003. "Sex and the Grand Old Party: An Experimental Investigation of the Effect of Candidate Sex on Support for a Republican Candidate." *American Politics Research* 31 (6): 595–612.

Koop, Royce. 2012. "Party Constituency Associations and the Service, Policy and Symbolic Responsiveness of Canadian Members of Parliament." *Canadian Journal of Political Science* 45 (5): 359–78.

Koopmans, Ruud. 2010. "Trade-Offs between Equality and Difference: Immigrant Integration, Multiculturalism and the Welfare State in Cross-National Perspective." *Journal of Ethnic and Migration Studies* 36 (1): 1–26.

– 2012. "The Post-Nationalization of Immigrant Rights: A Theory in Search of Evidence." *British Journal of Sociology* 63 (1): 22–30.

Koopmans, Ruud, Ines Michalowski, and Stine Waibel. 2012. "Citizenship Rights for Immigrants: National Political Processes and Cross-National Convergence in Western Europe, 1980–2008." *American Journal of Sociology* 117 (4): 1202–45.

Koopmans, Ruud, Paul Statham, Marco Giugni, and Florence Passy. 2005. *Contested Citizenship. Immigration and Cultural Diversity in Europe.* Minneapolis: University of Minnesota Press.

Krebs, Timothy B. 1998. "The Determinants of Candidates' Vote Share and the Advantages of Incumbency in City Council Elections." *American Journal of Political Science* 42 (3): 921–35.

Krishna, Anirudh. 2002. "Enhancing Political Participation in Democracies: What Is the Role of Social Capital?" *Comparative Political Studies* 35 (2): 437–60.

Kuklinski, James H., and Paul J. Quirk. 2001. "Conceptual Foundations of Citizen Competence." *Political Behavior* 23 (3): 285–311.

Kushner, Joseph, David Siegel, and Hannah Stanwick. 1997. "Ontario Municipal Elections: Voting Trends and Determinants of Electoral Success in a Canadian Province." *Canadian Journal of Political Science* 30 (2): 539–53.

Kymlicka, Will. 1995. *Multicultural Citizenship: A Liberal Theory of Minority Rights.* New York: Oxford University Press.

Lackey, Gerald. 2007. "'Trust in Context': A Study of Political Trust among Mexican Immigrants." Paper presented at the Latino National Survey Workshop for Young Scholars, Cornell University, Ithaca, NY, November.

Lawrence, Daniel. 1974. *Black Migrants, White Natives: A Study of Race Relations in Nottingham*. Cambridge: Cambridge University Press.

Leighley, Jan E. 2001. *Strength in Numbers? The Political Mobilization of Racial and Ethnic Minorities*. Princeton: Princeton University Press.

Leijenaar, Monique, Kees Niemöller, and Astrid van der Kooij. 1999. *Kandidaten gezocht: Politieke participatie en het streven naar een grotere diversiteit onder gemeenteraadsleden*. Amsterdam: Instituut voor Publiek en Politiek.

Le Lohe, Michel. 1998. "Ethnic Minority Participation and Representation in the British Electoral System." In *Race and British Electoral Politics*, edited by Shamit Saggar, 73–95. London: UCL Press.

Letki, Natalia. 2008. "Does Diversity Erode Social Cohesion? Social Capital and Race in British Neighbourhoods." *Political Studies* 56 (1): 99–126.

Levitt, Peggy, and Nina Glick Schiller. 2004. "Transnational Perspectives on Migration: Conceptualizing Simultaneity." *International Migration Review* 38 (3): 1002–39.

Lien, Pei-te. 1997. *The Political Participation of Asian Americans: Voting Behavior in Southern California*. New York: Garland Publishing.

– 2001. *The Making of Asian America through Political Participation*. Philadelphia, PA: Temple University Press.

– 2004. "Asian Americans and Voting Participation: Comparing Racial and Ethnic Differences in Recent US Elections." *International Migration Review* 38 (2): 493–517.

Lijphart, Arend. 1999. *Patterns of Democracy: Government Forms and Performance in Thirty-Six Countries*. New Haven, CT: Yale University Press.

Linz, Juan J. 2000. *Totalitarian and Authoritarian Regimes*. Boulder, CO: Lynne Rienner Publishers.

Linz, Juan J., and Alfred Stepan. 1996. *Problems of Democratic Transition and Consolidation: Southern Europe, South America, and Post-Communist Europe*. Baltimore: Johns Hopkins University Press.

Listhaug, Ola, and Matti Wiberg. 1995. "Confidence in Political and Private Institutions." In *Citizens and the State*, edited by Hans-Dieter Klingemann and Dieter Fuchs, 298–322. Oxford: Oxford University Press.

Long, J. Scott. 1997. *Regression Models for Categorical and Limited Dependent Variables*. Advanced Quantitative Techniques in the Social Sciences, no. 7. Thousand Oaks, CA: Sage Publications.

MacDermid, Robert. 2009. "Funding City Politics: Municipal Campaign Funding and Property Development in the Greater Toronto Area." Toronto: Centre for Social Justice and Vote Toronto. http://www.socialjustice.org/uploads/pubs/FundingCityPolitics.pdf.

MacLeod, Peter. 2006. "How to Organize an Effective Constituency Office." *Canadian Parliamentary Review* 29 (1): 9–12.

Malloy, Jonathan. 2003a. *To Better Serve Canadians: How Technology Is Changing the Relationship between Members of Parliament and Public Servants*. New Directions Series 9. Toronto: Institute of Public Administration of Canada.

– 2003b. "High Discipline, Low Cohesion? The Uncertain Patterns of Canadian Parliamentary Party Groups." *Journal of Legislative Studies* 9 (4): 116–29.

Mansbridge, Jane. 1999. "Should Blacks Represent Blacks and Women Represent Women? A Contingent 'Yes.'" *Journal of Politics* 61 (3): 628–57.

– 2003. "Rethinking Representation." *American Political Science Review* 97 (4): 515–28.

Marland, Alex. 1998. "The Electoral Benefits and Limitations of Incumbency." *Canadian Parliamentary Review* 21 (4): 33–6.

Marschall, Melissa J., Anirudh V.S. Ruhil, and Paru R. Shah. 2010. "The New Racial Calculus: Electoral Institutions and Black Representation in Local Legislatures." *American Journal of Political Science* 54 (1): 107–24.

Marshall, Thomas Humphrey. 1950. *Citizenship and Social Class: And Other Essays*. Cambridge: University Press.

Martin, Nicole. 2012. "Do Ethnic Minority Candidates Mobilise Ethnic Minority Voters? Evidence from the 2010 General Election." Paper prepared for the Elections, Public Opinion and Parties Conference, University of Oxford, 7–9 September.

Martin, Shane. 2011. "Parliamentary Questions, the Behaviour of Legislators, and the Function of Legislatures: An Introduction." *Journal of Legislative Studies* 17 (3): 259–70.

Matheson, Ian Andrew. 2005. "Seeking Political Inclusion: The Case of South Asian Political Representation in Peel Region." Master's thesis, Ryerson University, Toronto. *Digital Commons @ Ryerson, Theses and dissertations*. Paper 350. http://digital.library.ryerson.ca/islandora/object/RULA%3A460.

Matson, Marsha, and Terri Susan Fine. 2006. "Gender, Ethnicity, and Ballot Information: Ballot Cues in Low-Information Elections." *State Politics & Policy Quarterly* 6 (1): 49–72.

Matsubayashi, Tetsuya, and Michiko Ueda. 2011. "Political Knowledge and the Use of Candidate Race as a Voting Cue." *American Politics Research* 39 (2): 380–413.

Maxwell, Rahsaan. 2010a. "Evaluating Migrant Integration: Political Attitudes across Generations in Europe." *International Migration Review* 44 (1): 25–52.

– 2010b. "Political Participation in France among Non-European-Origin Migrants: Segregation or Integration?" *Journal of Ethnic and Migration Studies* 36 (3): 425–43.

– 2013. "The Geographic Context of Political Attitudes among Migrant-Origin Individuals in Europe." *World Politics* 65 (1): 116–55.

McAllister, Ian, and Toni Makkai. 1992. "Resource and Social Learning Theories of Political Participation: Ethnic Patterns in Australia." *Canadian Journal of Political Science* 25 (2): 269–93.

McAllister, Ian, and Juliet Pietsch. 2011. *Trends in Australian Political Opinion, 1987–2010: Results from the Australian Election Study*. Canberra: ANU Public Policy.

McDermott, Monika L. 1998. "Race and Gender Cues in Low-Information Elections." *Political Research Quarterly* 51 (4): 895–918.

Meissner, Doris, Deborah Myers, Demetrios Papademetriou, and Marc Rosenblum, eds. 2006. *Immigration and America's Future*. Washington, DC: Migration Policy Institute.

Merelman, Richard M. 1980. "Democratic Politics and the Culture of American Education." *American Political Science Review* 74 (2): 319–32.

Messina, Anthony. 1998. "Ethnic Minorities in the British Party System in the 1990s and Beyond." In *Race and British Electoral Politics*, edited by Shamit Saggar, 47–69. London: UCL Press.

Michelson, Melissa R. 2003. "The Corrosive Effect of Acculturation: How Mexican Americans Lose Political Trust." *Social Science Quarterly* 84 (4): 918–33.

Michon, Laure. 2011. "Ethnic Minorities in Local Politics: Comparing Amsterdam and Paris." PhD diss., Institute for Migration and Ethnic Studies, University of Amsterdam.

Michon, Laure, and Jean Tillie. 2003a. *Amsterdamse polyfonie: Opkomst en stemgedrag van allochtone Amsterdammers bij de gemeenteraads- en deelraads-verkiezingen van 6 maart 2002*. Amsterdam: IMES.

– 2003b. "Politieke participatie van migranten in Nederland sinds 1986." In *Politiek in de Multiculturele Samenleving*, edited by Huib Pellikaan and Margo Trappenburg, 126–59. Amsterdam: Boom.

Neuman, W. Russell. 1986. *The Paradox of Mass Politics: Knowledge and Opinion in the American Electorate*. Cambridge, MA: Harvard University Press.

Newton, Kenneth. 2007. "Social and Political Trust." In *Oxford Handbook of Political Behavior*, edited by Russell J. Dalton and Hans-Dieter Klingemann, 169–87. Oxford: Oxford University Press.

Nicholson, Stephen P., Adrian D. Pantoja, and Gary M. Segura. 2006. "Political Knowledge and Issue Voting among the Latino Electorate." *Political Research Quarterly* 59 (2): 259–71.

Nie, Norman H., Jane Junn, and Kenneth Stehlik-Barry. 1996. *Education and Democratic Citizenship in America*. Chicago: University of Chicago Press.

Niemi, Richard G., and M. Kent Jennings. 1991. "Issues and Inheritance in the Formation of Party Identification." *American Journal of Political Science* 35 (4): 970–88.

Niessen, Jan, Thomas Huddleston, and Laura Citron. 2007. *Migrant Integration Policy Index*. Brussels: Migration Policy Group.

Norris, Pippa. 2002. *Democratic Phoenix: Reinventing Political Activism*. New York: Cambridge University Press.

O'Neill, Brenda, Elisabeth Gidengil, and Lisa Young. 2012. "The Political Integration of Immigrant and Visible Minority Women." *Canadian Political Science Review* 6 (2–3): 185–96.

Panagopoulos, Costas, and Donald P. Green. 2011. "Spanish-Language Radio Advertisements and Latino Voter Turnout in the 2006 Congressional Elections: Field Experimental Evidence." *Political Research Quarterly* 64 (3): 588–99.

Pantoja, Adrian D., and Gary M. Segura. 2003. "Fear and Loathing in California: Contextual Threat and Political Sophistication among Latino Voters." *Political Behavior* 25 (3): 265–86.

Paquet, Mireille. 2013. "Les provinces et la fédéralisation de l'immigration au Canada, 1990–2010." Doctoral dissertation. Université de Montréal.

Paskeviciute, Aida, and Christopher J. Anderson. 2007. "Immigrants, Citizenship, and Political Action: A Cross-National Study of 21 European Democracies." Paper presented at the annual meeting of the American Political Science Association, Chicago, 30 August.

Pennings, Paul. 1987. *Migrantenkiesrecht in Amsterdam: Een onderzoek naar de participatie en mobilisatie van etnische groepen bij de gemeenteraadsverkiezingen van 19 maart 1986*. Amsterdam: Gemeente Amsterdam, Bestuursinformatie, Afdeling Onderzoek en Statistiek / Universiteit van Amsterdam, Subfaculteit Politicologie, Vakgroep Collectief Politiek Gedrag.

Phalet, Karen, and Marc Swyngedouw. 2003. "Measuring Immigrant Integration: The Case of Belgium." *Migration Studies* 40 (154): 773–803.

Phillips, Anne. 1995. *The Politics of Presence*. Oxford: Oxford University Press.

Philpot, Tasha S., and Hanes Walton, Jr. 2007. "One of Our Own: Black Female Candidates and the Voters Who Support Them." *American Journal of Political Science* 51 (1): 49–62.

Pitkin, Hannah F. 1967. *The Concept of Representation*. Berkeley: University of California Press.

Plante, Johanne. 2010. *Characteristics and Labour Market Outcomes of Internationally-Educated Immigrants*. Cat. no. 81-595-M – No. 084. Ottawa: Statistics Canada, Culture, Tourism and the Centre for Education Statistics.

Portes, Alejandro, and Rubén Rumbaut. 2006. *Immigrant America*, 3rd ed. Berkeley: University of California Press.

Portes, Alejandro, and Julia Sensenbrenner. 1993. "Embeddedness and Immigration: Notes on the Social Determinants of Economic Action." *American Journal of Sociology* 98 (6): 1320–50.

Price, Richard G., and Maureen Mancuso. 1995. "The Ties That Bind: Parliamentary Members and Their Constituents." In *Introductory Readings in Canadian Government and Politics*, 2nd ed., edited by Robert M. Krause and R.H. Wagenberg. Toronto: Copp Clark Pitman.

Putnam, Robert D. 1995. "Tuning In, Tuning Out: The Strange Disappearance of Social Capital in America." *Political Science & Politics* 28 (December): 664–83.

– 2000. *Bowling Alone*. New York: Simon and Schuster.

Ramakrishnan, S. Karthick. 2005. *Democracy in Immigrant America: Changing Demographics and Political Participation*. Stanford, CA: Stanford University Press.

Ramakrishnan, S. Karthick, and Thomas J. Espenshade. 2001. "Immigrant Incorporation and Political Participation in the United States." *International Migration Review* 35 (3): 870–909.

Ramakrishnan, S. Karthick, and Celia Viramontes. 2010. "Civic Spaces: Mexican Hometown Associations and Immigrant Participation." *Journal of Social Issues* 66 (1): 155–73.

Ramakrishnan, S. Karthick, Janelle Wong, Taeku Lee, and Jane Junn. 2009. "Race-Based Considerations and the Obama Vote: Evidence from the 2008 National Asian American Survey." *Du Bois Review* 6 (9): 219–38.

Ramírez, Ricardo. 2011. "Mobilization en Español: Spanish-Language Radio and the Activation of Political Identities." In *Rallying for Immigrant Rights*, edited by Kim Voss and Irene Bloemraad, 63–81. Berkeley: University of California Press.

Ramírez, Ricardo, and Luis Fraga. 2008. "Continuity and Change: Latino Political Incorporation in California since 1990." In *Racial and Ethnic Politics in California*, vol. 3, edited by Bruce Cain, Jaime Regalado, and Sandra Bass, 61–93. Berkeley, CA: Berkeley Public Policy Press.

Rasmussen, Jorgen. 1981. "Female Political Career Patterns & Leadership Disabilities in Britain: The Crucial Role of Gatekeepers in Regulating Entry to the Political Elite." *Polity* 13 (4): 600–20.

Rath, Jan. 1983. "Political Participation of Ethnic Minorities in the Netherlands." *International Migration Review* 17 (3): 445–69.

Rath 1985. "Immigrant Candidates in the Netherlands." *Cahiers d'Etudes sur la Méditerranée Orientale et le monde Turco-Iranien* 1:46–62.

– 1988. "Political Action of Immigrants in the Netherlands: Class or Ethnicity?" *European Journal of Political Research* 16 (6): 623–44.

- 1990. *Kenterend tij: Migranten en de gemeenteraadsverkiezingen van 21 maart 1990 te Rotterdam*. Utrecht: RUU, Vakgroep Culturele Antropologie.

Reitz, Jeffrey G., Rupa Banerjee, Mai Phan, and Jordan Thompson. 2009. "Race, Religion, and the Social Integration of New Immigrant Minorities in Canada." *International Migration Review* 43 (4): 695–726.

Roberts, Rebecca. 2011. "Ethnic Media Outlets Seek to Fill Coverage Gap." *Talk of the Nation*, NPR, 18 August.

Rosenstone, Steven, and John M. Hansen. 1993. *Mobilization, Participation, and Democracy in America*. New York: Macmillan.

Saalfeld, Thomas. 2011. "Parliamentary Questions as Instruments of Substantive Representation: Visible Minorities in the UK House of Commons, 2005–2010." *Journal of Legislative Studies* 17 (3): 271–89.

Saggar, Shamit. 2000. *Race and Representation: Electoral Politics and Ethnic Pluralism*. Manchester: Manchester University Press.

- 2001. *Race and Representation Reconsidered*. Kingsland Papers Series, vol. 2. London: Hansard Society.

Saggar, Shamit, and Anthony Heath. 1999. "Race: Towards a Multicultural Electorate?" In *Critical Elections: The 1997 British Election in Long-Term Perspective*, edited by Geoffrey Evans and Pippa Norris, 102–23. London: Sage.

Sainsbury, Diane. 2006. "Immigrants' Social Rights in Comparative Perspective: Welfare Regimes, Forms in Immigration and Immigration Policy Regimes." *Journal of European Social Policy* 16 (3): 229–44.

Sanbonmatsu, Kira. 2002. "Gender Stereotypes and Vote Choice." *American Journal of Political Science* 46 (1): 20–34.

Schatz, Robert T., Ervin Staub, and Howard Lavine. 1999. "On the Varieties of National Attachment: Blind versus Constructive Patriotism." *Political Psychology* 20 (1): 151–74.

Searing, Donald D., Joel J. Schwartz, and Alden E. Lind. 1973. "The Structuring Principle: Political Socialization and Belief Systems." *American Political Science Review* 67 (2): 415–32.

Searing, Donald, Gerald Wright, and George Rabinowitz. 1976. "The Primacy Principle: Attitude Change and Political Socialization." *British Journal of Political Science* 6 (1): 83–113.

Sears, David O., and Carolyn L. Funk. 1999. "Evidence of the Long-Term Resistance of Adults' Political Predispositions." *Journal of Politics* 61 (1): 1–28.

Sears, David O., and Sheri Levy. 2003. "Childhood and Adult Political Development." In *Oxford Handbook of Political Psychology*, edited by David O. Sears, Leonie Huddy, and Robert Jervis, 60–109. New York: Oxford University Press.

Sears, David O., and Nicholas A. Valentino. 1997. "Politics Matters: Political Events as Catalysts for Preadult Socialization." *American Political Science Review* 91 (1): 45–65.

Seidle, F. Leslie. 2014. "Local Voting Rights for Non-nationals: Experience in Sweden, the Netherlands and Belgium." *Journal of International Migration and Integration* 16 (1): 27–42.

Shane, Kristen. 2010. "Critics say MPs' offices turning into de facto immigration offices." *Hill Times* (Ottawa), 4 October.

Siemiatycki, Myer. 2011a. *The Diversity Gap: The Electoral Under-Representation of Visible Minorities: Diversity Institute in Management and Technology.* Toronto: Ryerson University.

– 2011b. "Governing Immigrant City: Immigrant Political Representation in Toronto." *American Behavioral Scientist* 55 (9): 1214–34.

Siemiatycki, Myer, and Sean Marshall. 2014. "Who Votes in Toronto Municipal Elections?" Toronto: Maytree. http://maytree.com/wp-content/uploads/2014/10/Who_Votes-final.pdf.

Sigel, Roberta, ed. 1989. *Political Learning in Adulthood: A Sourcebook of Theory and Research.* Chicago: University of Chicago Press.

Sigelman, Carol K., Lee Sigelman, Barbara J. Walkosz, and Michael Nitz. 1995. "Black Candidates, White Voters: Understanding Racial Bias in Political Perceptions." *American Journal of Political Science* 39 (1): 243–65.

Silvester, Jo. 2009. "Recruiting Politicians: Designing Competency-Based Selection for UK Parliamentary Candidates." In *The Psychology of Politicians,* edited by Ashley Weinberg, 21–38. Cambridge: Cambridge University Press.

Skuterud, Mikal. 2010. "The Visible Minority Earnings Gap across Generations of Canadians." *Canadian Journal of Economics* 43 (3): 860–81.

Smith, Matt, and Alan Walks. 2013. "Visible Minority Electability in Urban Local Government in Ontario." CERIS Working Paper No. 97. Toronto: CERIS – The Ontario Metropolis Centre. http://www.ceris.metropolis.net/wp-content/uploads/2013/02/CWP_97_Smith_Walks.pdf.

Sobolewska, Maria. 2013. "Party Strategies and the Descriptive Representation of Ethnic Minorities: The 2010 British General Election." *West European Politics* 36 (3): 615–33.

Soroka, Stuart, Erin Penner, and Kelly Blidook. 2009. "Constituency Influence in Parliament." *Canadian Journal of Political Science* 42 (3): 561–91.

Soysal, Yasemin Nuhoglu. 1994. *Limits of Citizenship: Migrants and Postnational Membership in Europe.* Chicago: University of Chicago Press.

Speaker's Conference. 2009. *Speaker's Conference on Parliamentary Representation.* London: House of Commons.

Stasiulis, Daiva K., and Yasmeen Abu-Laban. 1991. "The House the Parties Built: (Re)constructing Ethnic Representation in Canadian Politics." In *Ethno-cultural Groups and Visible Minorities in Canadian Politics: The Question of Access*, edited by Kathy Megyery, 3–99. Toronto: Dundurn Press.

Statistics Canada. 2007. *2006 Census of Population – Topic-Based Tabulations, Immigration and Citizenship Tables: Place of Birth, Age at Immigration, Period of Immigration and Sex for the Immigrant Population of Canada, Provinces and Territories, 2006 Census – 20% Sample Data*. Cat. no. 97-557-XCB-2006-023. Ottawa: Statistics Canada.

– 2008a. *Canada's Ethnocultural Mosaic, 2006 Census*. Cat. no. 97-562-X. Ottawa: Statistics Canada.

– 2008b. *2006 Census of Population: Federal Electoral District (FED) Profile, 2006 Census*. Cat. no. 92-595-XWE. Ottawa: Statistics Canada.

– 2008c. *Visible Minority Population and Population Group Reference Guide, 2006 Census*: Cat. no. 97-562-GWE2006003.

Stegmaier, Mary, Michael S. Lewis-Beck, and Kaat Smets. 2012. "Standing for Parliament: Do Black, Asian and Minority Ethnic Candidates Pay Extra?" *Parliamentary Affairs* 66 (2): 268–85.

Stevens, Daniel, Benjamin Bishin, and Robert Barr. 2006. "Authoritarian Attitudes, Democracy, and Policy Preferences among Latin American Elites." *American Journal of Political Science* 50 (3): 606–20.

Stolle, Dietlind, and Michele Micheletti. 2013. *Political Consumerism: Global Responsibility in Action*. New York: Cambridge University Press.

Strömblad, Per, and Per Adman. 2009. "Political Integration through Ethnic or Nonethnic Voluntary Associations?" *Political Research Quarterly* 63 (4): 721–30.

Swyngedouw, Marc, and Dirk Jacobs. 2006. "Qui a voté en 2003 pour les candidats d'origine étrangère en Flandre (Belgique)?" In *Penser l'immigration et l'intégration autrement : Une initiative belge inter-universitaire*, edited by B. Khader, M. Martiniello, A. Rea, and C. Timmerman, 159–76. Bruxelles: Bruylant.

Teorell, Jan. 2003. "Linking Social Capital to Political Participation: Voluntary Associations and Networks of Recruitment in Sweden." *Scandinavian Political Studies* 26 (1): 49–66.

Terkildsen, Nayda. 1993. "When White Voters Evaluate Black Candidates: The Processing Implications of Candidate Skin Color, Prejudice and Self-Monitoring." *American Journal of Political Science* 37 (4): 1032–53.

Tillie, Jean. 2000. *De etnische stem: opkomst en stemgedrag van migranten tijdens gemeenteraadsverkiezingen 1986–1998*. Utrecht: Forum.

– 2004. "Social Capital of Organisations and Their Members: Explaining the Political Integration of Immigrants in Amsterdam." *Journal of Ethnic and Migration Studies* 30 (3): 529–41.

Togeby, Lise. 1999. "Migrants at the Polls: An Analysis of Immigrant and Refugee Participation in Danish Local Elections." *Journal of Ethnic and Migration Studies* 25 (4): 665–84.

– 2004. "It Depends... How Organisational Participation Affects Political Participation and Social Trust among Second-Generation Immigrants in Denmark." *Journal of Ethnic and Migration Studies* 30 (3): 509–28.

Tolley, Erin. 2011. "Black and White or Shades of Grey? Racial Mediation in Canadian Politics." Presentation at the "Political Immigrant: A Comparative Portrait" conference, Concordia University, Montreal, 18–19 November.

Tolley, Erin, and Robert Young. 2011. *Immigrant Settlement Policy in Canadian Municipalities*. Montreal and Kingston: McGill-Queen's University Press.

Tossutti, Livianna S. 2007. *The Electoral Participation of Ethnocultural Communities*. Elections Canada Working Paper Series on Electoral Participation and Outreach Practices. Ottawa: Elections Canada.

Triadafilopoulos, Triadafilos. 2013. *Becoming Multicultural: Immigration and the Politics of Membership in Canada and Germany*. Vancouver: University of British Columbia Press.

Trounstine, Jessica. 2010. "Representation and Accountability in Cities." *Annual Review of Political Science* 13:407–23.

Trounstine, Jessica, and Melody E. Valdini. 2008. "The Context Matters: The Effects of Single-Member vs. at-Large Districts on City Council Diversity." *American Journal of Political Science* 52 (3): 554–69.

Uhlaner, Carole J., Bruce E. Cain, and D. Roderick Kiewiet. 1989. "Political Participation of Ethnic Minorities in the 1980s." *Political Behavior* 11 (3): 195–231.

UK. Electoral Commission. 2005. *Black and Minority Ethnic Survey*. Research Study Conducted for the Electoral Commission. London: MORI.

UK ONS (Office for National Statistics). 2001. "2001 Census." http://www .ons.gov.uk/ons/guide-method/census/census-2001/index.html.

UNDP (United Nations Development Programme). 2008. *Fighting Climate Change: Human Solidarity in a Divided World – Human Development Report 2007/2008*. Basingstoke: Palgrave Macmillan.

Valentino, Nicholas A., and David O. Sears. 1998. "Event-Driven Political Communication and the Preadult Socialization of Partisanship." *Political Behavior* 20 (1): 127–54.

van der Heijden, Teri, and Anja van Heelsum. 2010. *Opkomst en stemgedrag van migranten tijdens gemeenteraadsverkiezingen van 3 maart 2010*. Amsterdam: IMES.

van Heelsum, Anja. 2005. "Political Participation and Civic Community of Ethnic Minorities in Four Cities in the Netherlands." *Politics* 25 (1): 19–30.

van Heelsum, Anja, and Jean Tillie. 2006. *Opkomst en partijvoorkeur van migranten bij de gemeenteraadsverkiezingen van 7 maart 2006*. Amsterdam: IMES.

van Londen, Marieke, Karen Phalet, and Louk Hagendoorn. 2007. "Civic Engagement and Voter Participation among Turkish and Moroccan Minorities in Rotterdam." *Journal of Ethnic and Migration Studies* 33 (8): 1201–26.

van Rhee, Marn. 2002. *Analyse van de opkomst bij de gemeenteraadsverkiezingen in Rotterdam op 6 maart 2002*. Rotterdam: Centrum voor Onderzoek en Statistiek (COS).

van Tubergen, Frank, Ineke Mass, and Henk Flap. 2004. "The Economic Incorporation of Immigrants in 18 Western Societies: Origin, Destination and Community Effects." *American Sociological Review* 69 (5): 704–27.

Vedlitz, Arnold, and Charles A. Johnson. 1982. "Community Racial Segregation, Electoral Structure, and Minority Representation." *Social Science Quarterly* 63 (4): 729–36.

Verba, Sydney, Norman H. Nie, and Jae-on Kim. 1978. *Participation and Political Equality: A Seven-Nation Comparison*. New York: Cambridge University Press.

Verba, Sidney, Kay Lehman Schlozman, and Henry E. Brady. 1995. *Voice and Equality: Civic Voluntarism and American Politics*. Cambridge, MA: Harvard University Press.

Vermunt, Jeroen K. 1997. *LEM: A General Program for the Analysis of Categorical Data*. Tilburg: Department of Methodology and Statistics, Tilburg University.

Voss, Kim, and Irene Bloemraad, eds. 2010. *Rallying for Immigrant Rights*. Berkeley: University of California Press.

Wagner, Angelia. 2011. "On Their Best Behaviour? Newspaper Journalists' Coverage of Women Municipal Candidates in Alberta." *Canadian Political Science Review* 5 (1): 38–54.

Wals, Sergio. 2006. "Latino Immigrants' Political Participation and Partisanship: A Theory of Imported Socialization." Paper prepared for the annual meeting of the Midwest Political Science Association, Chicago, 20 April.

Wals 2007. "Mexican Immigrants' Political Suitcase: Partisanship and Democratic Values." Paper prepared for the annual meeting of the Midwest Political Science Association, 12–15 April.

– 2008. "Traveling Light? The Role of Latino Immigrants' Imported Socialization on the Intensity of Political Engagement." Paper prepared for the annual meeting of the Western Political Science Association, 3–6 April.

– 2011. "Does What Happens in Los Mochis Stay in Los Mochis? Explaining Post Migration Political Behaviour." *Political Research Quarterly* 64 (3): 600–11.

Wattenberg, Martin P. 2008. *Is Voting for Young People?* Toronto: Pearson Longman.

Webster, P. 1990. "Tory leaders move swiftly to back black candidate." *Times* (London), December 1990.

Weisberg, Robert. 1978. "Collective vs. Dyadic Representation in Congress." *American Political Science Review* 72 (2): 535–47.

Whelan, Christopher T., and Bertrand Maître. 2005. "Economic Vulnerability, Multidimensional Deprivation and Social Cohesion in an Enlarged European Community." *International Journal of Comparative Sociology* 46 (3): 215–39.

White, Stephen E., and Antoine Bilodeau. 2014. "Canadian Immigrant Electoral Support in a Comparative Perspective." In *Comparing Canada: Methods and Perspectives on Canadian Politics*, edited by Luc Turgeon et al., 123–46. Vancouver: University of British Columbia Press.

White, Stephen E., Antoine Bilodeau, and Neil Nevitte. 2015. "Earning Their Support: Feelings toward the Host Political Community among Recent Immigrants in Canada." *Ethnic and Racial Studies* 38 (2): 292–308.

White, Stephen E., Neil Nevitte, André Blais, and Joanna Everitt. 2006. "Making Up for Lost Time: Immigrant Voter Turnout in Canada." *Electoral Insight* 8 (2): 10–16.

White, Stephen E., Neil Nevitte, André Blais, Elisabeth Gidengil, and Patrick Fournier. 2008. "The Political Resocialization of Immigrants: Resistance or Lifelong Learning?" *Political Research Quarterly* 61 (2): 268–81.

Williams, Melissa S. 1998. *Voice, Trust, and Memory: Marginalized Groups and the Failings of Liberal Representation*. Princeton: Princeton University Press.

Wilson, Paul. 1973. *Immigrants and Politics*. Canberra: Australian National University Press.

Wolfinger, Raymond E. 1965. "The Development and Persistence of Ethnic Voting." *American Political Science Review* 59 (4): 896–908.

Wong, Janelle. 2000. "The Effects of Age and Political Exposure on the Development of Party Identification among Asian American and Latino Immigrants in the U.S." *Political Behavior* 22 (4): 341–71.

Wright, Matthew, and Irene Bloemraad. 2012. "Is There a Trade-Off between Multiculturalism and Socio-political Integration? Policy Regimes and Immigrant Incorporation in Comparative Perspective." *Perspectives on Politics* 10 (1): 77–95.

Yang, Philip Q. 1994. "Explaining Immigrant Naturalization." *International Migration Review* 28 (3): 449–77.

Young, Iris Marion. 2000. *Inclusion and Democracy*. Oxford: Oxford University Press.

Zaller, John. 1992. *The Nature and Origins of Mass Opinion*. Cambridge: Cambridge University Press.

Zhou, Min, and Guoxuan Cai. 2002. "Chinese Language Media in the United States: Immigration and Assimilation in American Life." *Qualitative Sociology* 25 (3): 419–41.

Contributors

Antoine Bilodeau is associate professor in the Department of Political Science at Concordia University and a member of the Centre for the Study of Democratic Citizenship.

Karen Bird is associate professor of political science at McMaster University.

Jerome H. Black is retired from the Department of Political Science at McGill University.

Pascal Delwit is full professor of political science at Université libre de Bruxelles.

Elisabeth Gidengil is Hiram Mills Professor in the Department of Political Science at McGill University and a member of the Centre for the Study of Democratic Citizenship.

Chris Haynes is assistant professor at the University of New Haven.

Marc Helbling is full professor of political science at the University of Bamberg and a senior researcher at the WZB Berlin Social Science Center.

Dirk Jacobs is full professor of sociology at the Université libre de Bruxelles.

Michael Jones-Correa is professor and Robert J. Katz Chair of the Department of Government at Cornell University.

Ian McAllister is professor of political science at the Australian National University.

Laure Michon is a researcher at *O+S*, Research and Statistics, Municipality of Amsterdam.

Juliet Pietsch is a senior lecturer in political science in the School of Politics and International Relations at the Australian National University.

S. Karthick Ramakrishnan is professor and associate dean of public policy at the University of California, Riverside.

Andrea Rea is full professor of sociology at Université libre de Bruxelles.

Tim Reeskens is assistant professor in the Department of Sociology at Tilburg University (the Netherlands).

Jason Roy is associate professor in the Department of Political Science at Wilfrid Laurier University.

Shamit Saggar is the director of the Understanding Society Policy Unit and professor of public policy at the Institute for Social and Economic Research, University of Essex.

Cameron Stark is a research coordinator with the City of Calgary.

Dietlind Stolle is professor in the Department of Political Science at McGill University and director of the Centre for the Study of Democratic Citizenship.

Celine Teney is professor of social policy at the Universität Bremen.

Jean Tillie is dean of the Faculty of Social Sciences and Law at the Amsterdam University of Applied Sciences and professor of electoral politics in the Department of Political Science at the University of Amsterdam.

Anja van Heelsum is assistant professor in the Department of Political Science at the University of Amsterdam.

Stephen E. White is assistant professor in the Department of Political Science at Carleton University.

Matthew Wright is assistant professor of political science at American University in Washington, DC.

www.ingramcontent.com/pod-product-compliance
Lightning Source LLC
Chambersburg PA
CBHW021856020426
42334CB00013B/353